# GETTING BETTER
## The Policy and Politics of Reducing Health Inequalities

Clare Bambra, Julia Lynch and Katherine E. Smith

First published in Great Britain in 2025 by

Policy Press, an imprint of
Bristol University Press
University of Bristol
1–9 Old Park Hill
Bristol
BS2 8BB
UK
t: +44 (0)117 374 6645
e: bup-info@bristol.ac.uk

Details of international sales and distribution partners are available at policy.bristoluniversitypress.co.uk

© Clare Bambra, Julia Lynch and Katherine E. Smith, 2025

British Library Cataloguing in Publication Data
A catalogue record for this book is available from the British Library

The digital PDF and ePub versions of this title are available open access and distributed under the terms of the Creative Commons Attribution-NonCommercial-NoDerivatives 4.0 International licence (https://creativecommons.org/licenses/by-nc-nd/4.0/) which permits reproduction and distribution for non-commercial use without further permission provided the original work is attributed.

ISBN 978-1-4473-7286-8 paperback
ISBN 978-1-4473-7287-5 ePub
ISBN 978-1-4473-7288-2 ePdf

The right of Clare Bambra, Julia Lynch and Katherine E. Smith to be identified as authors of this work has been asserted by them in accordance with the Copyright, Designs and Patents Act 1988.

All rights reserved: no part of this publication may be reproduced, stored in a retrieval system, or transmitted in any form or by any means, electronic, mechanical, photocopying, recording, or otherwise without the prior permission of Bristol University Press.

Every reasonable effort has been made to obtain permission to reproduce copyrighted material. If, however, anyone knows of an oversight, please contact the publisher.

The statements and opinions contained within this publication are solely those of the authors and not of the University of Bristol or Bristol University Press. The University of Bristol and Bristol University Press disclaim responsibility for any injury to persons or property resulting from any material published in this publication.

Bristol University Press and Policy Press work to counter discrimination on grounds of gender, race, disability, age and sexuality.

Cover design: Sean Collins
Front cover image: Sean Collins

To our children Harry, Charity, David; Kieran, Eli; and Aiisha. May things get better.

# Contents

| | | |
|---|---|---|
| List of figures, tables and boxes | | vi |
| Acknowledgements | | vii |
| 1 | Introduction: The holy grail of reducing health inequalities | 1 |
| 2 | The Great Society: social reform and health inequalities in the United States | 15 |
| 3 | Vote early, vote often: democratisation in Brazil and health inequalities | 35 |
| 4 | What belongs together will grow together: German reunification and health inequalities | 54 |
| 5 | Things can only get better: England's Health Inequalities Strategy | 72 |
| 6 | Waxing and waning: the four levellers of health inequalities | 92 |
| 7 | Conclusion: The politics of health inequalities | 116 |
| Notes | | 131 |
| References | | 133 |
| Index | | 169 |

# List of figures, tables and boxes

## Figures
| | | |
|---|---|---|
| 1.1 | Looking upstream: the political determinants of health inequalities | 6 |
| 1.2 | The U-shaped curve of health inequalities over the 20th and 21st centuries | 10 |
| 2.1 | Premature mortality rates (deaths under age 65), United States, 1960–2002, by county median family income quintile | 25 |
| 2.2 | Premature mortality rates (deaths under age 65), United States, 1960–2002, by county median family income quintile for the US White population (dashed lines) and populations of colour (solid lines) | 26 |
| 3.1 | The Regions and Federative Units of Brazil | 37 |
| 3.2 | Infant mortality rate (per 1000 live births) across five regions of Brazil, 1990–2015 | 42 |
| 3.3 | Infant mortality rate (per 1000 live births) across the municipalities of Brazil, ranked by income quartile, 1991–2010 | 42 |
| 3.4 | Life expectancy at birth (years) across the municipalities of Brazil, ranked by income quartile, 1991–2010 | 43 |
| 4.1 | Life expectancy for men and women in East and West Germany, 1956–2020 | 58 |
| 4.2 | Male life expectancy in the former USSR, 1959–2013 | 68 |
| 4.3 | Female life expectancy in the former USSR, 1959–2013 | 69 |
| 5.1 | Inequalities in infant mortality rates by English local authority, 1983–2017 | 85 |
| 5.2 | Income inequality in the UK from 1910 to 2010, income share of the wealthiest 1 per cent | 90 |
| 6.1 | Official and alternative US income poverty rates, 1963–2010 | 100 |

## Tables
| | | |
|---|---|---|
| 2.1 | Major programmes of the Great Society (1964–69) | 22 |
| 3.1 | An overview of some of the key policies implemented in Brazil during democratisation | 51 |
| 4.1 | Welfare state regimes | 66 |
| 5.1 | Main health inequalities policies and interventions in England, 1997–2010 | 81 |

## Box
| | | |
|---|---|---|
| 7.1 | The disappointingly limited insights of systematic reviews for identifying which policies are effective in reducing health inequalities | 117 |

# Acknowledgements

Bambra's time on the book was supported by a Wellcome Trust award [221266/Z/20/Z]; and we gratefully acknowledge Wellcome Trust funding for the Open Access version of the book. Lynch's time on the book was supported by a paid teaching leave from the University of Pennsylvania, supported by the Dean of the School of Arts and Sciences. Smith's time on the book was partially supported by UK Prevention Research Partnership funding for the System-Science Informed Public Health and Health Economic Research (SIPHER) Consortium [MR/S037578/1]. We thank Debra Lederman for literature searching and reviewing which informed Chapter 2. We thank Julija Simpson of Newcastle University for support with literature searching and reviewing which informed Chapter 4 and for drawing Figures 4.1, 4.2 and 4.2. We also thank Cara Leavy of Newcastle University for support with literature searching and reviewing which informed Table 5.1 and Chapter 5. We thank Sean Collins of the Northern Health Sciences Alliance for the front cover design and for drawing Figures 1.1, 1.2, 2.1, 2.2, 3.1, 5.1, 5.2 and 6.1. We thank Victoria Morgan for administrative assistance with the book, including help with formatting and references.

# 1

# Introduction: The holy grail of reducing health inequalities

Significant inequalities, inequities and disparities in health exist in every country in the world. On average, people in the highest-status occupational groups (for example, corporate executives) have better health outcomes than those in mid-ranking occupations (such as teachers), who in turn have better health outcomes than those in the lowest occupational groups (for example, factory or shop workers). Similarly, people with higher incomes or university-level education have, on average, better health outcomes than those with a lower income or lower educational qualifications (Bambra, 2016). In Brazil, people in the wealthy, Southern state of Santa Catarina can expect to live 8.5 years longer than in the poorer, Northeastern state of Piauí. And in the US city of New Orleans, there is a whopping 25-year gap in life expectancy between the richest and poorest neighbourhoods. Health inequalities are evident even in relatively equal Norway, where life expectancy varies by up to eight years between districts in the city of Oslo. There are also significant inequalities in health, well-being and mortality between men and women (many studies find that women have higher rates of illness, while men have higher mortality rates); between ethnic groups (for example, COVID-19 death rates are three times higher among Black Americans than other ethnic groups); by migration status (with migrant communities often prevented from easily accessing healthcare); and among other marginalised groups (for example, many studies find higher rates of mental ill health among LGBTQ+ groups). Universally, across time and place, people from more privileged social groups have, on average, better health than people from less privileged groups (Bambra, 2016).

These health inequalities have been increasing in recent decades in many countries (Mackenbach et al, 2016), with life expectancy stalling – even declining – in the most disadvantaged communities (Marmot, 2020; Walsh and McCartney, 2024). The COVID-19 crisis was experienced unequally and has exacerbated these trends, as has the post-pandemic global cost-of-living crisis (Bambra et al, 2020; Marmot and Bambra, 2024). Behind these statistics lies the reality that more and more people are dealing with the premature loss of loved family members and friends, and these losses are disproportionality experienced by people living in more marginalised and disadvantaged communities.

Reducing health inequalities has been described as the 'holy grail' of public health (Horton, 1997). However, we are clearly a very long way from achieving health equity in most countries, which means there are urgent questions about how best to accomplish this task. What will it actually take to get better? While most research focuses on trying to define, document or analyse health inequalities, this book engages head on with the question of what can be done to reduce health inequalities. Rather than taking a typical public health approach of reviewing research evidence to identify the most promising policies and intervention points, we instead ask what can be learnt from studying the historical experiences of countries that *have* successfully reduced health inequalities. This is important because politicians are only likely to put in the effort to reduce health inequalities if they believe it is possible to achieve reductions with policy change.

In his authoritative account of the history of economic inequality, Walter Scheidel (2017) uses multiple examples, from the stone age to the 20th century, to identify four 'great levellers' of inequality: mass-mobilisation warfare (for example, the First and Second World Wars); transformative revolutions (for example, the communist revolutions in Russia and China and the French Revolution); state collapse (for example, the collapse of the Tang dynasty in China and the Roman Empire); and global pandemics (for example, the Black Death in 14th-century Europe and the smallpox, measles and typhus epidemics in the Americas in the 16th century). Following Scheidel, this book examines four historical examples from across the world of when sizeable population-level reductions in health inequalities have been achieved: the Great Society of the 1960s in the USA; democratisation in Brazil in the 1980s–2010s; German reunification in the 1990s; and the English Health Inequalities Strategy in the 2000s. We identify four common 'levelling' mechanisms for reducing health inequalities that span the different examples: welfare state expansion, improved healthcare access, reduced income inequalities and enhanced democratic engagement (Bambra, 2022a). The book will also examine evidence of what happens to health inequalities when the converse situation occurs: when social safety nets are dismantled, accessing high-quality healthcare becomes more difficult, poverty and inequality increase, and political and civil rights begin to decay. Together, we argue, this 'waxing and waning' of attempts to equalise the social, economic and political determinants of health provide useful lessons about the political alliances and policy actions that will be required to reduce health inequalities in the future. The book concludes by arguing that reducing health inequalities requires the political will – and resulting policy action – to implement long-term and wide-reaching macro-level policies.

First, though, this introductory chapter lays out some pertinent conceptual, theoretical and empirical issues in the field. It starts by outlining the different perspectives about the causes of health inequalities – privileging the political economy perspective that will be taken in the rest of the book. It then examines trends in health inequalities, taking the long view over the last hundred years and highlighting the role of changing politics and policies in shaping these trends. It finishes by briefly overviewing the case studies that will be examined in the rest of the book.

## Unfair and avoidable: health inequalities, inequities and disparities

The term 'health inequality' is usually employed to refer to the systematic differences in health which exist between different population groups (for example, different social classes or ethnic groups). Traditionally, in the UK and Europe, discussion of health inequalities has focused on the distribution of health by social class and/or socio-economic position (Smith et al, 2015). In contrast, in the USA (and to some extent countries such as Canada, Australia and New Zealand), health inequalities research has tended to emphasise differences by race/ethnicity (for example, between Black and White Americans, or between indigenous and White Australians) (Lynch and Perera 2017). Recent research has highlighted the health disadvantages experienced by other social minorities such as substance users, members of the LGBTQ+ community or people with disabilities. The ways in which different elements of social identity and stratification (for example, socio-economic status, race/ethnicity, gender) interact to shape people's health experiences has also increasingly been integrated within health inequalities research, with researchers increasingly drawing on the concept of intersectionality (for example, Kapilashrami et al, 2015).

The term health inequalities also can be used to refer to both (a) inequalities in health outcomes (for example, mortality rates, life expectancy and so on) and (b) inequalities in access to healthcare and inequalities in the outcomes of healthcare. In some contexts, slightly different terms may be preferred. For example, in the USA and Canada, the term 'health disparities' is often employed, while in other countries and within some global organisations (for example, at the World Health Organization), the preferred term is 'health inequities' (avoidable differences in health between different groups of people with different levels of need). In this book, where our focus is on the 'big picture' of how different mixtures of macro-policy change impact overarching health patterns, we use the catch-all terms 'health inequalities' and 'social inequalities in health' to refer to 'systematic differences in the health of people occupying unequal positions in society' (Graham, 2009, p 3) that are socially produced, avoidable, and therefore unfair and unjust (Whitehead, 2007). These differences may occur across a variety of different social divides, including class, race or ethnicity, gender, sexual orientation or disability status. We also recognise the cumulative, additive, and integrated nature of health inequalities and the converging processes associated with different, intersecting categories of disadvantage.

## Looking upstream: politics, policies and health inequalities

This book is about the role politics and policies can play in reducing – or increasing – health inequalities. This section sets out our *political economy* approach to understanding health inequalities, contextualising it within the broader conceptual literature on the causes of health inequalities.

Over the last 50 years, a sizeable body of theoretical and empirical research has sought to explain the causes of (socio-economic) health inequalities. From this body of research six different explanations for health inequalities have emerged: the behavioural, materialist, psychosocial, life course, intersectionality and political economy paradigms (Bartley, 2017).

The 'behavioural–cultural' theory of health inequalities asserts that the causal mechanism generating health inequalities is the prevalence of health-damaging behaviours among individuals in lower socio-economic groups (Bartley, 2017). Such differences in health behaviour are often considered to be a consequence of or a coping mechanism for dealing with disadvantage, and as such unhealthy behaviours may also come to make up part of the culture or 'habitus' of deprived socio-economic groups.

The 'materialist' explanation for health inequalities argues that income itself determines access to health-benefitting goods and services (for example, healthcare access, schools, transport, social care) and the degree of exposure to particular material risk factors (for example, poor housing, inadequate diet, physical hazards at work, environmental exposures), and hence different income levels are consistently associated with different levels of health.

The 'psychosocial' explanation for health inequalities focuses on the adverse biological consequences of psychological and social domination and subordination, superiority and inferiority. Social inequalities in health are explained by the unequal social distribution of such psychosocial risk factors such as control at work and in the community, stigma and discrimination or social support, with these risk factors being concentrated among lower-status individuals.

The 'life course' approach to understanding health inequalities highlights the role of the accumulation of disadvantage over the totality of a person's life, reflecting the amount of time people have spent in more or less disadvantaged circumstances. Health inequality between social groups is therefore a result of inequalities in the accumulation of social, psychological, and biological advantages and disadvantages over time.

Intersectionality theory focuses on how socio-economic status, ethnicity, gender, and other axes of social identity are experienced in combination, as socially constructed structural and systemic experiences rather than demographic factors. So, for example, ethnic inequalities in health can arise through discrimination personally, institutionally and structurally. These inequalities also intersect with other axes of inequalities, meaning that they may play out differently for, say, a Black woman in precarious employment compared to a Black man in a senior professional occupation.

Finally, the political economy approach to health inequalities, which informs our research in this book, combines the materialist, psychosocial, life course and intersectional explanations with the recognition that risk factors for poor health such as low income, low social status and discrimination are themselves shaped by macro-level structural determinants of health: politics and policies, the economy, the state, the organisation of work and the labour market. A consequence of this view is that, even within the constraints of unequal societies, the social and behavioural determinants of health are amenable to public policy interventions.

Each of these approaches to understanding health inequalities privileges different causal mechanisms and puts emphasis at different scales – from micro-level individual risk factors (behavioural); through meso-level social factors (materialist, psychosocial, life course); and macro-level structural, political, economic and policy factors (intersectionality, political economy). Another way of thinking about these different approaches and how they fit together, is to imagine a river: downstream are the individual behavioural factors, mid-stream is the material, psychosocial and life course factors and upstream are the macro-level intersectional, political, economic and policy factors (Figure 1.1). If something polluting is put in the river upstream, then it will contaminate all the water in the river – mid-stream and downstream (McKinley, 1975). In terms of health, our political choices result in certain economic and social policies being pursued. These policies can be either salutogenic (health-promoting) or pathogenic (health-harming) to the people and places they touch as they influence all the other mid- and downstream determinants of health (Bambra, 2016). In this way, social inequalities in health and disease are produced by the structures, values and priorities of political and economic systems (Krieger, 2013).

While the wider public health literature is dominated by downstream, individual-focused behavioural approaches, it is the mid-stream and upstream approaches that are seen as the most important by the global health inequalities community as they highlight the *causes* of social inequalities in health. This growing scientific consensus on the importance of upstream determinants was exemplified in the World Health Organization's *Global Commission on the Social Determinants of Health* (2008) which concluded that health inequalities are driven by inequalities in 'growing, living and working conditions; the social and economic policies that shape growing, living, and working; the relative roles of state and market in providing for good and equitable health; and the wider international and global conditions that can help or hinder national and local action for health equity' (WHO, 2008, p vii).

**Figure 1.1:** Looking upstream: the political determinants of health inequalities

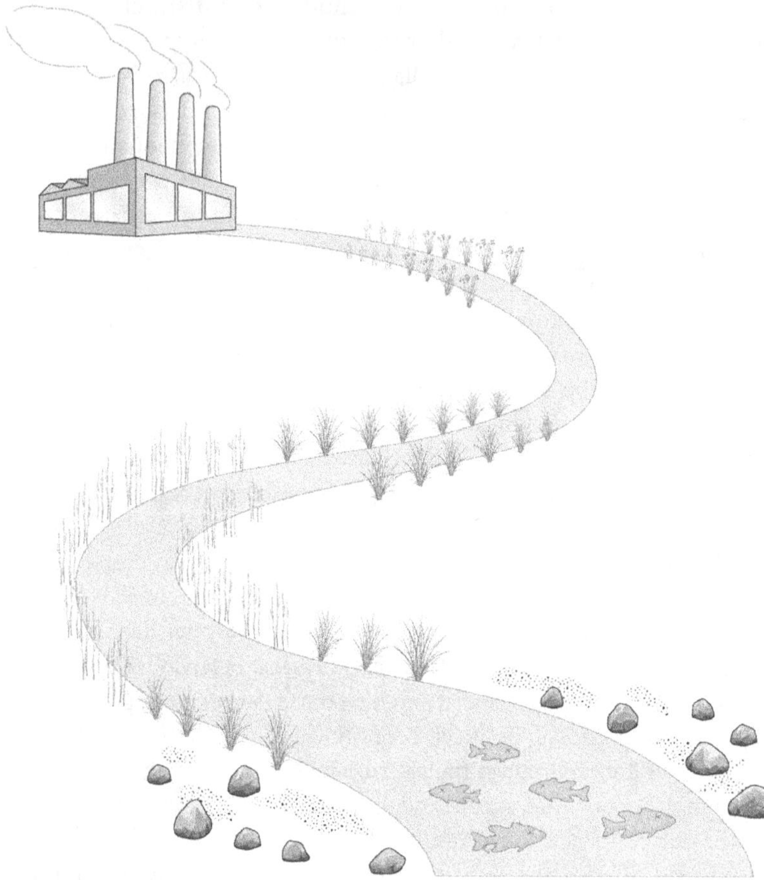

These social, political, and economic structures and relations are largely outside the control of the individuals or communities or places they affect. Why some places and people are consistently privileged by public policies while others are consistently marginalised is a political choice – it is about *where the power lies* and in whose interests that power is exercised (Bambra, 2016). Political choices can thereby be seen as the fundamental causes of health inequalities.

Let's take socio-economic inequalities in heart disease as an example. A downstream behavioural 'cause' could be poor diet, of which the midstream social 'cause' could be living on a low-income or in a deprived neighbourhood with limited access to affordable, healthy food. The causes of the latter are arguably structural: poverty exists because the economic system creates poverty and the political system *allows* it to exist. Public policies can be introduced to reduce poverty through social transfers or higher minimum wages, or food prices could be controlled or subsidised rather than left to the vagaries of the market. In other words, politics can make us sick – or healthy (Schrecker and Bambra, 2015; 2025).

In common with most of the other theories outlined previously, the political economy approach arose from a traditional focus on socio-economic inequalities in health. However, the importance of politics and policies is also relevant when examining other forms of social inequality in health. For example, in terms of gender, research has examined how social policies such as childcare, parental leave, active labour market programmes and long-term care policies can reduce the gendered burden of family care-work, strengthen gender equity and reduce women's morbidity burden (Bambra et al, 2021). Likewise, research combining an intersectional and political economy approach has highlighted the health impacts of the intersection of interpersonal, institutional (exclusionary processes, attitudes and behaviours in labour markets, the education system, housing provision and healthcare) and structural racism (produced and reproduced by laws, rules, and practices, sanctioned and even implemented by various levels of government, and embedded in the economic system as well as in cultural and societal norms) which has both direct and indirect health impacts – not least through increased rates of poverty (Nazroo, 2022). Similarly, the adverse health experiences of social minorities result from a heightened risk of poverty, caused by – or compounded by – stigma, trauma, social exclusion, discrimination and victimisation (Aldridge et al, 2018).

Politics and the balance of power between key political groups determine the role of the state and other agencies in relation to health and whether there are collective interventions to improve health and reduce health inequalities, and also whether these interventions are individually, socially or structurally focused. Public policies mean that not all high-income countries have the same levels of health inequality, with different political choices and public policies responsible for these differences (Beckfield and Bambra, 2016). In this way, politics (broadly understood) is a *fundamental* determinant of social inequalities in health because it results in the public policies which themselves shape the social, economic and cultural environment and the social and spatial distribution of salutogenic and pathogenic factors both collectively and individually (Bambra, 2016).

The next section of this introductory chapter further illustrates the role of politics and policies in shaping health inequalities through an examination of trends in high-income countries over the 20th and 21st centuries.

## The long view: trends in health inequalities over the 20th and 21st centuries

Historical epidemiological studies suggest that there is a U-shaped curve in socio-economic health inequalities in high-income countries (and in racial inequalities in the USA) over the 20th and 21st centuries.[1] While evidence from the early part of the 20th century is sparse, the historical data available from the USA and Sweden suggests declines in health inequalities from the 1920s. A larger body of work from the USA, the UK and Western Europe examines trends since the 1960s. These find that health inequalities further diminished from the mid-1960s until the early 1980s when they increased again – with an acceleration in the pace of increase in the early part of the 21st century. This section documents this U-shaped curve of health inequalities over the 20th and 21st centuries and shows how changes in politics and policies lie 'behind the curve'.

Data on early 20th-century trends in health inequalities are available in studies of infant mortality rates (IMR) in the USA and Sweden (Rodriguez et al, 2022; Burstrom, 2003). Overall, IMRs fell dramatically over the 20th century for all social groups. For example, in the USA IMR fell from an average of 61 per 1000 live births in 1935 to 6 per 1000 live births in 2020 and in Sweden from 50 to 2 (O'Neil, 2022a; 2022b). However, studies have noted a 'fall and rise' of inequalities in IMR in the USA over the 20th century (Krieger et al, 2008). For example, Rodriguez and colleagues (2022), in a study of state-level trends in IMR from 1925 to 2017, found that inequalities by race/ethnicity in the USA declined between 1925 and 1945, then increased slightly until the mid-1960s, before falling again until around 1980 when they increased again through to 2017 (with a period of slight decrease from around 2000 to 2010). A similar pattern has been found in analysis of historical trends in inequalities in IMR for Sweden. Socio-economic inequalities in IMR in Sweden first appeared in the late 1890s and then decreased steadily over most of the 20th century, through until 1980 when they were at their smallest (Burstrom and Bernhardt, 2001; Burstrom, 2003). In the early and mid-1980s, socio-economic inequalities in IMR in Sweden then increased between the most and least privileged groups (Ericson et al, 1993).

Research examining more recent historical trends in inequalities in IMR is available for the USA, Sweden, Norway, Denmark and England. Analysis by Krieger and colleagues (2008) of county-level trends in IMR in the USA between 1960 and 2002 found that absolute and relative racial/ethnic inequalities in IMR fell between 1966 and 1980 (and particularly between 1965 and 1971, Chay and Greenstone, 2000) but that relative inequalities rose again between 1980 and 2002, while absolute inequalities stagnated (Krieger et al, 2008). They also found similar trends for income inequalities in IMR in the USA: shrinking relative and absolute inequalities between the top and bottom quintiles of income before 1980, followed by their widening or stagnating thereafter (Krieger et al, 2008). Relative socio-economic inequalities in IMR also increased in Norway and Sweden between 1980 and 2001, and in Denmark absolute inequalities by socio-economic status increased in IMR in this period (Arntzen and Nybo Andersen, 2004).

Analysis of socio-economic trends in IMR in England from 1983 to 2017 also found that from the early 1980s to the late 1990s, absolute and relative inequalities in IMR increased; there was then a slight decline in inequalities in the early part of the 21st century (1999–2010) before inequalities increased again from 2011 to 2017 (Robinson et al, 2019).

This U-shaped curve is also evident in terms of trends in socio-economic inequalities in premature mortality in England, the USA, France and other European countries. Analysis by Thomas et al (2010) of trends in area-level deprivation in under-65 mortality in England from 1921 to 2007 found that the relative index of inequality in standardised mortality ratios (SMRs) declined from 2.50 in 1921–30, to a low of 1.92 in the early 1970s. From the 1980s onwards, it increased consistently rising to 2.79 in the mid-2000s. They found the same pattern for the SMR of best to worst of the most deprived 10 per cent to the least deprived 10 per cent (Thomas et al, 2010). A similar trend was noted by Krieger and colleagues' (2008) research in the USA. They found that inequalities by income and race/ethnicity in premature mortality rates (under 65 years) also present a U-shaped curve with absolute and relative inequalities by income and race/ethnicity falling between 1966 and 1980, with relative inequalities widening – while absolute inequalities stagnated – from 1980 onwards. Analysis of trends in educational inequalities in France in premature all-cause mortality rates (for men and women aged 30–64) from 1968 to 1996 also noted increases from the 1980s: the relative index of inequality increased from 1.96 (men) and 1.87 (women) in 1968–74, to 2.77 (men) and 2.53 (women) in 1990–96 (Menvielle et al, 2007). The rise in health inequalities since the 1980s is also evident in other European countries. For example, Mackenbach and colleagues' (2018) analysis of trends in relative educational inequalities in all-cause mortality for 17 European countries from 1980 to 2014 found that while mortality rates declined steadily among all educational groups over this period, relative inequalities increased considerably.

Looking into the early 21st century, evidence from the USA and the UK shows a further increase in socio-economic inequalities in health – to such an extent that they may be leading to a stall in overall health improvement (Marmot, 2020). Prominent research in mortality trends between 1999 and 2013 in the USA by Case and Deaton (2015) found an increase in all-cause mortality among middle-aged White non-Hispanics. These increases were concentrated among those without a four-year college or bachelor's degree (Case and Deaton, 2020). Since 2010, death rates have also risen among Black non-Hispanics and Hispanics without a degree. Overall, adult life expectancy in the USA over the last decade has risen for the college educated and fallen for the rest (Case and Deaton, 2021). Similarly, an analysis by Marmot (2020) of trends in inequalities in life expectancy in the UK has found that 'over the decade since 2010, the social gradient in life expectancy has become steeper and the inequalities by area-level deprivation greater'. So, this recent increase in health inequalities in the USA and the UK is due to stagnation or declines in lower socio-economic groups alongside continued improvement in higher groups. These recent trends in the UK and USA are examined further in Chapter 6 of this book.

In summary, the available historical studies reviewed here suggest that there is a U-shaped curve of health inequalities over the 20th and 21st centuries. In Sweden, the USA and the UK, there is a U-shaped curve in relative socio-economic (and racial in the USA) inequalities in infant mortality from the 1960s onward. This curve is also evident in studies of relative socio-economic inequalities in premature mortality in the USA, England, France and for all-cause mortality in Europe. There is also more recent evidence from the USA and the UK of an acceleration in the increase in socio-economic inequalities in health in the early part of the 21st century. These trends in health inequalities parallel changing politics and policy regimes, of which four key periods can be identified (Figure 1.2): the *interbellum era* (1920–50); the *trente glorieuses* (1950–80); *neoliberalism* (1980–2010); and the *crisis age* (2010 to date). We now chronologically examine how these distinct periods may lie behind the U-shaped curve.

The *interbellum era* – or between the two World Wars – was a period of social reform with the beginnings of welfare state systems in many countries. In Sweden, for example, Burstrom (2003) describes how improvements in water, sanitation, hygiene, social housing, nutrition, family policies and healthcare over the early part of the 20th century particularly benefitted children in the poorest families. Average incomes also increased in this period in many

**Figure 1.2:** The U-shaped curve of health inequalities over the 20th and 21st centuries

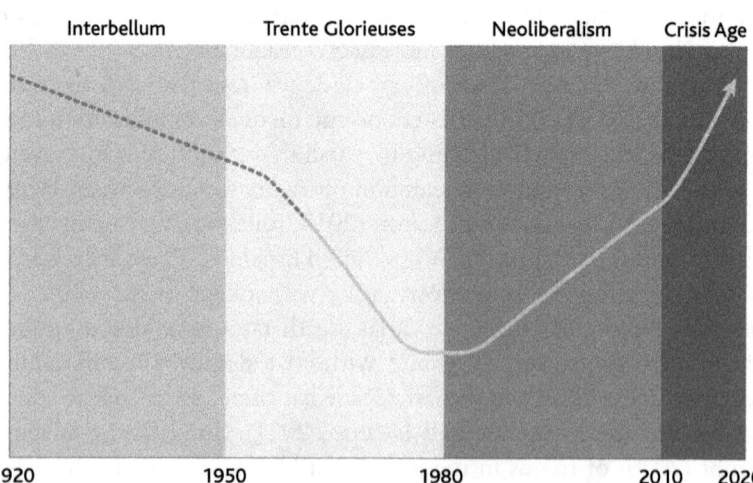

Note: The dashed line represents where there is less historical evidence.

countries, and income inequalities fell (Piketty, 2014). Likewise in the UK, the 1920s and 1930s saw the introduction of old-age and invalidity pensions, slum clearances and the start of social housing as well as an increase in the coverage of community-based health insurance schemes. Technical advances in medicine were also beneficial including better understanding of infectious diseases and more vaccination programmes (Burstrom, 2003). In the USA, this period has been labelled the 'Great Compression' as income inequality fell dramatically because of progressive taxation, stronger unions, strong economic growth and wage regulation under Roosevelt's New Deal (Bartles, 2004). The New Deal of this period also entailed public works projects; protection for labour organising; establishing minimum wages; public house-building; and the introduction of pensions, unemployment insurance and government cash transfers to some families with children (Hiltzik, 2011).

The *trente glorieuses* refers to the sustained period of economic growth experienced in Europe (and other high-income countries) from the late 1940s through to the late 1970s. This was a 'golden age' of welfare state capitalism – characterised (to a greater or lesser extent depending on the country) by central government intervention in society, universal social provision, and active macroeconomic management by the state (Keynesian economics). This last entailed interventionist fiscal policy, a large public sector, full (male) employment, high public expenditure, and the promotion of mass consumption via a redistributive tax and welfare system (Bambra et al, 2010). There was also a mainstream political consensus in favour of the welfare state and the redistribution it effected (Schrecker and Bambra, 2015). Western European countries experienced significant improvements to public housing, healthcare, and the other main social determinants of health (Bambra, 2011). This meant that from the 1950s and 1960s until the 1980s, income and wealth inequalities were historically at their smallest – and poverty rates the lowest (Piketty, 2014). In the USA in the 1960s, President Lyndon B. Johnson's 'Great Society' included policies that enhanced public healthcare coverage, protected voting rights and outlawed racial discrimination ('Jim Crow' laws) and segregation in public services, and reduced poverty through interventions in the labour market and cash transfers. This period in the USA is examined in more detail in Chapter 2 of this book.

This golden age of the welfare state effectively ended with the economic crisis of the 1970s and the subsequent rise of *neoliberalism* or 'market fundamentalism' (Schrecker and Bambra, 2015; 2025). The fundamental presuppositions of neoliberalism are that markets are the normal, natural and preferable way of organising the economy and society, and that the primary function of state institutions and policies is to ensure the efficient functioning of markets and market outcomes (Schrecker and Bambra, 2015). Initially in the Anglo-American countries under the Reagan and Thatcher administrations, but then more broadly (for example, under Kohl in West

Germany), the political consensus of the post-war settlement between labour and capital broke down as governments started to follow monetarist theories and dismantle and restructure the interventionist Keynesian welfare state (Scott-Samuel et al, 2014). Neoliberal 'reforms' were characterised by the privatisation and marketisation of state services and industries; the retrenchment of social security benefits and social housing; modified taxation arrangements that shifted the burden away from businesses; restrictions on labour organising; and the abandonment of the state's role in promoting full employment (Schrecker and Bambra, 2015; 2025). Wages fell and income inequality, poverty rates and unemployment all increased (Schrecker and Bambra, 2015). This period in the UK is examined in more detail in Chapter 5 of this book.

The *crisis age* started with the Global Financial Crisis (GFC) of 2007–08 which was sparked initially by a crisis in the financial markets for mortgage-backed securities in the USA. This led to a collapse in global financial markets, a huge rise in government debts, and increases in unemployment and poverty (Gamble, 2009). The GFC also led to large-scale cuts to public service budgets (austerity) in many countries, including for healthcare and welfare services and benefits for the poorest. Income and wealth inequality increased because of stagnating wages and higher poverty rates and tax cuts for the wealthy and corporations (Piketty, 2014). The period since 2008 has been a time of permanent crisis for most high-income countries, with simultaneous instability across political, economic, environmental, and health systems. This includes populist and far right threats to democracy and rolling wars in Europe and the Middle East; the return of protectionism and an apparent new 'cold war' with China; environmental disasters and evident impacts of climate change, with, for example, the highest ever recorded temperatures in Europe and China in summer of 2024; and the global COVID-19 pandemic that has resulted in over 7 million recorded deaths and led to social and economic upheaval across the world. The COVID-19 crash has since merged into the current 'cost of living crisis' characterised by rising inflation, interest rates and economic inactivity. Poverty rates and inequalities in income and wealth have increased in many countries in this period (Saez and Zucman, 2020). These recent international social policy trends are examined further in Chapter 6 of this book.

Looking back over trends in health inequalities over the 20th and 21st centuries and these four distinct policy periods, the *trente glorieuses* appears as an historic exception when health inequalities were at their lowest. This era teaches us that to break the U-shaped curve and reduce health inequalities requires large-scale policy action across all aspects of society. Chapter 2 of this book provides a case study of the USA in the 1960s which examines these issues in more detail. The other chapters of this book examine what can be seen as 'blips in the curve' – reductions in health inequalities in Brazil in the 1980s (Chapter 3), Germany in the 1990s (Chapter 4) and England in the 2000s (Chapter 5) *despite* wider trends in terms of increasing social inequalities. The next section of this introductory chapter provides a fuller preview of these case studies and the rest of this book.

## The rest of the book

From the preceding overview we get a sense of the multiple and interacting causes of health inequalities, how politics and policies have shaped them, and how they have increased over the last few decades. The rest of this book presents evidence from four real-world case studies of when politics has led to the implementation of large-scale progressive policies that have successfully reduced health inequalities. These case studies show what has worked in the past, and how we might learn for the future. The four cases have been chosen because they are from different time periods, in different countries, were implemented on a large scale, and have been evaluated in the scientific literature.

Chapter 2 examines the impact on health inequalities of the reforms that occurred during the 'Great Society' of the 1960s. The chapter provides an overview of the health, social policy and inequalities context before and after the reforms of the Great Society, which included programmes to address inequalities in medical care, civil rights, education and poverty. The chapter summarises the very large body of research that has amassed that examines the impact of policy reforms on health inequalities. A clear finding is that both racial and income inequalities in premature mortality and infant mortality declined between the mid-1960s and late 1970s as a result of the 'War on Poverty', investments in social welfare, extension of voting rights and other civil rights protections.

Chapter 3 examines the impact on health inequalities of the democratisation of Brazil from the 1980s to the 2000s. It provides an overview of the health, social policy and inequalities context before and after the reforms. In 1985, Brazil started a gradual transition from military dictatorship (1964–85) to become a relatively stable democracy by the mid-2000s. Increased political participation by lower-income groups, indigenous and Afro-Brazilian populations, was accompanied by an expansion of health and welfare programmes, including efforts to distribute income more fairly. The chapter brings together research examining the impact of these reforms on the social and economic determinants of health, showing that they led to reductions in poverty and inequality, which corresponded with significant improvements in key health indicators (including infant mortality rates) and a decrease in health inequalities.

Chapter 4 examines the impact on health inequalities of the fall of Communism in the former German Democratic Republic and the reunification of the East with democratic West Germany from 1990. It provides an overview of the health, social policy and inequalities context before and after the reforms. The German reunification process involved substantial changes in the East, including improvements in living standards, wage levels, nutrition, pensions and healthcare services. Research that has examined the impact of these reforms on regional health inequalities is summarised. In 1990 the life expectancy gap between the former East and the former West of Germany was almost three years for women and three and a half years for men. By 2010, this gap had disappeared for women and was around 18 months for men, showing the impact of improving living standards, integration into a fully functioning welfare state and democratic reforms on the health of the region.

Chapter 5 examines the impact on health inequalities of England's National Health Inequalities Strategy, which was enacted between 2000 and 2010. The strategy, led by a newly elected Labour government under Tony Blair, focused on supporting families, engaging communities in tackling deprivation, improving preventive health services, increasing access to healthcare and tackling the underlying social determinants of health. The chapter provides an overview of the health, social policy and inequalities context before and after the reforms. This chapter summarises research finding that these reforms led to reductions in health inequalities between the most deprived areas in England and the rest of the country.

Chapter 6 looks across the case studies and draws out four common levelling mechanisms for reducing health inequalities that are evident across time and space during periods of 'waxing' health equity: welfare state expansion, improved healthcare access, reduced income inequality and enhanced democratic participation. The chapter also examines evidence from across our case studies and beyond of what happens when the converse, 'waning', situation occurs – that is, the negative impact on health inequalities of fraying social safety nets, wider and increasing social and economic inequalities, limited healthcare access, high poverty, political alienation and a lack of labour rights.

The book concludes by arguing that reducing health inequalities is demonstrably feasible but requires strong political will to enact long-term, macro-level policies that aggressively target the social determinants of health in ways that have an equalising impact. Reflecting on the case studies presented, alongside theories developed to try to understand how and why political change occurs, we consider what is needed to build the political will required to reduce health inequalities in the future and how to get policymakers to act differently.

# 2

# The Great Society: social reform and health inequalities in the United States

In this chapter, we explore the programmes enacted in 1964–68 by US President Lyndon B. Johnson's administration as part of his 'Great Society' agenda. We show how these programmes, taken together, contributed to a more equal distribution of the social, economic and political determinants of health; improved the health of America's lower-income and non-White populations; and resulted in a reduction of health inequalities.

Soon after Johnson succeeded President John F. Kennedy, who had been assassinated in November of 1963, the new president announced his administration's intention to build a Great Society based on 'abundance and liberty for all' and 'an end to poverty and racial injustice' (Johnson, 1964a). The Johnson administration proposed, and the US Congress passed, a series of policies addressing poverty, malnutrition, substandard housing, lack of access to education and healthcare, unemployment, racial discrimination and barriers to political representation that affected previously excluded groups in American society. These policies touched the lives of working and non-working poor people living in both rural and urban areas, but most particularly in the areas where everyday racism against Black Americans was most entrenched.

This ambitious progressive legislative agenda was feasible because Johnson's Democratic Party had substantial majorities in both houses of Congress, which allowed for swift legislative action without significant Republican opposition. In addition, the ongoing movement for civil rights for Black Americans, which in 1964 enjoyed the support of many progressive White Americans, created a permissive environment for passing new and expanded social welfare initiatives. During this brief window of opportunity, implementation of a coherent, large-scale policy agenda led to a measurable reduction of health inequalities in the US, whether defined by SES (socio-economic status) or ethnicity.

## What came before: poverty and inequality in a land of plenty

To understand why the Johnson administration prioritised policies designed to reduce poverty and increase equality in America, we need to understand the immediate political and economic circumstances surrounding the passage of these policies. During the 1950s, the United States had experienced a period of dramatic economic growth and had the second highest per capita gross domestic product (GDP) in the world (World Bank, 2024). Yet almost one fifth of the population, and four in ten Black Americans, lived in poverty (Haveman et al, 2015).

In the early 1960s many poor families in the US, particularly racial minority families, were also undernourished and housed in poor conditions. Even more alarmingly, in a society grounded in ideals of equal opportunity, many citizens lacked access to the education, job prospects, medical care, and political voice that could allow them to partake fully in America's success in the future. Oral histories from this era (for example, Charlton et al, 2008) provide some sense of how such blatant inequalities contributed to the growing social pressure for change:

> In 1964, a racially mixed team of young organizers ... came to Indianola. ... 'My mother looked at them, she said, "you know, I've lived my whole life, worked all my life for nothing." ... She said, "It's time now for a change to come about, and it's time for y'all to take an active role in it." I said, "You mean that?" She said, "Yes, I do"'
>
> Cora Fleming went to the church meeting that night and spoke publicly to the crowd, which included a number of sharecroppers from the plantations that surrounded Indianola. She remembered:
>
> 'I said, "You've been working in the fields all your days. Now you're suffering for fifteen dollars a week. I'm working for the same thing. ... And what can you do with fifteen dollars? Nothing." Children in bare feet, hungry half the time, but that was the best they could do at that time. And a lot of people who were going to that meeting ... was scared, but they went anyway. Lost their jobs. My sister lost her job.' (Extract from Charlton et al, 2008)

When considered through the lens of the social, economic and political determinants of health, then, it is little surprise that inequalities in health status between the poor and the better-off, and between Black and White communities, were large as the 1960s dawned.

Health inequalities were particularly stark for children. For example, in 1960, in the poorest 5 per cent of counties in the US, an average of 38 children per 1000 died before their first birthday, while in the wealthiest counties, the rate was only 20 per 1000 (Turner et al, 2020, p 2). A total of 47 out of every 1000 infants born to Black women perished during their first year of life, while only 24 of 1000 White babies did (Almond et al, 2006). At the other end of the age spectrum, White men (women) could expect to live an average of 66 (73) years in 1960 America, while life expectancy for non-White men (women) was only 61 (66) (Highsmith, 2022, p 21).

These marked gaps in life expectancy and mortality are linked to broader patterns of inequalities in the distribution of the social, economic, and political determinants of health across class and ethnic groups in the 1950s and 1960s in the US. Income and poverty, nutrition, housing, education, employment, and access to healthcare and political rights all varied in ways that contributed to worse health among Americans of colour and those with lower incomes.

For example, while roughly 15 per cent of White families lived below the poverty line in 1960, an astonishing half of all households headed by persons of colour were poor as the 1960s dawned. Beginning in 1963, poverty in the US was measured in official statistics with reference to a basic food budget. By this measure, more than one in five Americans was not only poor at the start of the 1960s but also potentially hungry, with income insufficient to meet minimal nutritional needs alongside expenses for housing and transportation. Archival research into this era notes that investigations by a Senate Sub-Committee advised President Johnson, in April 1967, that they had 'heard testimony and observed, first-hand, conditions of malnutrition and widespread hunger in the Delta counties of Mississippi' (De Jong, 2005, p 397). This research goes on to describe how

> [D]octors sent by the Field Foundation to study the healthcare needs of rural poor children graphically described conditions resembling what some of them had seen in developing nations of Asia and Africa. 'We saw children whose nutritional and medical condition we can only describe as shocking,' they wrote. 'They are living under such primitive conditions that we found it hard to believe we were examining American children of the twentieth century. ... They are suffering from hunger and disease and directly or indirectly they are dying from them – which is exactly what "starvation" means.' (Extract from De Jong, 2005, p 397)

The results of a government survey on malnutrition carried out in ten states in 1968–70 found evidence of low weight-for-age and height-for-age, which went unreported due to a lack of standardised value for comparison at the time (Graham, 1985, p 120).

In addition to low incomes, many poor, Black and Latino families in the US had housing that was below the standards of a prosperous post-war society. In 1960, while only 12 per cent of White families lived in units without a private toilet, 31 per cent of Black families lacked basic in-home sanitation (Olsen and Ludwig, 2013, p 209). 'White flight' from urban centres meant that by the 1960s large numbers of non-White families were becoming concentrated in high-poverty areas that were segregated by race. Residential segregation was reinforced through policies and practices that made it difficult for non-White families to secure mortgage loans in majority White areas, while poor housing quality in minority neighbourhoods was reinforced via banking practices that resulted in underinvestment (Ellen and Steil, 2019, pp 11, 41). Racial inequalities in wealth were then exacerbated further as White owners bought up real estate in urban areas and rented it, at high prices, to Black tenants. An account by Dr Kenneth Clarke (cited In Taylor, 2012) summarises the situation: 'Exploiters come into the ghetto, from outside, bleed it dry, and leave it economically dependent on the larger society. ... [T]he white power structure has collaborated in the economic serfdom of Negros by its reluctance to give loans and insurance to Negro businesses' (Taylor, 2012, p 196).

One of the factors contributing to household poverty and inequality in the US at the start of the 1960s was a lack of employment. Despite a booming economy, according to a 1964 economic report discriminatory employment practices meant that the unemployment rate for non-Whites was double that for Whites (Johnson, 1964b). Moreover, farm and domestic workers, many of whom were Black, were not eligible for unemployment insurance benefits, leaving their families at risk of poverty should they become unemployed. Low unemployment insurance benefits meant that a lack of employment was an important cause of low income even among working-aged Whites, though: 1.6 million households with a White head who was unemployed for part of the year had total earnings under US$3000 (a bit less than half the median income of US$5660) (Bureau of the Census, 1964). A lack of employment for older people also left many senior-headed households in poverty: 65 per cent of households headed by a non-White male over age 65, and 75 per cent of those headed by a non-White female over age 65, had incomes under US$3000 (Bureau of the Census, 1964).

Primary and secondary education in the US is funded mainly through local property taxes. As a result of the segregation of minorities into lower-income neighbourhoods, school districts with majority–minority student populations also tended to have fewer resources, including textbooks and qualified teachers. In 1960, the US was, moreover, still in the process of trying to overcome a history of racially segregated schooling, which had been overturned in a ruling of the country's highest court in 1954 but was still prevalent. There is little doubt, then, that the education provided to White and racial minority children in the US in 1960 was often of markedly different quality. An oral history testimony provided by a high school principal, looking back on his time working in schools in North Carolina in the 1950s and 1960s, recounted how he felt some local managers, 'wanted to run the school systems as they would a plantation you know. You know, like give the slaves enough to survive on and don't provide them too much by way of elevating experiences or expanding their opportunities' (Mask, 1991). A student in the early 1960s recalled that:

> We didn't have textbooks of any kind. We held classes in the church. The white schools sent us their used textbooks just before they were ready to put them in the trash. Pages were torn out; they were old, worn, and so marked up that there wasn't any space to write our names.
> (Etta Joan Marks, cited in Foster, 1998, p xxxii)

The quantity of education received also differed markedly by race. According to the US Census department, the median school years completed in 1960 was 10.6 (11.1) for White males (females) but only 8.4 (8.9) for racial minority males (females) (United States Census Bureau, 1962). Accordingly, only 40 per cent of people of colour, versus 70 per cent of Whites, completed high school in 1964 (Johnson, 1964b). The segregated, unequal education system played a key role in the growing civil rights movement. One large-scale example of the growing push for change came in Mississippi in the summer of 1964, when 41 grassroots Freedom Schools were established by educators seeking to confront the vastly unequal conditions of White and minority students (Hale, 2011). Over 2000 middle and high school students attended, with classes focusing on Black history and literature, the history of the civil rights movement and (to strengthen students' democratic engagement) how to engage in non-violent protests and how local, state and national governments operated.

Along with education, access to healthcare is often seen as a guarantor of equal opportunity to live a full life. In early 1960s America, neither was equal. When it came to healthcare, there was no national government insurance against the costs of medical care, so patients were left to pay out-of-pocket for whatever care they received, or enrol in private insurance plans. By 1959 only two thirds of Americans had insurance to cover the costs of hospitalisation (Cohen et al, 2009). The one third of the population that was uninsured included many workers of colour employed in sectors such as agriculture and domestic service, where health insurance was rarely offered as an employment benefit. The cost of medical care, however, was not the only problem for minorities in need of health services. In 1960 hospitals and doctors were still legally allowed to turn away patients based on their race, a practice that was common in many southern states and northern cities (Smith, 1990). Even where hospitals were not formally segregated, it was common practice for White patients to be treated by White doctors in separate (usually better equipped) wards. A Black doctor practising in South Carolina and Georgia in the 1950s–60s recalled being isolated with Black patients, 'in somewhat second-rate black wards' and reflected that his White colleagues, 'didn't want me to treat white women' (Ranzy Weston, cited in Beardsley, 1986, p 384).

Legal segregation of education and healthcare were but two examples of a broader system of structural racism that grew out of the failed efforts at 'reconstruction' after the Civil War that ended slavery in the US. For roughly 20 years after the end of the Civil War in 1865, Black Americans gained voting rights and representation in state and national legislatures. However, by 1877 US political elites from the north and south agreed on an unwritten bargain that allowed southern states to reimpose restrictions on the social and political inclusion of Black Americans. Poll taxes, literacy tests, and felon disfranchisement laws were passed and maintained through the 1950s, such that as of 1956, the percentage of eligible Blacks who were registered to vote was as low as 5 per cent in Mississippi, and only 37 per cent in Texas, the southern state with the largest share of registered Black voters (Coleman, 2014, p 12). The Civil Rights Acts passed in 1957 and 1960 were intended to undermine efforts to restrict political participation by Blacks but 'had only minimal effect' according to Lyndon B. Johnson's Attorney General (quoted in Coleman, 2014, p 11). Only five US states had elected a Black member of Congress between the end of Reconstruction and the start of the War on Poverty, and there would not be a post-Reconstruction Black US senator until 1967. Meanwhile, working-class people (defined as employees on a farm, in an industrial setting, or in a union) commanded a small and clearly under-representative, but relatively stable, 2 per cent of US legislative seats for most of the 20th century (Carnes, 2012, p 7).

## The Great Society as a war on inequality

The Great Society proposed programmes that would target the root causes of poverty and of socio-economic and racial inequalities. These policies supported children growing up in poverty with nutrition and education programmes to ensure that their futures would not be permanently marked; provided job training and sheltered employment for young adults; increased pensions for the disabled and elderly; insured against the growing costs of medical care; and tore down racist rules that created unequal access to a range of societal and political institutions.

A tidal wave of legislation beginning in 1964 established the central programmes of the Great Society. The centrepiece of the War on Poverty was the 1964 Economic Opportunity Act, which created the Office of Economic Opportunity to oversee roughly 40 new and expanded anti-poverty programmes. Other major pieces of legislation during the period that had direct benefit for low-income individuals and families included the Food Stamp Act (1964); the Elementary and Secondary Education Act (1965); the Social Security Act (1965); the Housing and Urban Development Act (1965); and several upgrades to the federal minimum wage. Other significant legislative steps on the road to the Great Society came in the form of expansions of federal support for access to higher education via the Higher Education Facilities Act (1963) and Higher Education Act (1965); banning discriminatory practices in education, private and public services, and politics in the Civil Rights Act of 1964 and the Voting Rights Act of 1965; and a raft of consumer and environmental protection acts.

The major programmes introduced as part of the Great Society are summarised in Table 2.1. The programmes of the Great Society addressed many of the major downstream social determinants of health, including access to healthcare, nutrition, housing, education, income, and environmental quality. In addition, policies sought to make headway on some important structural determinants of health, such as labour market conditions and gender, racial and ethnic discrimination. Still other programmes aimed to make more equitable the distribution of key political determinants of health, such as constitutional rights, access to legal advice and representation, and voice in decisions about local priorities. A final array of policies targeting environmental and consumer product safety had the potential to impact health inequalities by reducing exposures to hazards that likely disproportionately affected lower-income people – although very few of these have been evaluated with those outcomes in mind.

## Outcomes of the Great Society

### The overall impact

At the aggregate level, spending on the War on Poverty programmes grew from $60 billion in 1965 to $185 billion in 1972 (both in 2024 dollars) (based on Haveman et al, 2015). This resulted in major reduction in poverty over the near term, especially for non-White families headed by men. Overall, the share of Americans in families with incomes below the Federal Poverty Line declined from 15.6 per cent in 1965 to 11.9 per cent in 1972, a drop of 3.7 percentage points. However, poverty fell by a whopping 16.3 (8.8) percentage points for minority males (females) (Haveman et al, 2015, p 600).

Almost a half million new units of housing were built for low- and moderate-income families during the Great Society, primary and secondary schools were finally desegregated (a decade after the Supreme Court's *Brown v. Board of Education* ruling), and the gap in earnings between White and minority workers began to close due to policies mandating non-discrimination in employment. Hospitals, too, were successfully desegregated, and health insurance coverage increased to nearly 100 per cent among the elderly. Low-income people enjoyed expanded access to healthcare through Community Health Centers (CHCs) and Medicaid, the public health insurance programme for poor families.

Great Society programmes also increased political participation and efficacy among minority citizens. The Voting Rights Act re-enfranchised

**Table 2.1:** Major programmes of the Great Society (1964–69)

| Determinant of health | Policy response | Policy purpose |
|---|---|---|
| Poverty | Equal Pay Act (1963) | Protected against wage discrimination on the basis of sex. |
| | Special Programmes to Combat Rural Poverty (Title III of Equal Opportunity Act [EOA]) (1964) | Provided federal guaranteed loans to low-income rural residents and local cooperatives for purchase of assets to permanently increase earning capacity. |
| | Income tax changes (1964, 1965) | Marginal tax rate for lowest tax bracket reduced. |
| | Amendments to 1935 Social Security Act (1965, 1967) | 1965: Made it easier to apply for disability and retirement benefits, increased cash benefits by 7%. 1967: Increased benefits by 13%, introduced minimum monthly benefit for a person retiring at or after age 65 (or receiving disability benefits). |
| | Amendment to 1938 Fair Labour Standards Act (1966) | Raised federal minimum wage and extended coverage to workers in public schools, nursing homes, laundries, construction and large farms. |
| Nutrition | Food Stamp Act (1964) | Made permanent a 1961 nutrition assistance programme. Food stamps allowed poor families (with eligibility set by state governments) to purchase food produced in the US at subsidised prices. |
| | Child Nutrition Act (1966) | Created federally funded School Breakfast Programme and allocated funding for expanded National School Lunch Programme, which were to provide nutritionally balanced, low-cost or free meals to eligible children each school day. Eligibility and funding were determined at the state level. |
| | Amendment to National School Lunch Act (1969) | Provided expanded funding to states conditional on guaranteeing free school lunches for any student whose family earned less than 125% of the federal poverty line. |
| Housing | Housing and Urban Development Act (1965) | Provided rent subsidies for low-income people, grants for low-income homeowners to rehabilitate their homes, grants to rehabilitate blighted urban property. Set goal of replacing all 'slum' housing by building 6M new dwellings for low- and moderate-income families. Provided federal funds to cities for urban renewal conditional on establishing minimum housing standards; provided easier access to home mortgages. |
| | Demonstration Cities Act (1966) | Established comprehensive neighbourhood renewal programme that emphasised housing renovation and neighbourhood facilities. |
| | Fair Housing Act (1968) | Banned racial discrimination in housing, subsidised construction and rehabilitation of low-income housing. |
| Education | Head Start Programme (1964) | Promoted school readiness of young children from low-income families by providing comprehensive early childhood education, health, nutrition, and parent involvement services. |

(continued)

**Table 2.1:** Major programmes of the Great Society (1964–69) (continued)

| Determinant of health | Policy response | Policy purpose |
|---|---|---|
| | Upward Bound (1964) | Provided enrichment programmes for poor students interested in attending college. |
| | Federal Work-Study Programme (1964) | Provided matching funds to subsidise employment for low-income college students. |
| | Elementary and Secondary Education Act (1964) | Title I Provided significant federal aid for public primary and secondary education, especially schools with a high concentration of low-income children. |
| | Higher Education Act (1965) | Created scholarships and low-interest loans for lower-income students, established national Teacher Corps to provide teachers in high-poverty areas. |
| Employment | Job Corps (1964) | Provided minimally paid full-time work and job skills training in a residential setting to low-income people aged 16–21 who had not completed high school. |
| | Neighbourhood Youth Corps (1964) | Provided paid part-time work for low-income people aged 16–22 to build skills and enable them to stay in school or return to school. |
| | Job Opportunities in the Business Sector (JOBS) Programme (1968) | Provided federal funding for job retraining and subsidised employment for long-term unemployed in 50 US cities. |
| Access to healthcare | Neighborhood Health Centers (1964) | Provided federal grants for hospitals, medical schools, community groups, and health departments to plan and administer free or low-cost health centres in low-income areas. |
| | Medicare (1965) | Part A: Covered costs of hospital care for the elderly. Mandatory, funded via payroll taxes. Part B: Covered doctor bills for the elderly via a voluntary insurance programme funded by individual premia. |
| | Medicaid (1965) | Provided federal money to states to create optional programme to cover healthcare costs for the blind, disabled, poor elderly people, children without support from their parents and those children's caretakers. |
| | Desegregation of hospitals (1966) | Hospital eligibility for Medicare payments required ending discriminatory practices. Johnson administration made clear that Title VI of 1964 Civil Rights Act barring federal spending on racially segregated facilities would apply to hospitals, and sent teams of federal employees to hospitals to ensure compliance. |
| Political representation | Community Action Programmes (CAP) (1964) | CAPs require 'maximum feasible participation' of the people who would be affected in making decisions about how federal funds would be spent in their community. |
| | Volunteers in Service to America (VISTA) (1964) | Employed middle-class people to work in poor areas to assist with community organizing and legal and social empowerment efforts. |

(continued)

**Table 2.1:** Major programmes of the Great Society (1964–69) (continued)

| Determinant of health | Policy response | Policy purpose |
|---|---|---|
| | Legal Services for the Poor (1964) | Provided federal funding via the EOA for legal services organisations that were required to include poor people on their boards of directors and have offices located in poor neighbourhoods. |
| | Civil Rights Act (1964) | Banned discrimination and segregation in elections, schools, the workplace, and public accommodations based on race, colour, sex, religion, and national origin. |
| | Voting Rights Act (1965) | Enacted to guarantee enforcement of the 14th and 15th Amendments by eliminating voter literacy tests and discriminatory practices that kept minority populations from voting. |
| | Immigration and Nationality Act (1965) | Ended immigration nationality quotas, creates preference system based on skills and family connections in the US (while maintaining limits on immigrants per country and total immigration). |
| | Indian Civil Rights Act (1968) | Extended many Constitutional protections to Native Americans on reservations. |
| Environment | Clean Air Act of (1963), Motor Vehicle Air Pollution Control Act (1965), Air Quality Act (1967) | Mandated that state develop plans to control air pollution, set automobile emissions standards, established federal government oversight of air quality. |
| | Water Quality Act 1965 | Set national water quality standards. |
| | Land and Water Conservation Fund Act (1965) | Provided matching funds for federal, state and local governments to purchase land and water to establish parks and recreation areas. |
| | Solid Waste Disposal Act (1965) | Established regulatory framework for control of solid waste disposal and minimum safety requirements for landfills. |
| | National Environmental Policy Act (1969) | Required federal government agencies to evaluate the environmental impacts of their actions and decisions. |
| Regulation of potentially health-harming products | Cigarette Labeling and Advertising Act (1965) | Required cigarette packages to display health warning labels. |
| | National Traffic and Motor Vehicle Safety Act (1966) | Empowered federal government to set safety standards for motor vehicles and road traffic safety. |
| | Wholesome Meat Act (1967), Wholesome Poultry Products Act (1968) | Required state meat and poultry safety standards to meet or exceed those of the federal food safety inspection service. |
| | Gun Control Act (1968) | Introduced strongest federal gun control legislation to date, regulating interstate commerce and transportation of guns across state lines. |
| | Public Health Cigarette Smoking Act (1969) | Required health warning labels in print advertising for cigarettes. |

the Black population, Legal Services Programmes provided direct legal aid and advocacy, and Community Action Programmes – including CHCs – harnessed local-level leadership and trained a new generation of leaders through their insistence on the mandated 'maximum feasible participation' (Rubin, 1969) of beneficiaries in the running of these programmes.

Laws put in place during the Great Society to regulate tobacco and automobile safety and to limit air and water pollution and protect green space did not have an immediate effect on Americans' exposure to commercial or environmental hazards, but they did set the stage for longer-term achievements in these areas.

How did all of these changes affect health inequalities? At the aggregate level, it is easy to see that something happened during the late 1960s and early 1970s in the US that substantially narrowed inequalities in health by both income and race, albeit temporarily. Since 1959, there has been a gradual increase in life expectancy in the US, with the fastest rate of improvement in the period 1969–79 (Woolf and Schoomaker, 2019, p 11). Infant mortality also dropped by nearly half between 1966 through 1981 (Singh and Yu, 1995, p 958). And while life expectancy and infant survival rates improved across the board, for a brief period in the late 1960s to early 1970s, they improved even faster for low-income people (Krieger et al, 2008; and Figure 2.1). The poorest counties in the US experienced exceptionally large gains in infant survival as compared to wealthier counties between 1960 and 1970 (Turner et al, 2020).

Racial gaps in mortality, particularly infant and maternal mortality, also closed substantially during the Great Society. In 1965, 4 per cent of Black infants in the United States died within one year of birth. By 1971, the mortality rate for Black infants had dropped to 2.8 per cent, with even

**Figure 2.1:** Premature mortality rates (deaths under age 65), United States, 1960–2002, by county median family income quintile

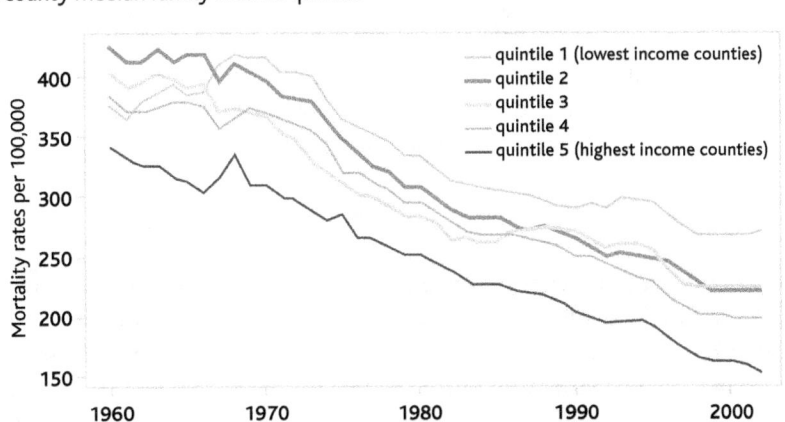

**Figure 2.2:** Premature mortality rates (deaths under age 65), United States, 1960–2002, by county median family income quintile for the US White population (dashed lines) and populations of colour (solid lines)

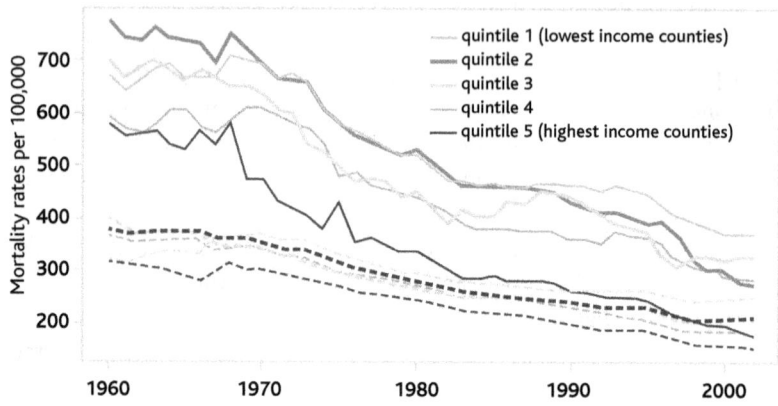

steeper declines in the deep south. Meanwhile, White infant mortality declined less steeply during the same time period, resulting in more than half of the gap in survival between White and Black babies being closed (Chay and Greenstone, 2000; Anderson et al, 2020). Between 1960 and 1980, the gap in mortality between Black and White Americans overall also shrank, driven by substantial mortality gains among Black women of child-bearing age (Satcher et al, 2005; see Figure 2.2).

It is not immediately obvious to what specific programmes, if any, we ought to attribute these narrowing health inequalities during and immediately following the Great Society. However, scholars have shown that cohorts of Black Americans who spent most of their childhood in the better conditions prompted by the Great Society had decreased chronic disease mortality relative to White Americans, as compared to earlier cohorts whose lifetime health was influenced by childhoods spent under Jim Crow (Masters et al, 2014). Anderson et al (2020) surmise that 'declining fertility among lower-income Blacks after passage of the Civil Rights Act of 1964, the economic progress made by Blacks throughout the 1960s, and the rollout of CHCs and Medicaid programmes' could be responsible.

### *Measuring the impact of specific Great Society policies on health*

Many new programmes were introduced in a short period of time during the Great Society, making it hard to determine which programme or programmes were effective, and which were not. Many Great Society programmes were universal, providing benefits to all people meeting certain eligibility criteria, which means that there is no 'control group' of similar individuals who did not receive the same benefits. Selection into or out of the 'treatment' of a programme is also an issue for making causal inferences, since few programmes mandated enrolments or provided benefits automatically. Many Great Society programmes might have had an impact on health equity had they been fully funded, but in reality they were underfunded or progressively de-funded and hence may have produced results too small to detect. Some programmes were never fully implemented; for example, the Fair Housing Act was undermined by nearly immediate Supreme Court decisions that made it difficult to enforce the Act's anti-discrimination provisions. Still other programmes had unintended negative consequences: For example, applying a minimum wage to previously excluded sectors depressed the labour force participation of Black men working in some low-wage jobs, even while it ultimately boosted the earnings of many Black women.

For all of these reasons, it is hard to know for certain how much, or indeed whether, any one specific Great Society programme had an effect on health equity. However, modern techniques of econometric analysis, which take advantage of moments when 'treatment' by individual policies was assigned essentially randomly to otherwise similar groups of individuals, allows us to understand a bit more than we otherwise might about the causal impact of Great Society programmes on the distribution of the determinants of health, and on health outcomes. We examined every study we could locate that identified an effect of a specific policy enacted during the Great Society period on either social determinants of health or on health outcomes. Our key takeaway from this body of research is that the expansion of healthcare access, although a good in itself, was not the main cause of most of the improvements in health equity brought about by the Great Society. Instead, concerted action on the social, economic and political determinants of health, through policy efforts aimed at reducing poverty, eliminating racial discrimination across multiple domains of society, and enhancing the political efficacy of previously marginalised low-income and minority populations in both urban and rural areas of the country, was likely responsible for the narrowing of health inequalities.

The expansion of anti-poverty programmes such as Aid to Families with Dependent Children (AFDC) and Social Security benefits during the Great Society had notable effects on household income, a key social determinant of health. Between 1965 and 1975, social benefits as a percentage of personal income increased from about 6 per cent to over 10 per cent (Haveman et al, 2015). The reduction of tax rates on lowest-income families also contributed to reduction in after-tax rates of poverty (Meyer and Sullivan, 2012). We found no studies examining health effects of these types of cash transfers during the Great Society period. However, a study of mothers in the late 1970s found that household income (but not participation in

AFDC per se) predicted higher infant birthweight of their infants (Currie and Cole, 1993).

Nutrition programmes, too, were expanded or enacted during the Great Society. Because they were rolled out at varying times during the period it is possible to get sharper estimates of the causal effects of programme participation on the distribution of social determinants of health such as nutrition, income and education. Expansion of Food Stamps and other nutritional supplements were found to have contributed to reduced poverty, increased spending on food, and economic self-sufficiency in later life (Almond et al, 2011; Hoynes et al, 2009; 2016). One study found that both employment and hours worked fell in concert with the roll-out of Food Stamps, suggesting that the programme may have allowed mothers to spend more time with children as a result (Hoynes and Schanzenbach, 2018). School breakfast and lunch programmes also increased food security among low-income families, with one study of such a programme in the early 2000s finding as much as a 20 per cent reduction in food insecurity (Huang et al, 2016). Evidence from the rollout of school breakfast and lunch programmes during the Great Society also suggests a positive impact on educational outcomes for children (Bitler and Karoly, 2015; Frisvold, 2015). Nutrition programmes appear to have had a long-term impact on the distribution of the social determinants of health, too. Without the Great Society era's expansion of food stamps and other nutrition programmes, estimates one study, the child poverty rate in 2010 would have been three percentage points higher (Olsen and Ludwig, 2013).

Because food insecurity is known to be associated with chronic disease (Seligman et al, 2010), it does not come as a surprise that nutrition programmes that increased access to food generally have been found to have a positive impact on health. Exposure to the newly expanded Food Stamp programme in the first trimester of a pregnancy led to increases in birth weight, with larger impacts at the bottom of the birth weight distribution, and reduced the incidence of low birth weight among those treated by 7 per cent for Whites and between 5 per cent and 11 per cent for Black mothers (Almond et al 2011). School meal programmes have been found to reduce obesity and other poor health outcomes (Bhattacharya et al, 2004; Gundersen et al, 2012). In the longer term, exposure to Food Stamps from birth to age five led in later life to a decreased incidence of obesity, high blood pressure and diabetes, all major causes or correlates of early death among US adults (Hoynes et al, 2016).

Housing is another social determinant of health that was the subject of numerous interventions during the Great Society. Here the effects of policies on health and health equity are, however, less clear. Housing quality and security are known to have important impacts on health (Acevedo-Garcia and Osypuk, 2006; Krieger and Jacobs, 2011; Bess et al, 2023), and living in a segregated neighbourhood is associated with worse health outcomes (Williams and Collins, 2001; Wang et al, 2022). Some of the housing programmes initiated during the Great Society did have a positive impact on housing quality, families' disposable income and employment, and housing segregation (Orfield, 2015; Abramovitz and Smith, 2021). However, the Fair Housing Act, arguably the period's signature policy in the housing area, was essentially dead on arrival. The Act had not been expected to pass at all, and once it did, its most progressive features were either limited to certain segments of the housing market or stripped out by US Supreme Court rulings (Orfield, 2015). In fact, one study evaluating policies of the period used housing policy as a key example to make the point that 'unless implemented, civil rights are promises without benefit' when it comes to reducing racial and ethnic inequalities in health (Hahn et al, 2018, p 23).

In the area of employment, the Great Society had a more substantial impact on the distribution of key social determinants of health: jobs, wages and earnings. Great Society-era job training programmes appear to have had a positive impact on the distribution of social determinants of health. Evaluations of the residential Job Corps programme have found substantial enough positive effects on education, employment and wages of graduates to justify the expense (Schochet et al, 2008; Holzer, 2013). However, a direct impact on health has not been established.

Pay disparities, including gender pay disparities, can contribute significantly to higher rates of depression and anxiety (Platt et al, 2016), underscoring the potential importance of equitable pay for mental health and well-being. The Equal Pay Act of 1963 reduced wage disparities and especially benefited Black women (Neumark, 2023). Prior to the act, in 1960, Black women earned only 66 per cent of what White women earned. However, by 1980, this figure had risen to 92 per cent (Satcher et al, 2005). Non-discrimination in employment, mandated by Title VII of the Civil Rights Act, led to a desegregation of the labour market in the US South. Black women began to enter pink and white-collar jobs, and Black men were able to move into higher-paid industrial and white-collar professions. Civil rights legislation in the 1960s thus led to a (temporary) narrowing of the wage gap between Black and White workers between 1965 and 1980 (Heckman and Payner, 1989; Donohue and Heckman, 1991; Card and Krueger, 1993). Whether this had a direct causal effect on the reduction in health inequalities between Black and White Americans during this period has not been studied.

The effects of minimum wage increases on health in general appear to be somewhat mixed (Neumark, 2023). The Fair Labour Standards Act (FLSA) of 1966, which increased the federal minimum wage and applied it to several sectors that were previously excluded from national-level legislation, also appears to have had a mixed impact on the social determinants of health.

It increased average wages by 6.5 per cent, and substantially narrowed the racial wage gap over a period of just a few years since the changes mainly affected Black workers (Bailey et al, 2021a; Derenoncourt and Montialoux, 2021). However, it also led to a reduction in employment and hours worked by Black men, as employers reduced hours due to the additional costs of the higher minimum wage (Bailey et al, 2021a). Despite these mixed results however, the one study that rigorously examined the causal impact of the FLSA on health found that it did contribute to reducing the racial infant mortality gap (Musen, 2023).

Education was one of the top priorities of the Great Society. The early education Head Start programme began as a local Community Action Program. Expanded quickly, although never funded at levels sufficient to meet actual need, Head Start participation improved children's test scores in the short run (Gibbs et al, 2013). A number of long-term programme evaluations have found that participation in the Head Start programme improved life chances for children in low-income families by reducing inequalities in the distribution of social determinants of health. The programme also contributed to participants' long-term educational achievement and earnings growth later in life (Gibbs et al, 2013). Head Start participation closed one third of the gap in a summary index of young adult outcomes between children with median and bottom quartile incomes (Deming, 2009), and scores on an index of adult human capital rose by 18 percent of a standard deviation among Head Start participants relative to children born in the same county who were ineligible because of age when the programme began (Bailey et al, 2021b). Participation in Head Start relative to other preschool environments also reduced the chances of later criminal legal system involvement by around 12 percentage points (Garces et al, 2002). While Head Start appears to have a robust impact on multiple important social determinants of health in childhood and later life, estimates of its direct health impact are scarce. The one study to date that has assessed health outcomes relative to Head Start participation found that compared to all non-participants, Head Start participants born in 2001 were less likely to be overweight than children in other forms of non-parental care (Lee et al, 2013).

The Elementary and Secondary Education Act (ESEA), particularly Title I, affected both educational equity and health equity in the United States. Despite the landmark Supreme Court ruling in Brown v. Board of Education in 1954, school segregation persisted with little change until the late 1960s, at which point substantial desegregation began and continued until the mid-1980s (Reardon and Owens, 2014). The federal government leveraged Title I funding to incentivise desegregation, particularly in Southern school districts during the 1960s (Cascio and Reber, 2013). The overall impact of Title I on student educational achievement has been modest. A 1996 meta-analysis reviewed 17 federal evaluations of Title I and found a small impact on educational attainment, but the effect grew as the programme matured (Borman and D'Agostino, 1996). While increases in federal funds sometimes led to corresponding declines in state and local funding (Bitler and Karoly, 2015), Title I did help narrow the spending gap between richer and poorer states, although it was insufficiently funded to eliminate the gap entirely (Cascio et al, 2013). Additionally, Title I funds were tied to improvements in educational opportunities for Black children. In turn, improved school quality for Black students contributed to about one-fifth of the reduction in the Black–White earnings gap between 1960 and 1980 (Card and Krueger, 1992).

Beyond its effects on education and income, both among the most important determinants of health, the ESEA also influenced the provision of health services for disadvantaged students. Title I programmes have addressed numerous health needs by expanding the use of school nurses and dental hygienists, increasing home visits, and enhancing access to psychologists and speech therapists (Ratchick, 1968).

The most substantial impacts on healthcare during the Great Society came from the implementation of the public, tax-funded Medicare and Medicaid health insurance programmes and the introduction of federally funded CHCs. Medicare created near universal eligibility for Americans aged 65+ for hospital and outpatient insurance. In 1963, two years before Medicare was enacted, about 56 per cent of persons 65 years of age and over had insurance for hospital care. With the implementation of Medicare in 1966, 98–99 per cent of the elderly population enrolled in hospital insurance coverage, and nearly all also enrolled in coverage for outpatient services (Gornick et al, 1996). This coverage increased hospital utilisation among the elderly population as a whole (Lubotsky et al, 2010), despite the fact that '[w]hen Medicare was passed into law, the average African American man did not live long enough to become eligible for Medicare' (Satcher et al, 2005, p 462). The implementation of Medicare also led to a rapid and thoroughgoing desegregation of hospitals. Of the more than 7000 hospitals certified as eligible to receive Medicare funds, only 214 Southern hospitals opted to remain racially segregated (Anderson et al, 2020, p 1).

The impact of Medicare introduction on health inequalities between income and racial/ethnic groups has not been well studied, likely because the universal nature of the programme meant that there was not a control group to which to compare Medicare beneficiaries. And because advances in medical treatment were occurring at the same time, it is impossible to attribute gains in mortality or life expectancy during this period to the programme's introduction. What we can say for sure is that by the 1980s large Black–White gaps in Medicare utilisation remained, despite effective desegregation of hospitals, and the federal government was far less vigilant about desegregating nursing homes than hospitals (Gornick, 2000; Yearby et al, 2022). Hospital desegregation, initially thought to have had a large effect on neonatal mortality among Black infants in the South, was later found not to have produced a measurable effect after controlling appropriately for period effects (Almond et al, 2006; Anderson et al, 2020).

Medicaid, unlike Medicare, was not a universal entitlement but instead limited eligibility to low-income families and gave state governments wide discretion over setting other restrictions. This allowed states to limit eligibility in ways that kept racial minority groups from qualifying (Yearby et al, 2022). Even so, the introduction of Medicaid appears to have had positive consequences for access to healthcare and healthcare utilisation (Goodman-Bacon, 2018; Currie and Duque, 2019). One study even found improved labour market outcomes later in life for cohorts that were exposed to Medicaid during childhood (Goodman-Bacon, 2021). Because states chose when to implement Medicaid (all states except Arizona did so between 1966 and 1972), it has been possible to estimate the effects of the programme on health by leveraging temporal variation. Studies of Medicaid rollout have found that the introduction of the programme in a state improved birth outcomes (particularly for racial minorities) and reduced childhood mortality (Goodman-Bacon, 2018; Noghanibehambari, 2022). It also had a positive impact on health in later life: adult disability, high blood pressure, diabetes, heart disease and obesity were all lower among those exposed to Medicaid in childhood (Boudreaux et al, 2016; Goodman-Bacon, 2021).

Access to low-cost or free healthcare at federally funded CHCs, was, like Medicaid, a limited rather than universal entitlement. Only some Community Action Programmes chose to implement CHCs, such that after the first decade of the programme's existence, CHCs existed in only 117 out of the roughly 3000 counties in the US. However, unlike Medicaid, CHCs did more than provide medical care: they were also attentive to social and structural causes of health, and created jobs in the communities they served (Chowkwanyun, 2018). A study of the rollout of CHCs from 1965 to 1977 found marked effects on age-adjusted mortality rates in counties with CHCs, driven by reductions in death from cardiovascular disease among adults aged 50 and over (Bailey and Goodman-Bacon, 2015). Notably, while these positive effects were concentrated among people eligible for Medicare, there was no increase in Medicare enrolment or spending at the county level during this time period, suggesting that the declines in mortality were attributable to the presence of a CHC rather than access to services covered under Medicare. Adding to the credibility of this attribution, older, poor adults were more likely to report having both a regular source of healthcare and lower out-of-pocket spending on medications in areas with a CHC (most CHCs had their own subsidised pharmacies). In a less robust design, CHCs were found to have an impact on infant mortality, with stronger effects on Black than on White infant mortality from 1970 to 1978.

In sum, by the 1970s the combination of Medicare, Medicaid, and CHCs had led to a substantial reduction in Black–White disparities in healthcare utilisation and healthcare spending (Dickman et al, 2022). There is no evidence, however, for a direct effect of Medicare introduction on health equity, while Medicaid and CHCs appear to have contributed in a rather minor way to a narrowing of both income- and race-related health inequalities. But if the direct impacts on health of improved equity in healthcare provision during the Great Society were small, the effects of changes in the political sphere were substantial.

We have described previously some of the effects of the 1964 Civil Rights Act and the end of Jim Crow-era segregation on social determinants of health. The Voting Rights Act, too, not only expanded the political participation and representation of Black Americans (Chapa, 2015; Bernini et al, 2023); it also resulted in a more equal distribution of many social determinants of health. For example, counties where voting rights were more strongly protected experienced larger reductions in the Black–White wage gap between 1950 and 1980, a result of both expanded public sector employment among Black workers and of more aggressive enforcement of affirmative action and anti-discrimination laws (Aneja and Avenancio-Leon, 2019). Overall, analysts have concluded that the Voting Rights Act resulted in improved labour market and social outcomes for Black Americans above and beyond what would have occurred only as a result of anti-discrimination legislation (Donohue and Heckman, 1991). In other words, political participation had a direct effect on the distribution of social determinants of health. The value placed on 'maximum feasible participation' of participants in programmes sponsored by the Office of Economic Opportunity also led to enhanced political voice and efficacy. For example, evaluations from the first ten years of the VISTA programme showed that it was successful in enhancing efficacy and self-sufficiency in communities where the programmes took place (Corporation for National & Community Service Office of Research & Evaluation, 2018).

The political changes brought about by the Great Society appear also to have had measurable effects on health equity. Some of this impact is likely mediated by changes in the distribution of social determinants of health, but political changes may have more direct effects as well. Experiencing discrimination and disempowerment can lead to poor health outcomes (Williams et al, 2019; Morey et al, 2021), while civic and political participation may also lead directly to better health (McSorley et al, 2023; US Department of Health and Human Services, 2024). Several studies link the narrowing of Black–White gaps in infant mortality to the end of Jim Crow segregation (Krieger et al, 2014, 2013) and to federal intervention in support of voting rights after passage of the Voting Rights Act (Rushovich et al, 2024).

## Conclusion

While it is complicated to identify the exact pathways and mechanisms linking the Great Society to improvements in health equity, something clearly happened to reduce health inequalities by both and race during the period of greatest effort. The Great Society was linked to a significant, albeit temporary, narrowing of income-related and racial/ethnic disparities in health outcomes due to a combination of policy efforts aimed at reducing poverty, eliminating racial segregation and discrimination across multiple domains of society, and enhancing the political voice and efficacy of previously marginalised low-income and minority populations. It is likely that the policy package as a whole – which demonstrated that the American polity was serious about inclusion and equality – had an effect that was greater than the sum of its parts. One thing that is clear is that expansion of healthcare access, although a good in itself, was likely not responsible for most of the improvements in health equity that sprang from the Great Society.

By the mid-1970s, the Great Society initiative had come to an end. This was caused by a combination of a sharp, economy-wide economic recession caused by rapidly rising oil prices, White backlash against the increased participation and voice by racial and ethnic minorities (which included a wave of protests in urban areas beginning in the late 1960s), and the rise of neoliberal policy approaches among the US political establishment on both the left and right (Berman 2022). The result was a rollback of many of the programmes implemented during the Great Society, and an end to the brief narrowing of health inequalities in the US. The country would not see another similar effort to bridge health gaps until the early 2020s, when the COVID-19 pandemic sparked another quite effective, but even more short-lived, set of initiatives to reduce health inequalities.

# 3

# Vote early, vote often: democratisation in Brazil and health inequalities

This chapter explores how an era of democratisation in Brazil impacted on health inequalities. Between 1985 and the early 2000s, Brazil underwent a gradual transition from a military dictatorship, which had ruled from 1964 to 1984, to a relatively stable democracy. The increased political participation that democracy brought was accompanied by an expansion of health, welfare, employment and anti-poverty policies which, collectively, helped distribute resources more equitably across the population. This enabled Brazil – which had, under military dictatorship, become one of the most unequal countries in the world – to successfully reduce economic and health inequalities. Although there were gaps and limitations in Brazil's democratic transformation, the mixture of policies introduced as part of the transition proved remarkably effective at simultaneously improving population health and reducing health inequalities.

The chapter begins by briefly outlining Brazil's intersecting inequalities. The next section considers what life was like in Brazil during the 1964–84 military dictatorship, delving into some of the issues that led to Brazil becoming an extreme example of socio-economic inequality. We show how these inequalities underpinned increasingly widespread social movements that worked to challenge the military regime and push for a return to democracy. In this section, we cite some of the research that documents health improvements. The way in which policies were rolled out – often simultaneously and at a large, sometimes universal, scale – means that it has been difficult for researchers to identify the specific contributions of particular policies. However, the available evidence suggests that, collectively, the policies implemented in Brazil's new democratic era, especially in the 2000s, have been associated with significant improvements in maternal and child health outcomes and in life expectancy. Moreover, recent data suggest that Brazil also managed to achieve a reduction in health inequalities. These combined successes make Brazil a particularly interesting case study, since population level health improvements are often associated with increases in health inequalities as the health of better-off groups improves more rapidly. The aim of the remaining sections is to explore how Brazil managed to simultaneously improve population health and reduce health inequalities.

The chapter goes on to document the major policy changes introduced after 1985, particularly during the first presidency of Luiz Inácio Lula da Silva, and consider how these reshaped social, economic and commercial determinants of health. The penultimate section considers what might explain the intersecting pathways connecting democratic politics to population health improvements. The conclusion summarises what the Brazilian case can teach us about tackling health inequalities, highlighting the centrality of democracy to Brazil's achievements. In the context of a subsequent shift to a populist, right-wing presidency, with the 2019 election of Jair Bolsonaro as president, and an associated increase in socio-economic inequalities, the conclusion also briefly considers some of the limitations of, and challenges to, Brazil's social reforms. Arguably, these factors contributed to declining popular support for Brazil's progressive, pro-poor policies in the late 2010s, paving the way for Bolsonaro's election. These limitations are explored further in Chapter 6.

## Brazil's intersecting health inequalities

Like many countries, Brazil has significant, intersecting health inequalities. The wealthier southern states typically perform better across a wide range of health indicators, while the poorer, more rural, northern states tend to have worse health outcomes (see Figure 3.1 for a map of Brazil's states and regions). In 2022, of Brazil's 27 sub-national districts, the state of Santa Catarina (in the centre of Brazil's Southern region) had the highest life expectancy (at 82.51 years), while Piauí, in the Northeast, had the lowest life expectancy (at 74.00 years) – a gap of 8.51 years. Infant mortality rates followed a similar pattern: Espirito Santo, in south-eastern Brazil, had the lowest rates (at 5.4 infant deaths per 1000 live births), while rates in Amapá in the north of Brazil were nearly four times higher (at 20.37 infant deaths per 1000 live births).

Intersecting with these regional inequalities, Brazil also has marked economic and ethnic inequalities. World Bank data show the Gini coefficient, a widely used measure of income inequality,[1] rose from 0.53 in 1960 to 0.61 in 1972, making Brazil one of the most unequal countries in the world during the military dictatorship. By 2024, Brazil's Gini coefficient had declined to 0.53. While this still marked Brazil as the ninth most unequal country in the world, this was a substantial reduction in income inequalities, most of which was achieved in the 1988–2014 period.

Despite lessening economic inequality, the country's history of colonialism and slavery continues to cast a long shadow for Brazil's Indigenous populations, whose communities were decimated by colonisers, and for those descended from people who were enslaved. Brazil was the last country in the Americas to outlaw slavery, in 1888, and in the 1880s the Brazilian slave

**Figure 3.1:** The Regions and Federative Units of Brazil

population was about 1 million – in a country with just over 3.5 million people (Palma et al, 2021). Both Indigenous people and those descended from people who were enslaved currently experience higher infant mortality and maternal mortality rates, and a higher chronic disease burden, yet often face barriers in accessing healthcare services (Santos et al, 2022).

In sum, Brazil has multiple, often stark, intersecting social and economic inequalities that reflect the country's historical legacy and help to explain the country's significant contemporary health inequalities. As we will see, many of the policies pursued by the military dictatorship, in power 1964–85, reinforced and exacerbated these historical inequalities.

## The 1964 coup and unequal economic gains under military dictatorship

In 1964, in a context of social unrest and economic crisis, a military coup ended the Fourth Brazilian Republic (1946–64) and commenced a 20-year period of military dictatorship (1964–85). The coup was quick; in the early hours of 31 March 1964, General Olímpio Mourão Filho ordered a military advance on Rio de Janeiro, where democratically elected President João Goulart was visiting. The next day, Goulart returned to Brasilia before beginning a 14-year period of exile in Uruguay. The speed with which the coup succeeded reflected initial support from the military, many politicians, businesses, religious and civil society organisations and, crucially, the USA. It followed claims that the president's planned programme of progressive reforms to tackle Brazil's social and economic inequalities risked enabling a communist revolution (Chiro, 2018). However, rather than handing power to their political allies on the right, as had been expected, the military remained in power.

This period of military dictatorship was characterised by political and social repression, censorship and human rights abuses. Although the military regime kept up a pretence of democracy, with elections and a rotating system of presidents, they threatened and even closed Congress if it did not reflect the military regime's interests. The government imposed strict censorship on the media, arts and education. Political opponents, activists, trade unionists and intellectuals faced surveillance, arrest, torture and exile. Brazil's subsequent *Comissão Nacional da Verdade* (National Truth Commission) report, presented in 2014, details the state torture, state-sponsored sexual violence and murder, and the 'disappearing' of bodies that occurred under the dictatorship.

While the military regime focused on maintaining political power, control of economic policy was largely entrusted to technocrats, who pursued a programme of export-driven growth and urbanisation. Real GDP per capita increased an average of 4.6 per cent per year between 1960 and 1980 (Ayers et al, 2019). However, this astonishing growth was unequally distributed. World Bank data show the Gini coefficient rose from 0.53 in 1960 to 0.61 in 1972, making Brazil one of the most unequal countries in the world in the 1970s. Moreover, macroeconomic instability was recurrent, with a deep recession in the early 1960s and growing national debts following the 1973 oil crisis (Ayers et al, 2019).

By the early 1970s, researchers were already questioning the reality of Brazil's so-called 'economic miracle': 'There now seems to be agreement that the income distribution did worsen during the 1960s. The picture is not a pretty one. Every decile of the population except the first experienced a relative decline in income' (Fishlow, 1973).

At the same time, large-scale rural–urban migration and a political decision to prioritise infrastructure, especially road-building, over housing (Martine and McGranahan, 2012), created severe housing shortages and contributed to the growth of make-shift urban housing developments, known as *favelas* (Amaral De Sampaio, 1994). The legacy of extensive poor-quality urban housing, and the highly unequal nature of housing, remains evident in Brazil today (Martine and McGranahan, 2012).

The focus on national economic development and infrastructure involved internal colonisation of Brazil's rural areas (Perz et al, 2007). The Amazon rainforest was framed as an important resource for the regime's economic development, which resulted in large-scale occupation, including the building of hydro-electric dams, re-purposing of land for farming (including cattle ranches), timber extraction, new mines and roads (Fearnside, 1984; Haller et al, 1996; Perz et al, 2007). As a consequence, tens of thousands of Indigenous people lost their lands and their lives, and dozens of tribes were obliterated. In 1967, an official report (not publicly released at the time) documented the many crimes perpetrated against Indigenous people in Brazil in this period, including individual and collective murder, forced prostitution, slave labour, alienation, confinement and land removal (Sant'Anna et al, 2018). Many of the surviving Indigenous people moved to peripheral urban areas in search of work and affordable housing (Martine and McGranahan, 2012).

The jobs available in urban areas were often poor quality and had negative health impacts. Political authoritarianism was mirrored in workplace conditions for many Brazilians. Manufacturing jobs in poorly regulated factories tended to have inadequate health and safety standards: over 1.3 million work accidents were officially registered in the country in 1971 (Fontes and de Macedo, 2013). This contributed to growing dissatisfaction among the working classes and laid the foundations for a social uprising that played a major role in ending Brazil's military dictatorship. In 1978, metalworkers in São Bernardo do Campo folded their arms in front of their machines and refused to work, breaking the 'decade of silence imposed by force on the Brazilian working class' (Fontes and de Macedo, 2013, p 99) and paving the way for thousands of subsequent strikes across the country.

While small examples of workplace resistance occurred throughout military rule, the strikes of 1978–80 were far greater in scale and visibility, attracting broad support from other social sectors favouring democratisation (Fontes and de Macedo, 2013). Alongside workplace resistance, a strong ecological and social justice movement was arising, several strands of which were headed by Indigenous community leaders (Garfield, 2001). Supported by an arm of the Catholic church, representatives from different Indigenous communities came together for annual meetings that built awareness of shared experiences of abuse and theft of land by private entities headed by White Brazilians. In 1980, an Indigenous youth movement, *União das Nações Indígenas*, was established and, over time, these two groups came together as a Union of Indian Nations (Rita, 2010). During its 12-year existence, the Union forged links with other social movements and non-governmental organisations (NGOs) to challenge the military government and the treatment of Indigenous populations (Rita, 2010).

In short, the authoritarian military dictatorship left Brazil with 'strong hierarchies of gender, race, and class, which sustained enormous and persistent social and political inequalities', combined with 'a strong repressive apparatus capable of promoting serious human rights violations and perpetuating inequalities, both territorial and racial in nature' (Rios, 2020, p 26). Despite the risks, a multitude of politicised groups emerged in the late 1970s and early 1980s, reflecting diverse social and economic interests such as workers' rights, constitutional land rights and the rights of historically stigmatised groups, including Indigenous communities and the descendants of people who had been enslaved. While they had disparate interests, these groups were united by a desire to end the military dictatorship and return Brazil to democracy (Garfield, 2001; Rios, 2020).

Multi-faceted social resistance paved the way for Brazil's re-democratisation. Luiz Inácio Lula da Silva, who would go on to become President of Brazil, played a key role in this organised resistance, leading a series of strikes in his then role as President of a Steel Workers' Union. In January 1985, after more than two decades of military rule, Tancredo Neves was elected as president. Neves died in April 1985 before taking office, so the vice president, José Sarney, assumed the presidency. This marked the official end of the military regime and the beginning of the New Republic, a return to civilian rule and democratic governance. The democratic transition was solidified with the adoption of a new constitution in 1988, which established the framework for Brazil's current political system, guaranteeing civil liberties, political rights and the separation of powers. The first direct presidential election in over 30 years was held in 1989, resulting in the election of Fernando Collor de Mello as President.

## Brazil's transition to democracy: a health 'miracle'?

Brazil's 1988 Constitution established that:

> Health is a right to be enjoyed by all and a duty of the State; it shall be guaranteed by economic and social policies that aim to reduce the risk of disease and other maladies and by universal and equal access to all activities and services for its promotion, protection, and recovery.
> (Article 196)

Since 1989, multiple social, health and economic policies have been introduced that aim to realise the ambitions of Brazil's new constitution and tackle the widespread social and economic inequalities. These policies enabled Brazil to simultaneously improve average population health outcomes and reduce health inequalities. For example, the Brazilian IMR has decreased from 69.2 deaths per 1000 live births in 1990 to 16 deaths per 1000 live births in 2010 (Coelho and Dias, 2019). By 2022, this had reduced further to 11 deaths per 1000 live births. Life expectancy also increased nationally from 62.5 years in 1980 to 76.8 years in 2024. These overall improvements in population health were accompanied by decreases in health inequalities. For example, longstanding inequalities in in infant mortality between Brazil's five regions decreased between 1990 and 2015: in 1990 the IMR was 2.7 times higher in the poorest Northeast region than in the highest income South region, but by 2015 this had fallen to 1.4 times (Szwarcwald et al, 2020) (see Figure 3.2). Reduction in inequalities is also visible at the municipal scale: the IMR gap between the lowest and highest income municipalities had narrowed from 2.7 times higher in 1991 to 2.1 times by 2010 (Coelho and Dias, 2019) (Figure 3.3).[2] Similar improvements in inequalities occurred in overall life expectancy, at the regional as well as municipal scale (Coelho and Dias, 2019) (Figure 3.4).

At the same time, Brazil managed to reduce inequalities in health between regions (Arretche, 2016; Boing et al, 2019), and between poorer and richer segments of the population (Szwarcwald et al, 2020). For example, Boing et al's (2019, p 713) analysis of data from the last three national censuses (1991, 2000 and 2010), computed for the 5565 Brazilian municipalities, finds 'a remarkable decrease in regional and socioeconomic inequality' in life expectancy between 1991 and 2010: While there was a gain of around seven years of life in the richest municipalities, the gain was around 12 years in the poorest municipalities. Similarly, Szwarcwald and colleagues' (2020) analysis of infant mortality data finds a marked decrease in inequalities in infant mortality rates when comparing municipalities, regions and income deciles.

## Social, economic and health policy change under democracy

The following sections outline five key policy areas that research suggests have played an important role in improving population health and reducing health inequalities in Brazil. After this, the chapter briefly considers areas of policy where efforts to address inequalities have been less successful, before summarising evidence of the overarching impacts that this mixture of policies has had on health and health inequalities.

### *Introducing a right to health*

Brazil's 1988 constitutional commitment to the 'right to health' directly informed the creation, two years later, of the *Sistema Único de Saúde (SUS)*, Brazil's unified health system. This largely tax-funded health system aims to provide comprehensive healthcare services for everyone in Brazil, regardless of their socio-economic status, ethnicity, gender, income or employment. It is the largest government-run public healthcare system in the world, and covers preventative health services (for example, vaccinations campaigns and health education), primary care

**Figure 3.2:** Infant mortality rate (per 1000 live births) across five regions of Brazil, 1990–2015

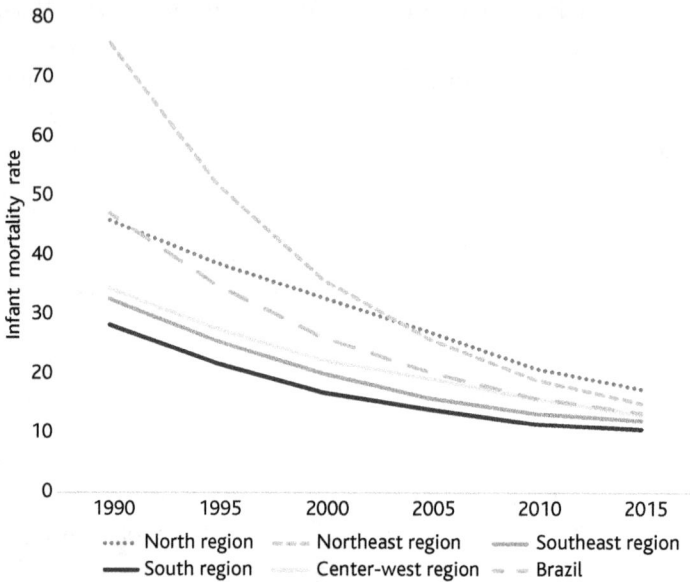

Source: Drawn using data from Landmann-Szwarcwald et al (2020).

**Figure 3.3:** Infant mortality rate (per 1000 live births) across the municipalities of Brazil, ranked by income quartile, 1991–2010

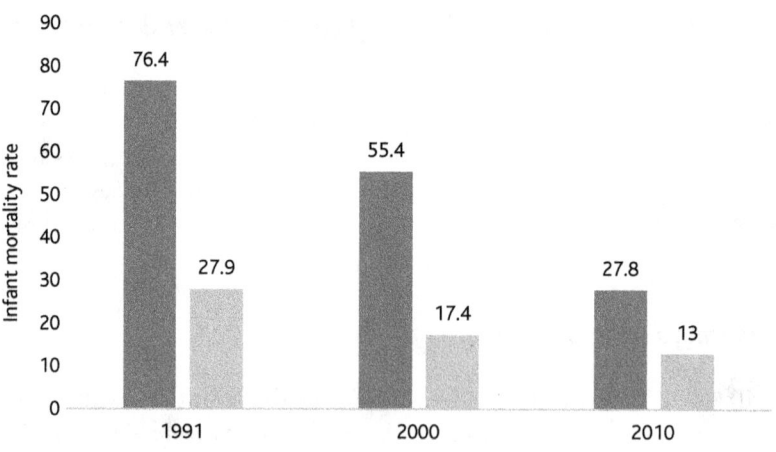

Source: Drawn using data from Coelho and Dias (2019).

**Figure 3.4:** Life expectancy at birth (years) across the municipalities of Brazil, ranked by income quartile, 1991–2010

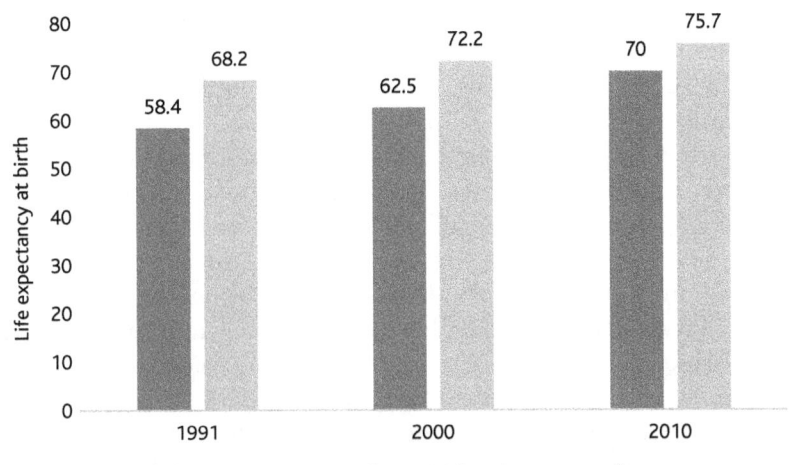

■ Lowest income quartile  ■ Highest income quartile

Source: Drawn using data from Coelho and Dias (2019).

(with particularly significant investments in family health programmes and maternal and child health), secondary and tertiary care (specialised medical services and hospital care, including emergency care) and support for accessing essential medicines. While responsibility for achieving the constitution's 'right to health' sits at federal level, a regionalised system enables the health system to be adapted to suit local population needs. There is also some civil society and public involvement, via health councils and conferences, as we discuss later.

Thirty-five years of Brazil's unified health system have created significant gains. From 2000 to 2014, total health expenditure rose from 7.0 per cent to 8.3 per cent of GDP; population healthcare coverage increased from 7.6 per cent to 58.2 per cent; vaccination rates increased substantially (against tuberculosis, from 79 per cent in 1990 to 99 per cent in 2015, measles from 78 per cent to 96 per cent, and polio from 58 per cent to 98 per cent, all in the same period); and the population eligible for free medications expanded from 27.2 per cent in 1998 to 46 per cent in 2008 (Ortega and Pele, 2023). As we have seen, health outcomes improved dramatically, and inequalities decreased, in the period since the SUS was established. There is evidence that the expansion of healthcare funding and coverage contributed to these health improvements. For example, Macinko et al (2006) found that the Family Health Programme of primary care (*Programa Saude da Famiia* or PSF) was associated with declines in infant mortality, even when controlling for other factors such as access to clean water and hospital beds per 1000: a 10 per cent increase in Family Health Programme coverage was associated with a 4.5 per cent decrease in IMR. The impact of the programme was also more pronounced in the lower income North and Northeast regions (Macinko et al, 2006).

Brazil's constitutional commitment to health as a right also enabled the country to successfully confront and resolve global barriers to accessing anti-retroviral drugs (ARVs) for the treatment of HIV/AIDS (Lee et al, 2010), earning Brazil worldwide respect among public health advocates (see, for example, Galvão, 2005). Supported by pharmaceutical companies and the government of the USA, the Agreement on Trade-Related Aspects of Intellectual Property Rights (TRIPS) made ARVs and other drugs unaffordable in low-income countries. Brazil developed a multifaceted response, combining investments in local pharmaceutical production with public reframing of the spread of HIV/AIDS as a public health emergency. This enabled use of a TRIPS clause that allowed generic versions of some patented medicines to be manufactured and imported under certain conditions. Brazil also actively participated in international forums to advocate for the rights of countries to access essential medicines, and contributed to the 2001 Doha Declaration on the TRIPS Agreement and Public Health, which affirmed the right of World Trade Organization members to protect public health and promote access to medicines for all. This enabled Brazil to become the first country not classed as 'high income' to offer free ARV treatment to HIV/AIDS patients, which led to a dramatic decline in AIDS-related morbidity and mortality (Lee et al, 2010).

## Pro-poor cash transfer programmes linked to health and education

Under the leadership of Fernando Henrique Cardoso (1995–2002) and the first presidency of Luiz Inácio Lula da Silva (2003–11), Brazil adopted a large-scale programme of pro-poor cash transfers. The first, flagship policy was the *Bolsa Escola* (School Grant), which provided a monthly payment to low-income parents of school-aged children, with the aim of bringing the family up to the minimum standard of living, on the condition that their children attend school. The *Bolsa Escola* was piloted in the district of Paranoá in 1995 and, following positive performance, was gradually extended to cover the whole of Brazil (Buarque, 2001).

By the end of 2003, the scheme had been implemented in almost all of the country's 5561 municipalities and had distributed almost US$500 million in grants to over 5 million families, reaching 8.6 million children (Buarque, 2001). An early World Bank assessment of the *Bolsa Escola* programme concluded that it was successful in helping to achieve improvements in education and poverty, and was having an equalising impact for those who could access it, though it raised concerns about the extent to which residency requirements were excluding the poorest families (World Bank Group, 2001). Other countries in the region followed suit and, in May 2001, UN Trade and Development were promoting it as a key poverty eradication programme.

In 2003, Lula became Brazil's first president to bring personal experience of growing up in poverty. At his inauguration, Lula attracted international attention for his pledge to end hunger: 'If, by the end of my term of office, every Brazilian has food to eat three times a day, I shall have fulfilled my mission in life' (Bellos, 2002). His administration's initial attempt to consolidate the *Bolsa Escola* with other social safety net programmes targeting nutrition, cooking gas costs and child labour was called *Fome Zero* (Zero Hunger) (Hall, 2006). However, after a series of targeting and implementation problems, in October 2003, the newly labelled *Bolsa Família* programme was launched to bring about deeper cross-programme alignment (Hall, 2006).

Under *Bolsa Família*, 'very poor' households were initially awarded a fixed monthly stipend of US$23 per month and were eligible for additional, variable payments based on family composition; while 'poor' households (initially categorised as those earning between R$51–120 per month) were eligible only for variable payments (Hall, 2006). To receive these cash transfers, families had to provide proof that their children were attending school and health checks regularly and receiving vaccinations; while pregnant and nursing women were required to follow specific public health guidelines. The aims were to provide immediate relief from extreme poverty and to help achieve improved health and education outcomes, with a view to breaking the intergenerational cycle of poverty. Although municipalities are the main providers of public services in Brazil, centrally set requirements (for example, the eligibility criteria for *Bolsa Família*) aim to ensure that local decision-making does not inadvertently widen regional inequalities, while federal fiscal transfers to poorer areas are explicitly used to help reduce regional inequalities (Arretche, 2016).

In March 2023, 21.1 million families received an average of US$127, the highest *Bolsa Família* value ever. Although funded predominantly via taxation, the scheme quickly attracted additional financial support from other sources, including private companies, the International Monetary Fund (IMF), the World Bank and the International American Development Bank. Evaluations of *Bolsa Família* have been broadly positive, crediting the programme with significant reductions in poverty and income inequality and improvements in education outcomes (Soares et al, 2010) and healthcare access (Shei et al, 2014). This has also translated into better health for recipients, with evaluations noting improved nutritional status and less malnutrition, reduced infant mortality and mortality from cardiovascular disease, better engagement and access to health services for children, and lower tuberculosis incidence (Rasella et al, 2013; Shei et al, 2014; Nery et al, 2017). An evaluation by Rasella et al (2013) found that the under five mortality rate – particularly that resulting from malnutrition and diarrhoea – decreased as *Bolsa Família* coverage increased. Similarly, analysis of data from the 100 Million Brazilian Cohort, comparing mortality rates among adults who received *Bolsa Família* with those who did not (Pescarini et al, 2022), found that *Bolsa Família* receipt was associated with reductions in premature all-cause mortality and cardiovascular disease mortality. This study also found that *Bolsa Família* receipt was consistently associated with mortality reductions for people living in the lowest income municipalities (Pescarini et al, 2022).

## *Employment expansion and minimum wage increases*

Although a minimum wage policy has been in place in Brazil since 1940, the real value has fluctuated substantially over time (Barbosa de Melo, 2015). Lula's administration initially only implemented small increases in the minimum wage, but 2004–09 national campaigns by trade unions resulted in more substantial increases (Barbosa de Melo, 2015). At the end of 2006, an agreement between the unions and the government led to a policy to regularly increase Brazil's minimum wage (Barbosa de Melo, 2015). Although this agreement only became law in 2011, Lula's administration implemented increases that aligned with the new agreement from 2006 onwards (Barbosa de Melo, 2015). The impacts were significant: 40–55 per cent of the decline in inequality in household incomes in 1995–2012 has been attributed to changes in labour earnings (Ferreira et al, 2016). Earlier analysis focusing on the impact of the minimum wage on the reduction in income inequality between 1995 and 2005 found that 64 per cent of the improvement at the household level was due to increases in the minimum wage (Saboia, 2007). Hence, the 2004+ increases in Brazil's minimum wage were a crucial policy development that contributed to greater economic equality.

Since the minimum wage is not always applied in the informal sector, it is also important to note the decline of the proportion of workers employed informally in this period, which fell 13 percentage points in a decade (from 57.39 per cent in 2002 to 44.38 per cent in 2012) (Romanello, 2017). Brazil achieved this shift from informal to formal employment through three key policy changes (Berg, 2010; Cardoso, 2007): (1) the SIMPLES law, implemented in 2007, reduced bureaucracy and lowered the rate of taxation for small businesses, with the specific intention of formalising informal businesses; (2) education policies (notably *Bolsa Escola* and *Bolsa Família*) reduced the number of young people with limited schooling, who typically occupied precarious jobs; and (3) improved labour inspection practices, combined with greater legal awareness among workers (likely shaped by the Lula administration's strong connections to labour unions).

Berg (2010) also argues that macroeconomic performance in the 2000s was an external factor contributing to economic equality: a growth in exports, combined with an increase in internal demand, helped achieve more inclusive growth and the emergence of a sizeable middle class. These developments also reflected economic policy decisions taken by the Brazilian government.

## Civic participation

The 1988 Brazilian constitution makes citizen and stakeholder participation a pillar of the democratic system, reflecting the strong advocacy of those seeking to prevent a return to authoritarianism and to enable locally appropriate responses to inequalities and poverty (Barth, 2006). Successive political administrations have experimented with methods of increasing civic participation in public policy decisions (Barth, 2006). President's Lula's party, *Partido dos Trabalhadores* (the Workers' Party), was particularly committed to 'efforts to use participatory governance as a means to transfer resources into low-income communities, to expand the number and range of voices in the political system, and to habituate citizens into democratic practices' (Wampler, 2012). There are at least four elements to Brazil's efforts to increase civic participation in decision-making: (1) participatory budgeting; (2) the creation of national councils for key policy areas; (3) the introduction of Brazil's Public Policy Management System (*Sistema de Gestão de Políticas Públicas*), which aimed to integrate different levels of government and civil society into the policy-making process; and (4) funding and other support for non-governmental organisations and civil society organisations. This section briefly outlines each of these in turn.

Perhaps the most famous and central component has been Brazil's use of participatory budgeting, which is designed to give interested citizens a means of shaping local policy decisions. During Lula's first presidency, 25 per cent of Brazil's population were living in a municipality that made some use of participatory budgeting (Wampler and Avritzer, 2005). It has been described as one of the 'most significant innovations in Latin America for increasing citizen participation and local government accountability' (Souza, 2001, p 159). Early assessments were broadly positive; while noting variation and the possibility that Brazil's poorest communities may not always be involved, Souza (2001) concluded that participatory budgeting helped enable formerly excluded groups to decide on investment priorities in their communities, reduced clientelist practices, and helped institutionalise Brazil's transition to democracy.

In addition, tens of thousands of public policy management councils (*conselhos*) were created to support decision-making in key areas of social policy (Avritzer, 2009). During Lula's first presidency, numerous *conselhos*, comprising representatives from civil society, government, and other stakeholders, were established as platforms for dialogue and decision-making on health, education, and social development. The aim of the councils was to facilitate broad participation and to ensure diverse perspectives were considered during policy formulation. For the *Bolsa Família* programme, outlined earlier, each municipality is required to set up a social council (*Conselho de Controle Social*) to take responsibility for data collection, registration of potential beneficiaries, and monitoring of adherence to conditionalities. Members are chosen by the local mayor from public and civil society sectors.

Beyond the creation of *conselhos*, successive administrations have implemented institutional changes designed to improve public administration and civic governance. While Lula's presidency (2003-11) focused on institutionalising participatory budgeting and enhancing the coordination of multi-level policies, President Dilma Rousseff's presidency (2011-16) built on these efforts by launching the Transparency Portal (*Portal da Transparência*) and other digital platforms to improve public access to government data and facilitate civic engagement, and by institutionalising principles of transparency, accountability, and civic participation via the Open Government Partnership. Collectively, these ongoing reforms came to be referred to as *Sistema de Gestão de Políticas Públicas*; a framework for institutional reforms designed to create a more integrated and participatory public policy management system in Brazil.

Finally, Lula, with his background as a union leader, sought to support social and civil movements, including trade unions, NGOs, Indigenous community groups and other civil society organisations. By providing funding and other support, Lula's government empowered these organisations to play a more significant role in policy advocacy and implementation. These groups were actively involved in policy discussions, including via national conferences and other policy forums on specific policy issues, where policymakers engaged with diverse social groups and the public. Recommendations from these conferences often informed legislative and executive actions.

### *Tackling commercial determinants of health*

In the post-1980 democratic era, Brazil also emerged as a leader in taking action to address some key commercial determinants of health (a term used to refer to the commercial actors that profit from manufacturing, marketing and selling health-harming products such as alcohol, tobacco and ultra-processed food). For example, Brazil was one of the earliest countries to take a comprehensive approach to tobacco control, via the National Programme for Tobacco Control (NTCP), which was established in 1986 (Portes et al, 2018) and paved the way for multiple tobacco control measures to be introduced.

Cigarette packs have displayed health warnings since 1988, with Brazil mandating graphic warning labels in 2001 and expanding coverage in 2018. Since the 1980s, smoking in public places has been increasingly restricted, culminating in a 2011 ban on smoking in enclosed public spaces (Portes et al, 2018). Between 2000 and 2014, tobacco advertising was gradually banned across various media, including sponsorships and point-of-sale advertising (International Tobacco Control Project, 2022). Tax increases were also employed in this period; by 2009, tobacco taxes were raised to 65 per cent of the retail price (International Tobacco Control Project, 2022). In 2012, Brazil became the first country to ban additives and flavours, including menthol, in tobacco products (Portes et al, 2018).

Brazil leveraged its success in overcoming TRIPS barriers for anti-retroviral drugs and strong domestic tobacco control to become a key player in WHO's Framework Convention on Tobacco Control negotiations (Lee et al, 2010). These achievements, which influenced other low- and middle-income countries, are particularly notable, given Brazil's status as a major tobacco producer and exporter.

Evaluations show that Brazil's comprehensive tobacco control approach was highly successful, with smoking rates dropping significantly across all education groups between 1989 and 2013 (Bandi et al, 2020). However, as elsewhere, these reductions were uneven, leading to significant inequalities in smoking rates.

While Brazil has not yet matched its success in tobacco control with alcohol or ultra-processed food, it has made progress. Alcohol regulations include age limits, marketing restrictions, and sales hour limitations. For ultra-processed foods, Brazil has subsidised healthy foods (including school meals), sponsored public health campaigns, taxed sugary drinks and restricted advertising, especially to children. Despite these efforts, obesity rates have continued to rise in recent decades (Estivaleti et al, 2022).

## *Housing and land reform*

In 2009, Brazil launched *Minha Casa, Minha Vida*, one of the world's largest government housing programmes. By 2017, 4.7 million housing units had been contracted across 3663 municipalities (Bueno et al, 2018). The programme is complex and involves multiple government levels and a tiered eligibility system. It works by financing home building and then using a favourable loan system, which the beneficiaries have to pay off over time (though, for the lowest income participants, researchers report that 'the terms are so generous that they approach an outright handout' – Bueno et al, 2018). Due to high demand, lower-income applicants are selected via a public lottery. Through a massive investment of US$55 billion, this programme helped reduce the housing deficit from 10.4 per cent in 2009 to 7.3 per cent in 2013 (Kopper, 2021) and was initially framed as a success. However, as we explore in Chapter 6, the programme experienced a range of implementation challenges which have resulted in more critical recent analyses.

## How did these policies affect health inequalities?

As Brazil transitioned into a democracy, health inequalities in infant mortality rates and life expectancy significantly declined. However, identifying which of the policies summarized in Table 3.1 were most influential in achieving these improvements is challenging because many were implemented simultaneously and aimed broadly at reducing poverty and socio-economic inequalities, rather than focusing specifically on health. This means that available research is often restricted to analysing associations (for example, between changes in patterns of income and patterns of health). Analysis by Coelho and Dias (2019) finds a strong association between growth in municipalities' mean income and lower infant mortality rates in Brazil, and a statistically significant association between growth in municipalities' mean income and higher life expectancy in Brazil. There was also a strong association between these health indicators and women's education (Coelho and Dias, 2019).

While changes in income and the broader mix of social, economic and health policies implemented in Brazil help explain the country's success in reducing health inequalities in the post-1985 era, it seems plausible that the transition to democracy was also a fundamental factor. Multiple health inequalities researchers have argued that power is a fundamental cause of health inequalities or, as some term it, a 'cause of the causes' (for example, Friel et al, 2021; McCartney et al, 2019; Popay et al, 2021). From this perspective, we can understand Brazil's transition to democracy as an example of addressing a fundamental driver of health inequalities.

There are at least three pathways via which Brazil's democratisation process plausibly impacted on health inequalities: (1) substantive: democratically elected administrations, who depended on popular support for electoral success, introduced policy changes that better reflected population needs and interests and were, therefore, more likely to favour the masses; (2) social: democratisation builds social solidarity and social support, and helps foster a sense of social connectivity that facilitates and enables policies that reflect population interests (as opposed to policies that reflect elite interests at the cost of others); and (3) psychosocial: democratisation can provide people with a sense of hope, fostering a belief that change is possible and that people can effect change in positive ways.

Of course, not all democracies are equal and there are many examples of countries that have democratically elected governments and yet do not appear to have policies that favour the masses, which lack a sense of social solidarity, and where people are lacking hope (see, for example, Smith and Stewart, 2024). This suggests we should pay attention to the specific approaches used to foster democracy in Brazil, notably the multi-stranded efforts to increase civic participation (which Hirono, 2023 identifies as an important mechanism for improving health outcomes). Institutionalising a

Table 3.1: An overview of some of the key policies implemented in Brazil during democratisation

| Determinant of health | Policy response | Policy purpose |
|---|---|---|
| Healthcare access | A constitutional commitment to a 'right to health' and the introduction of *Sistema Único de Saúde (SUS)*, Brazil's unified health system | The introduction of the tax-funded healthcare system, *Sistema Único de Saúde (SUS)*, was an ambitious attempt to improve healthcare access across the Brazilian population. This was supplemented by targeted outreach programmes focusing on poorer families and by a pro-poor cash transfer programme that incentivised poorer families to engage with public health and healthcare. Brazil also engaged in global negotiations to secure access to key pharmaceuticals. |
| Income | The introduction of pro-poor cash transfers, incentives for employers to move into the formal economy and increases in the minimum wage | Brazil implemented pro-poor cash-transfer programmes (*Bolsa Escola* and later, *Bolsa Família*) which were designed to incentivise poorer families to engage with education and public health. The government also made policy changes to encourage employers to move from the informal into the formal economy (requiring payment of the minimum wage), and increased Brazil's minimum wage. These policies contributed to reducing Brazil's extreme income inequalities. |
| Education | Large-scale investments in education, with federal rules guiding state spending on education, combined with incentives for poorer families to send their children to school | Following re-democratisation, Brazil made substantial investments in education, across primary, secondary and tertiary levels. Federal rules set requirements on state expenditure to ensure that these funds were invested in education. The *Bolsa Escola/Bolsa Família* cash transfer programmes were used to encourage poorer families to send their children to school, with payments dependent on school attendance. |
| Housing | *Minha Casa, Minha Vida* is one of the largest government-run housing programmes in the world | A large-scale investment of government resource to facilitate house building was accompanied by a tiered, government-subsidised loan system to enable people to buy the new houses and gradually pay the state back over time (requirements for people in the poorest tier to pay back the loan were more limited). |
| Commercial determinants | Helped negotiate the WHO Framework Convention on Tobacco Control and introduced a National Programme for Tobacco Control (NTCP) | Brazil was one of the first countries to take a comprehensive approach to tobacco control, via its National Programme for Tobacco Control (NTCP). This reduced people's exposure to tobacco and to tobacco industry influence, a key commercial determinant of health. Internationally, Brazil played a leading role in negotiating the WHO Framework Convention on Tobacco Control, which includes a clause (Article 5.3) requiring signatories to protect health policy from tobacco industry interference. |
| Democratic engagement | Participatory budgeting; the creation of national councils for key policy areas; the introduction of Brazil's Public Policy Management System (*Sistema de Gestão de Políticas Públicas*); and support for non-governmental organisations, trade unions and civil society organisations | Participatory budgeting, which is now used across the world to engage local communities in decisions about the allocation of public funds, was developed in Brazil during the 1980s. A system of councils also functioned to support public and civil society engagement in discussions and debates about key policy areas. More broadly, President Lula implemented multiple measures to integrate civil society, including trade unions, into the policy-making process, and to provide these organisations with resources to support their engagement. |

more inclusive and civic approach to governance can improve policy decisions both directly, via policy decisions that better reflect public preferences, and indirectly, via decision-maker awareness of, and responsiveness to, strong policy scrutiny (for example, from trade unions, civil society organisations and a free media – see Melo, 2016).

## Conclusion

This chapter argues that Brazil is a positive example of how democratisation can contribute to health gains and reductions in health inequalities. Two generations of Brazilians have now grown up knowing nothing other than democracy and the policies introduced in this era have, collectively, enabled Brazil to simultaneously improve average population health and reduce health inequalities. While public health researchers often seek to unpack, and even quantify, the contribution of specific policies and programmes to changes in health outcomes, the example of Brazil suggests it may be more fruitful to consider: (1) the mixture of social, economic and health policies required to simultaneously achieve these dual health goals; and (2) the governance mechanisms that enabled this mixture of policies to be successfully formulated and implemented.

On the first of these points, in the post-1985 democratic period (especially the 2000s), Brazil implemented policies that substantially increased and equalised healthcare and pharmaceutical access, redistributed resources (notably income) more equitably, which included pro-poor cash-transfer policies that were also designed to achieve positive social impacts (notably via incentivising families to send children to school and engage with primary healthcare), increased the minimum wage while also expanding those impacted by this policy by taking measures to formalise work in the informal economy, and tackled tobacco, and tobacco industry policy influence, in ways that substantially reduced tobacco use. In short, Brazil introduced policies that sought to improve equity via a broad combination of healthcare, economic, employment, welfare, education, public health and trade policies.

It seems likely that many of these specific policies depended on the multiple changes to the governance of Brazil, introduced in the post-1985 democratic era, particularly in the administrations led by President Lula (2003–11) and President Rousseff (2011–16). This included mechanisms to institutionalise civic participation in policy processes, to strengthen the community/non-government sector, to increase the opportunities for a wide range of stakeholders and publics to influence policy, and to strengthen the public and media scrutiny of policy decisions, including via greater transparency.

So far in this chapter, we have focused on the mixture of policies that research and data suggest helped achieve positive social, economic and health impacts. What we have not yet explored are some of the challenges that Brazil's democratic governments have struggled to overcome. Moreover, since Brazil managed to simultaneously achieve health gains and reductions in health inequalities, we have also avoided a need to explore any trade-offs between average population improvements and inequalities. Yet, as we bring this chapter to a close, it is important to acknowledge some of the limitations in Brazil's policies, and to underline the extent to which social inequalities continue to negatively, and unequally, impact on population health outcomes.

It would be impossible to comprehensively address all policies negatively impacting on health and inequalities but five policy areas stand out in assessments of Brazil's post-1985 performance (and are discussed further in Chapter 6). The first is Brazil's disappointing progress with human rights (Muñoz, 2017) and the consequences in terms of violence, crime and police brutality. The second, stark limitation to the mixture of social policies pursued by Brazil's democratic administrations relates to housing, where bold ambitions were frustrated by a series of implementation challenges (see Chapter 6). The third limitation relates to education. Here, despite the success of *Bolsa Escola* in increasing the percentage of children regularly attending school, the (2003–11) Lula administrations were less successful in raising levels of student learning (Arends-Kuenning, 2009). The fourth is workplace safety where, despite an increased trade union presence helping to improve workplace safety in some settings, poor practices have persisted, especially (though not only) in Brazil's large informal sector, leading to relatively high (and almost certainly under-reported) rates of workplace accidents and fatalities (Mogensen, 2006; Mendeloff, 2015). The fifth relates to the environment, where promising progress to curb deforestation in the democratic era were first strengthened by innovative policies introduced by Lula, early in his first presidency, but then progressively weakened over time (Hochstetler, 2017).

If we consider the series of health threats that the Brazilian state has had to respond to over the past decade, including an ongoing rise in obesity, the 2015–16 Zika virus outbreak, and the 2020 COVID-19 pandemic outbreak, we can perhaps better understand Brazil's recent decline in life expectancy. Layered on top of this, there are global economic pressures and a shift from mass to social media, which is changing the way people get information, including information about policy and politics. In Chapter 6, we argue that, in the 2019 election, these issues combined in ways that threatened to reverse some of the successes described in this chapter.

# 4

# What belongs together will grow together: German reunification and health inequalities

Regional health inequalities occur in many countries. This chapter examines what can be done to reduce them by considering the successful case of post-reunification Germany. Before reunification in 1990, there was a three-year life expectancy gap between women living in communist East Germany and women living in liberal democratic West Germany. For men, the life expectancy gap was three and a half years. Post-reunification, these life expectancy gaps rapidly reduced: East German women now have a higher life expectancy than West German women and the gap between life expectancy among East and West German men has reduced to around 18 months. Germany went from having the largest regional health inequalities among high-income countries in 1990 to having the lowest for women and modest ones for men in 2020 (Raalte et al, 2020). This chapter examines how the German health gap was closed so quickly and draws out the wider lessons that can be learnt from this for reducing health inequalities elsewhere.

The German reunification process involved substantial changes in the East, including improvements in living standards, wage levels, nutrition, pensions and healthcare services. This chapter assesses the impact of these reforms on health. We begin, as in previous chapters, with a description of the intersecting axes of inequality in Germany before reunification. Next we examine the policies put in place during the reunification process and explore the effects of these policies on health and health equity. To close, the chapter examines what happened in other former Eastern bloc countries where, in contrast to East Germany, there was a 'post-communist mortality crisis'.

## East and West: Germany 1945–90

After the Second World War, Germany was split into two separate states: the German Democratic Republic (GDR/East Germany) – a communist totalitarian state, part of the Warsaw pact and Soviet bloc; and the Federal Republic of Germany (FRG/West Germany) – a liberal democratic, capitalist state, and a founder member of the European Union and part of the North Atlantic Treaty Organization (NATO). The partition of Germany also included, and was symbolised by, the division of Berlin into two halves – East and West – by the Berlin Wall. In 1989 tentative political reforms led to a peaceful 'velvet revolution' in many Eastern bloc countries. The GDR, arguably one of the most repressive and ideological of the Eastern bloc countries (Fulbrook, 2005), delayed political reforms. But when a hole in the 'Iron Curtain' around the Eastern Bloc was created between Hungary and Austria, thousands of East Germans fled into West Germany via Hungary and Austria. The Berlin Wall was literally torn down in November 1989, leading to the GDR's first free elections and to the creation of a unified Germany in 1990 (Fulbrook, 2005).

Between 1949 and 1990, though, East Germans inhabited a different world from West Germans (and the citizens of other wealthy democracies). The GDR was dominated by a single political party, the Socialist Unity Party of Germany (SED), which enforced a state communist ideology across all parts of society. The economy, education, working life, domestic life, housing and healthcare were all under state control (Fulbrook, 2005) The infamous Stasi suppressed deviance from party orthodoxy (Fulbrook, 2005). For example, a participant in a study of people's experiences of state control in the GDR recalled:

> [P]eople were being put in jail for saying their opinions, telling jokes or whatever and that there was no freedom of speech, no freedom of expression, no freedom of the press. There was, in fact, no public voice in the GDR, eine Öffentlichkeit [public discourse] did not exist in the GDR. This did not exist, nothing that was not dictated by the party. (Frau M., quoted in Neuendorf, 2017, p 132)

This participant had been supportive of the GDR at the time, even working as an undercover spy providing the Stasi with information about close family and friends – including her husband. Neuendorf (2017) notes that this was not unusual; many East Germans were encouraged (and sometimes blackmailed) to spy on the people around them, fostering a sense of deep social unease and distrust. Another participant in the same study reflected that the sense of state control started early, with nursery and primary school:

> Even as a child, you noticed that you were living in a divided world. At home, you felt sheltered, that's where you are protected, where everything is ok. And then there's the state side: school, kindergarten ... also friends. (Frau D. quoted in Neuendorf, 2017, p 159)

Under this system, East Germany fell behind the West in terms of economic development, healthcare provision and medical technology, living standards, environmental standards and in terms of public health. The GDP of the GDR in 1990 was $9,679 per head, but 50 per cent higher ($15,300 per head) in the West (CIA, 2003). Manufactured and luxury goods were in a short supply. There were long waiting lists for cars, which cost 25,000 East German marks in 1988 – equivalent to two years of average wages (Krueger and Pischke, 1992). Basics such as food and rent (as well as alcohol and cigarettes) were, however, very cheap in East Germany, as they were subsidised by the state. For example, rents were only about 6 per cent of the average salary, although housing standards were also considerably less good than in the West (for example, many East Germans lived in overcrowded, poorly built houses, all allocated by the state) (Krueger and Pischke, 1992). Import restrictions affected the national diet, limiting access to 'exotic' produce like bananas and oranges (Fulbrook, 2005).

The natural environment in the East was also more pathogenic due to minimal regulation of air pollution and a dependency on domestically produced but highly polluting 'brown coal' (Fulbrook, 2005). In the Leipzig region, for example, a report from the late 1980s details almost unbearably poor air quality: 'These towns are falling apart, drab and grey, creating an oppressive impression of filth in this poisoned atmosphere. The buildings are black with smoke and soot, and crumbling plaster on the facades … show the clear signs of thick layers of dust' (cited in Ault, 2015, pp 37–8).

The East German economy was dominated by industry, which took a heavy toll on the environment. Many rivers were highly polluted, leading to around 13 per cent of the population consuming drinking water that had dangerously high levels of nitrates (Fulbrook, 2005). Life in the shadow of such significant pollution was tough, as a letter from a woman living with her three children in the village of Dorndorf, in southwestern East Germany, attests. The letter, which pleads with local authorities to take action, captures the experience of living with significant pollution from a local chemical plant: 'If there is a northeasterly wind, it is impossible to remain outside in the garden. Even opening the windows is barely an option, because it results in a thorough and demanding cleaning of living area' (cited in Ault, 2015, p 95).

Workplace accidents and occupational health problems were also rife with exposure to lead pollution, asbestos and mercury far higher than in Western countries (Ault, 2015). In one East German uranium mine, for example: '[M]iners were forced to undertake severe manual labour in narrow spaces with poor ventilation because there were no legal regulations for the protection of health, work, and the environment related to uranium mining. … On July 15, 1955, thirty-three miners died in a cable fire inside the pit' (Kido, 2019, p 63). One East German authority estimated that by the end of the 1980s, around 20–40 per cent of all morbidity in the GDR was work-related (Kido, 2019).

Healthcare provision in the East was state funded and state run. Until the late 1970s it was broadly comparable in terms of outcomes with other state-run systems in the West (such as the National Health Services in the UK or Sweden). However, from the 1980s onwards it was starved of investment as a result of economic problems and barriers to trade across the East–West border, and healthcare provision fell significantly behind Western norms (Fulbrook, 2005). The 1985 observations of an American researcher, who spent time studying the healthcare system in the GDR and the FDR, capture some of the resulting frustrations experienced by medical professionals:

> I had the opportunity to observe the work of a physician in a rural ambulatorium. ... Like other doctors throughout the GDR he complained to me about the general lack of medication, technology and equipment especially that from the West. Specific complaints he noted about an ambulatorium practice were that all laboratory studies had to be sent out, that he frequently had difficulty scheduling radiologic studies and that the nearest ambulance was located one-half hour away. (Regenstein, 1985, p 25)

Healthcare in the GDR increasingly suffered from under-investment, resulting in less well-equipped hospitals, fewer hospital beds, less well-trained and fewer medical professionals and less spending per head on healthcare provision. This situation was exacerbated by healthcare professionals escaping to the West; between 1985 and 1989, an estimated 4000 doctors sought asylum in West Germany (Hicks, 2010), prompting the GDR's leader, Honecker, to warn that, 'if we let out all doctors who want to leave, public health would collapse' (Hiepko, 2019, p 217).

By 1990, about a fifth of hospitals in East Germany were in a poor state of repair, a third of hospital beds were unusable, medical technology was 15 to 20 years behind usual practice in the West, the range of drugs available in the East was only 2000 compared to 40,000 in West, only 30 per cent of the equipment needed for heart surgery were provided in 1988, and there were severe shortages of day-to-day medical essentials such as rubber gloves, syringes and scalpels (Gjonça et al, 2000; Fulbrook, 2005). Inadequacies in the amount and quality of medical-technical equipment were a common feature of reports from GDR doctors and the Ministry of Health (Hiepko, 2019). The East German system also rationed healthcare with explicit preferences for the healthcare of 'productive and reproductive citizens' (working age men and women – with for example considerable investment in maternity care), over older people and people with long term health problems or disabilities (Fulbrook, 2005).

Health behaviours also differed significantly between the two countries: higher rates of smoking among men in the East – although lower rates among women – and considerably higher rates of hazardous alcohol consumption among both men and women in the East (Luy, 2004). Indeed, Fulbrook (2005, p 102) comments that in contrast to falling rates in Western countries – and a concentration among lower socio-economic groups there – 'in the GDR, smoking appears to have remained an accepted way of life across a far wider spectrum of society' and was 'endemic'. Consumption of large amounts of alcohol – particularly beer and cheap spirits – was also an important element of daily life, both socially and at work. In 1982, for example, East Germans consumed, on average, 9.7 litres of wine, 147 litres of beer, and 12.7 litres of spirits. These rates were more than double what the consumption had been in East Germany in 1960. The 1982 consumption of spirits in the East (arguably the most harmful form of alcohol for health) was twice the rate in West Germany at that time (Fulbrook, 2005). In 1987, it was estimated that around 12 per cent (or 1 in 8 people) of the East German adult population were alcoholics (Fulbrook, 2005). Alcohol was subsidised in East Germany, and the rising rates of alcohol consumption since 1960 may be interpreted as 'anaesthetising the strain' of living in a totalitarian dictatorship and an ailing economy (Fulbrook, 2005).

The impact of the GDR's policies on public health is demonstrated in Figure 4.1, which shows life expectancy trends between East and West from 1956 (earliest available data) to 2020 (most recent available data). Until the 1970s life expectancies for men and women living in the East and the West of Germany were very similar. But in the 1970s a gap emerged and by the fall of the GDR in 1990, it stood at around three years (2.8 years for women and 3.4 for men [Human Mortality Database, 2023]). This health

**Figure 4.1:** Life expectancy for men and women in East and West Germany, 1956–2020

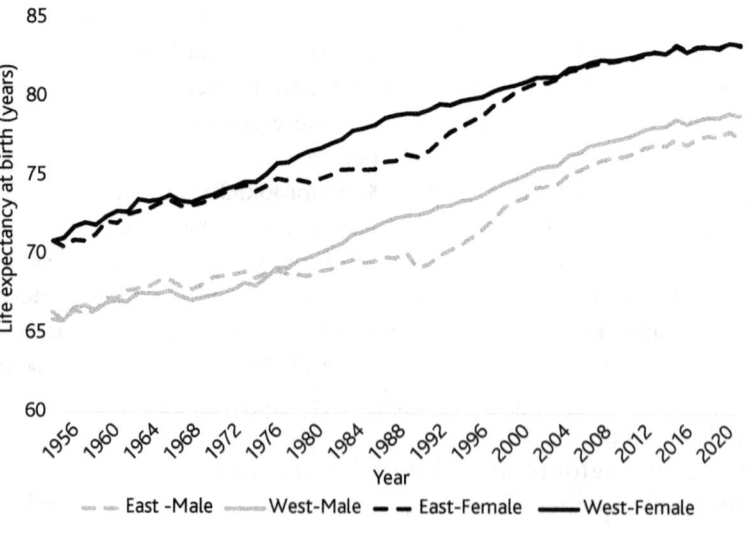

gap has rapidly narrowed in recent decades – particularly for women. By as early as 1999, the West–East health divide for women was only around six months and by 2017, female life expectancy in the East exceeded that in the West by around six months (West: 82.8 years; East: 83.4 years) (Human Mortality Database, 2023). Among men, the health gap also decreased post-reunification – but less impressively: by 1999, the West–East life expectancy gap had decreased to just over one year but even today, life expectancy for men in the East is still lagging that in the West, with a gap of around 18 months (West: 78.9 years; East: 77.5 years) (Lampert et al, 2019; Human Mortality Database, 2023). Most of the gains in life expectancy were in older groups – precisely where the gap between East and West had grown in the 1980s (Luy, 2004). In younger age groups, there had been no gap between East and West even before reunification (for example, in 1989, and infant mortality rates were the same between the two countries at around 8 per 1000 live births) (Luy, 2004).

The increasing life expectancy gap between the East and the West from the 1970s has been attributed by researchers mainly to a higher incidence of cardiovascular diseases in the East (particularly among the elderly, which was almost 1.5 times higher than Western levels [Grigoriev and Pechholdová, 2017]). Analysis suggests that this occurred because of the lower pension and healthcare spending in the East, and to a lesser extent, to higher rates of adverse health behaviours in the East such as poorer quality diets and higher rates of smoking (Gjonça et al, 2000; Luy, 2004). What is less clear is what led to the rapid post-reunification reduction in the health gap. The next section examines this in more detail.

## Reunification: what belongs together will grow together

How did reunification lead to such rapid improvements in the health of East Germans? There are three main factors that have been explored in the literature: economic reunification, improved living conditions, and better healthcare services. To this, we add the matter of democratisation and political incorporation. This section examines each of these factors in turn.

### *Economic reunification*

At reunification, Germany faced huge regional economic inequalities. While West Germany had participated in international trade and was one of the world's strongest economies, the GDR had a centrally planned economy isolated from international competition, with outdated machinery and inefficient businesses, and was on the verge of bankruptcy by 1989 (Vaizey, 2014; Enenkel and Rösel, 2023). Economic reunification therefore focused on trying to improve the economy in the East by rapidly transferring West

German economic and political institutions and processes (Michelsen and Weiß, 2010).

The impacts of reunification on the economy in the East were mixed. On one hand, the wages of East Germans improved significantly with a currency union in which the West German Deutsche Mark (a strong internationally traded currency) replaced the East German Ostmark (considered almost worthless outside of the Eastern bloc) as the official currency on a mark-for-mark basis. Salaries and savings in the East were thus protected and replaced by the much higher value Deutsche Mark, and as early as 1996, wages in the East had already reached around 75 per cent of Western levels, from less than 40 per cent in 1990 (Parkes, 1997; Lenhart, 2019). Accordingly, there was a rise in average incomes from 61 per cent to 84 per cent of Western levels (Burda and Hunt, 2001). On the other hand, the currency union also led to a collapse of the Eastern economy as low-quality East German goods could not compete internationally when priced at Western levels, resulting in a 30 per cent decrease in GDP between 1989 and 1992, and mass unemployment (15 per cent by 1992) (Nolte and McKee, 2000). Even decades later, unemployment in the East is significantly higher than in the West (Viazey, 2014).

Economic reunification was also accompanied by rapid de-industrialisation and privatisation of previously state-owned Eastern companies. In 1989, the level of industrialisation in East Germany was 50 per cent higher than in West Germany and 98 per cent of its businesses were state owned (Gornig and Häussermann, 2002). After reunification, however, the manufacturing industry in the former GDR collapsed almost overnight with, for example, employment rates in mining and manufacturing industries falling to a quarter of their pre-unification levels (Carlin, 1992). Previously state-owned East German companies were also rapidly privatised: by 1994, all 8000 previously state-owned East German companies were either closed or in private hands (Zeevaert, 2020). Cleaning up dirty East German industries and applying Western environmental standards increased overheads and led to further job losses (Viazey, 2014).

These processes further exacerbated unemployment in the former East Germany in the immediate aftermath of reunification. Women were particularly impacted by job losses. In the GDR, 90 per cent of women worked full time and were supported by a highly developed network of childcare support, which enabled women to work night shifts (Neuendorf, 2017). In the context of reunification, many women lost their jobs as well as the state support (such as childcare) that they had grown accustomed to. They also experienced a cultural shift in expectations regarding women's role in society. The GDR positioned men and women as equals, with everyone expected to work, and provided generous paid maternity leave. Unification with the more socially conservative West German society left many women from the former GDR struggling to combine motherhood and paid work, in the context of shorter paid maternity leave, more limited childcare and a lack of secure employment (Finzel, 2003).

Subsequently, there were high rates of East to West migration (particularly of younger and more educated people) and concurrent population losses in the East in this period (Finzel, 2003). However, over time, owing to new public and private investments and infrastructure development, labour productivity grew rapidly in the East – from less than 45 per cent of the Western level in 1991 to only 7 per cent lower in 2000 (Burda and Hunt, 2001). This was accompanied by an increase in GDP per capita from 42 per cent to 65 per cent of West German levels during the same period (Burda and Hunt, 2001). However, unemployment remained high in the East – consistently roughly double that of the West (Burda and Hunt, 2001).

Overall, 40 years on from reunification, while there has been 'substantial progress' in improving the economy of the former East Germany, there is still a considerable gap with the West. The states of the former East Germany are still poorer and experience higher levels of structural unemployment than in the West (van Raalte et al, 2020, p 487). Put in a wider context, while East Germany still lags the West, it has a relatively good economic performance by European standards – several states in Eastern Germany have higher GDPs than other regions in Western Europe (such as the North of England) and the per capita GDP in Eastern Germany, overall, is higher than that of countries such as Portugal (Bambra et al, 2014; Rehnberg, 2020; Eurostat, 2023).

## Improved living and working conditions

Economic reunification – or the 'Westernisation of the GDR' – was also accompanied by large-scale social transfer payments by the West German government, largely financed by Western German employees and companies. West Germany's well-established and comparatively generous social security system was also transferred to the East and provided a safety net to East Germans during the turbulent economic changes (Hall and Ludwig, 1994). As a result, pensions and unemployment benefit levels improved and relative poverty rates fell – although income inequalities and the cost of living increased (Vaizey, 2014).[1] Housing quality and the natural environment were also improved.

In 1985, retired households in the East had only 36 per cent of the income of employed households, while retirees in the West received 65 per cent (Gjonça et al, 2000; Wolle, 2019). After reunification and the extension of the West German pension system into the East, there were huge increases in income among older East Germans: in 1990 the monthly pension of an East German pensioner was only 40 per cent that of a Western pensioner, but by 1999 it had increased to 87 per cent of West German levels (Vogt and Kluge, 2015). This meant that retired people were one of the groups that benefited most from reunification – particularly East German women as they had, on average, considerably longer working histories and much greater labour force participation rates than their West German counterparts (for example, in 1989, the female labour force participation was 89 per cent in the East compared to only 56 per cent in the West [Rosenfeld et al, 2004]). East Germans also inherited generous unemployment supports which helped cushion the negative material consequences of mass unemployment (Snower and Merkl, 2006). Research by the Max Planck Institute for Demographic Research in Rostock has suggested that the rapid improvement in life expectancy in 1990s East Germany was largely a result of falling death rates among pensioners – particularly women (Gjonça et al, 2000). Similarly, a study by Vogt and Kluge (2015) specifically investigated the effects of increasing welfare spending on mortality differentials between East and West Germany during the period before and after reunification (1980–2000). They estimated that for every euro invested in East German pensions, three additional hours in life expectancy were gained. Similarly, Simpson and colleagues (2024) found that for every 10 per cent increase in the value of social security benefits, life expectancy at birth increased by an additional month for men and by two weeks for women in East relative to West Germany.

Relative household poverty levels also fell in the East post-reunification from 25 per cent in 1991 to 16 per cent in 2000. In the same period, it rose from 10 per cent to 13 per cent in the West (Federal Government Commissioner for the New Federal States, 2018). Housing quality in the former East German states was also improved post-reunification (Noll and Weick, 2014). Before 1990, the availability and quality of housing was much lower in the East than it was in West Germany. For example, in 1986 there were 1.6 rooms for each person in the GDR, compared to 1.9 in the West and 27 square metres per person, compared to 37 square metres (Noll and Weick, 2014). East German housing stock was also physically inferior and older than that in the West: 20 per cent of houses in the East were judged to require urgent and fundamental repairs and less than 50 per cent had been constructed post-war, compared to 70 per cent in the West (Noll and Weick, 2014). Post-reunification, wide-scale, publicly funded renovation programmes were implemented and now housing standards in the East have become more comparable with those in the West – but rents also increased (Noll and Weick, 2014). Housing improvements also led to reductions in air pollution levels in East Germany through the introduction of central heating. Deindustrialisation was also beneficial from an environmental perspective (Schulz et al, 2007).

The East German state had subsidised basic foods, but there were often shortages, especially of imported foods (Vaizey, 2014). After reunification, access to a variety of foods and consumer goods also increased as West German shops and companies set up in the East. With the state rent and food subsidies removed the cost of living also increased: rents were five to ten times higher and household expenditure on food increased from 5 to 20 per cent of earnings (Viazey, 2014). Despite higher costs, this helped to improve the diets of East Germans in ways that were potentially beneficial in terms of cardiovascular-related risk factors. Winkler and colleagues (1997) found that after reunification, the diets of East Germans improved, both in terms of variety and quality (Winkler et al, 1997). Obesity rates, initially higher in the East, also began to converge in the early 2000s (Lampert et al, 2019). Likewise, alcohol consumption declined in the 1990s in both East and West Germany, and drinking behaviour became more similar across the two regions (Bloomfield et al, 2005). In contrast, however, smoking rates among women from East Germany increased following reunification, likely reflecting Germany's weak tobacco control measures (Vogt et al, 2017).

*Better healthcare services*

Immediately after reunification, considerable financial support was given by the West German state to modernise the hospitals and healthcare equipment in the East and to increase nursing, screening and pharmaceutical services (Dörr et al, 2021). Due to the poor economic performance of the command communist economy, East Germany's healthcare system had been underfunded for decades before the fall of the Berlin Wall. As a result, there were widespread medical equipment shortages, a reliance on outdated technology and treatments, and dilapidated hospitals and health clinics. East Germany had one ultrasound device per 32,000 people compared to one per 2500 in the West; and there were 0.46 heart operations per 1000 East Germans (aged 60+) compared to over 7 per 1000 in the West (Schroeder and Deutz-Schröder, 2008; Grigoriev and Pechholdová, 2017). In the immediate post-reunification period, per capita funding of healthcare was tripled in the East so that it matched Western levels (Vogt and Kluge, 2015; Rehnberg, 2020). This influx of funds was used to quickly update the whole healthcare system and within just a few years, the East's healthcare system reached the standards of the West, with to up-to-date diagnostic and treatment technologies, medical training, clinical care pathways and modern treatments (Nolte et al, 2002).[2]

This healthcare system investment and modernisation had notable impacts on a variety of healthcare related outcomes. There were significant improvements, for example, in perinatal and neonatal mortality in the East after reunification (Nolte and McKee, 2000). Decreases in deaths from conditions amenable to prevention and medical treatment accounted for 36 per cent (men) and 37 per cent (women) of the overall increase in life expectancy to age 75 in East Germany in the 1990s (Nolte et al, 2002). The healthcare improvements also accelerated reductions in cardiovascular mortality in the East from almost 1.5 times higher than the West in 1990 to near convergence by 2000 (Luy, 2004; Grigoriev and Pechholdová, 2017). These reductions in deaths from cardiovascular disease account for a further 10 per cent (women) and 17 per cent (men) of the overall increase in life expectancy to age 75 in East Germany in the 1990s (Nolte et al, 2002). A study by Vogt and Vaupel (2015) found that improvements in life expectancy at older ages (65+) in the East were first seen in towns with university hospitals, where state-of-art services first became available and a study by Grigoriev and Pechholdová (2017) found that post-reunification there were significant reductions in mortality from cerebrovascular and chronic heart diseases – potentially related to improved healthcare access (and diet – as noted in the previous section). These improvements in healthcare outcomes particularly benefitted older East Germans, partly because older people generally are more likely to need healthcare interventions but also because pensioners had been neglected by the GDR medical system for decades in favour of working age people who could contribute more to the economy (Rehnberg, 2020).

## *Democratisation and political incorporation*

Under the totalitarian East German state there was no freedom of expression, of assembly, of movement, or the judiciary, or elections. While there were elections in the GDR, these consisted of approving the one available candidate from the ruling party (the Socialist Unity party or SED) (Vaizey, 2014). This changed in March 1990 when the first free democratic elections since 1933 were held in East Germany. Over 40 per cent of the electorate supported the Christian Democrats, who proposed a speedy reunification (Vaizey, 2014). The ensuing economic, political and social transformation of Eastern Germany has been described in the previous sections. What has been less considered in the research literature on the health improvement in East Germany post-reunification is the potential role of the *democratisation* of the GDR itself. However, by looking at the wider international literature on politics and health outcomes, it seems likely that the political incorporation of East Germans did play a role in improving public health and reducing health inequalities between the two regions.

A recent analysis of data from over 100 countries from 1960 onwards examined the health impacts of the spread of democracy. It concluded that 'democracy does improve health' on the basis that an increase in the level of democracy in a country – regardless of other factors such as a country's wealth or economic development – is associated with an increase in life expectancy and decreases in infant mortality, child mortality and mortality rates (Oyèkọ́lá, 2023, p 105). Earlier cross-national research studies, such as Besley and Kudamatsu (2006), similarly found that life expectancy is higher in democracies than in autocracies (by between 3.5 and 5 years) and that infant mortality is lower (by an average of 17 per 1000 since the 1950s). Safaei (2006) found that democracies have higher life expectancies at birth (of 3.6 years for men and 4.1 years for women), at age 60 and higher healthy-life expectancies than autocratic countries; and Wang et al (2019) found that since 1900 democracy improves IMR.

A review by Beckfield and Krieger (2009) examined how different political systems shape health inequalities. They concluded that political incorporation – extending democratic rights and participation to previously excluded and subordinated groups such as racial/ethnic/indigenous or women – can help to reduce health inequalities. By way of example, the extension of civil and political rights to BlackAmericans in the USA in the 1960s (as analysed in Chapter 2 of this book) has been associated with sharp reductions in inequalities in infant mortality and premature mortality (Krieger et al, 2008). Research examining the health effects of the dismantling of apartheid in South Africa post-1990 has had more mixed results depending on the time frames studied. Two short term studies looking at changes from the late 1980s to the late 1990s found no association between increased democratic rights in South Africa and reductions in racial/ethnic inequalities in infant mortality and morbidity (Cameron, 2003; Burgard and Treiman, 2006). Another study – which took a much longer time frame examining data from 1970 to the late 1990s did find that racial/ethnic disparities in South African infant and child mortality declined after the end of Apartheid (Nannan et al, 2007). With regards to women's' political incorporation, an analysis of 51 countries reported that increases in female autonomy and maternal education reduced socio-economic inequalities in child mortality (Houweling et al, 2007).

However, while these studies suggest that democratic societies do better than other forms of government in terms of health and that the extension of democratic rights to previously excluded social groups can reduce health inequalities, what they also show is that it is not just democracy *per se* that is 'better for health', but the nature of the democratic society and how it is organised and the services it delivers (Navarro et al, 2006; Beckfield et al, 2015). In fact, the literature on the relationship between types of democracy in high-income countries (broadly speaking, Liberal-, Social Democratic- and Conservative-dominated polities) and health outcomes has suggested that the latter two lead to better health outcomes. This is because while most Western countries are in economic terms capitalist, in that their economic activity is organised primarily through the operation of markets, and in political terms liberal democracies, they nevertheless differ in important ways in terms of how they implement, manage and structure their societies. These different forms of economic and societal organisation led to important differences in the distribution of social determinants of health (see Chapter 1). These differences are usefully captured through the concept of *welfare state regimes* (Esping-Anderson, 1990).

Modern welfare states can be considered a particular form of democratic capitalist state, which emerged in advanced market democracies, including Germany, during the early post-Second World War period (Esping-Anderson, 1990). To a greater or lesser extent in different countries, the 'golden age' of welfare state capitalism was characterised by centralism, universalism and Keynesian economics (active macroeconomic management by the state such as interventionist fiscal policy, a large public sector and a mixed economy), full (male) employment and high public expenditure, and the promotion of mass consumption via a redistributive tax and welfare system (see Chapter 1). There was also a mainstream political consensus in favour of the welfare state and the redistribution it effected. During this age of welfare state expansion (1940s to 1970s), Western countries experienced significant improvements to public housing, healthcare, and the other main social determinants of health. Welfare states themselves shape society and influence stratification (Bambra, 2011), and are therefore potentially an important macro-level political and economic determinant of health. However, golden age welfare states varied considerably in the services they provided and the generosity and coverage of social protection. To understand why reunification in Germany resulted in a reduction of health inequalities between the East and West, we need to understand that when West Germany exported its institutions to the East it was not just exporting any old political democracy or capitalist economy but rather a full-fledged Conservative welfare state.

Welfare states can be divided into three different types or regimes (Esping-Anderson, 1990): liberal, conservative, and social democratic, with the main distinctions summarised in Table 4.1. Comparative research on the social determinants of health has concluded that population health is most enhanced by the more generous and universal welfare provision of the social democratic countries, followed by the conservative countries, and lowest in the liberal welfare states (Bambra, 2012). For example, Navarro and colleagues (2003,

**Table 4.1:** Welfare state regimes

| Liberal | Conservative | Social Democratic |
|---|---|---|
| Anglophone countries[1] | Continental Europe[2] | Nordic countries[3] |
| Minimal state benefits | Benefits related to prior earnings | Universal benefits |
| Strict entitlement criteria | Social insurance managed by social partners | Generous social transfers |
| Private (market) provision of insurance, care | Generous benefits | Active redistribution |

[1] Australia, Canada, Ireland, New Zealand, United Kingdom, United States of America.
[2] Austria, Belgium, France, Germany, Italy, Switzerland, Netherlands.
[3] Denmark, Finland, Iceland, Sweden, Norway.

2006) and Coburn (2004) found that those countries which were the least neoliberal in their economic and social policy orientation (that is, the social democratic and conservative welfare states) had significantly lower infant mortality, lower overall mortality rates, increased life expectancy at birth, and less mortality at younger ages. These studies also suggested that welfare state regime type might be the mediating link between national economic wealth (GDP per capita), democracy and health (Navarro et al, 2003; 2006; Coburn, 2004). These findings were reinforced by Chung and Muntaner's (2007) analysis of welfare state regimes, which found that around 20 per cent of the difference in infant mortality between rich democratic countries, and 10 per cent of differences in low-birth-weight babies, could be explained by the type of welfare state.

After reunification, the newly democratised East Germany became part of the conservative welfare regime type. It is therefore plausible, and in keeping with the earlier discussion in this chapter of improvements in social security, living conditions and healthcare provision, that being part of this type of democratic regime – rather than just being democratic *per se* – has contributed to the post-1990 health gains in the East.

## The post-communist mortality crisis

The success of German reunification in terms of the rapid health improvement in the former East is highlighted by what happened in most of the other former Eastern Bloc countries after the collapse of Soviet communism. The experiences of these countries show what *could* have happened to health in East Germany if there had not been such extensive economic and social reunification and healthcare investment.

The political and economic collapse of the Soviet Union and the Eastern Bloc between 1989 and 1991 had a dramatic effect on population health in the region. Life expectancy in Russia for example, already lagging far behind the West since the 1960s, fell even further (Leon et al, 1997). There were various reasons for this: increases in unemployment because of radical economic changes such as mass privatisation; the removal of the Soviet-era social security safety nets; increases in income inequalities, crime and poverty; and – particularly in Russia – a huge, related, increase in consumption of cheap and highly concentrated alcohol (Bessudnov et al, 2012). The economic and political transition to capitalism in these countries was coupled with dramatic changes in mortality patterns, particularly among the former USSR countries (see Figures 4.2 and 4.3). For example, during a four-year period between 1991 and 1995, life expectancy in Russia fell by 5 years for males and by 2.6 years for females, and by 4 and 1.8 years in Latvia, respectively (Scheiring et al, 2019). Such reductions in life expectancy were unprecedented outside of the World Wars (Scheiring et al, 2019).

**Figure 4.2:** Male life expectancy in the former USSR, 1959–2013

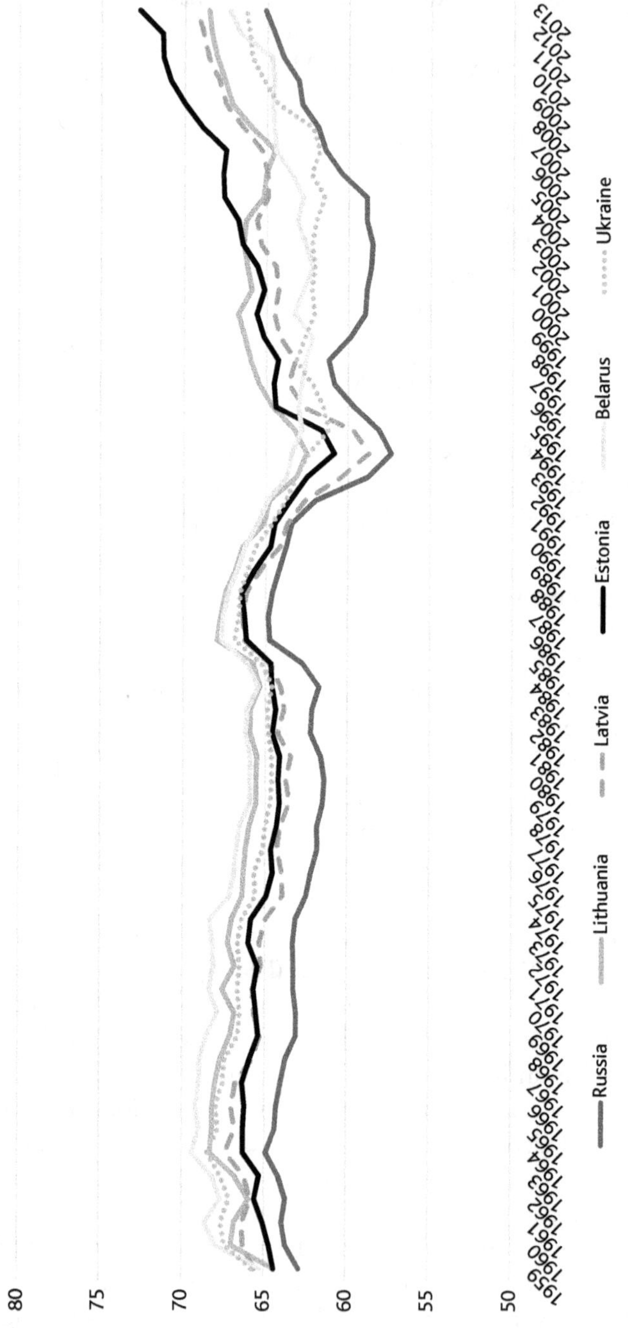

What belongs together will grow together

**Figure 4.3:** Female life expectancy in the former USSR, 1959–2013

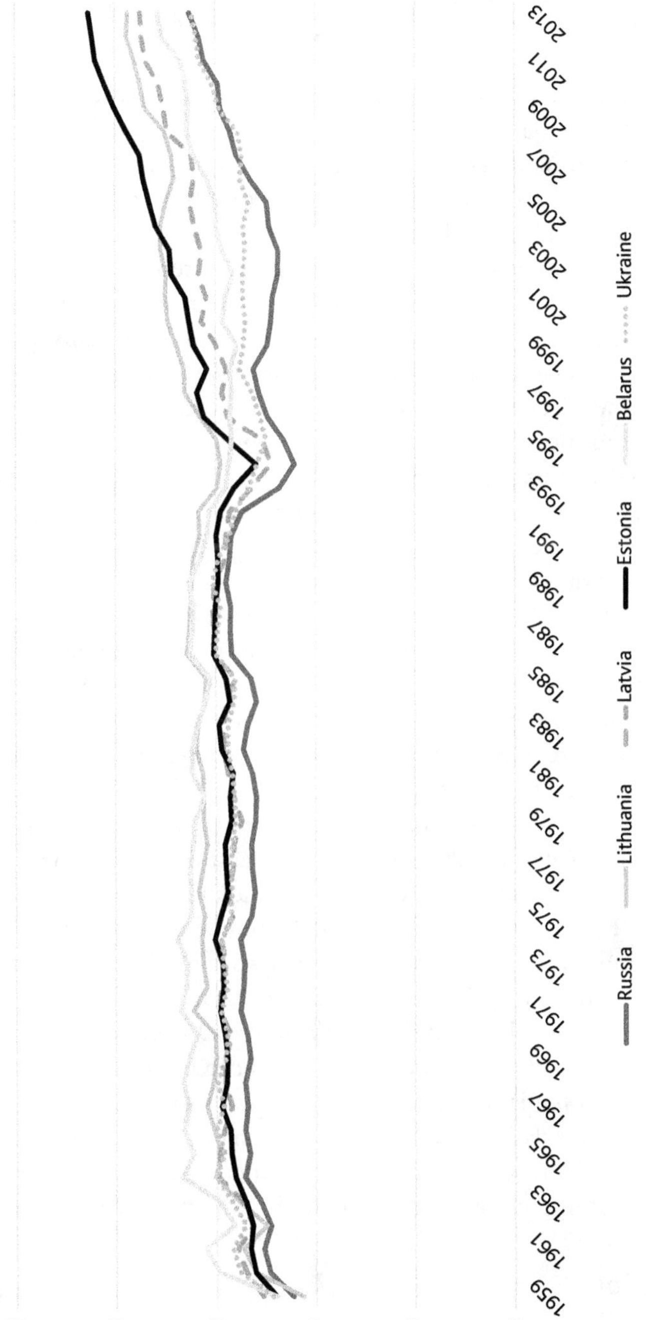

The rapid rises in mortality after the fall of communism were not shared equally across the population, which led to increasing health inequalities. For example, while there were large educational inequalities in mortality in Russia even in the late 1970s, these gaps widened from the mid-1990s onwards and life expectancy fell among the least educated. The health of low-skilled, manual workers suffered the most in this period with substantial increases in mortality rates among men and an increase in the mortality gap with male managers and professionals (Shkolnikov et al, 1998; Bessudnov et al, 2012). Similarly, in Estonia and Czech Republic, mortality rises were also more pronounced among the least educated (Leinsalu et al, 2003; Shkolnikov et al, 2006). Likewise, in Poland, occupational health differences were not significant until the early 1990s when a mortality gap between manual and non-manual workers developed (Watson, 1998). A comparative study of the Czech Republic, Estonia, the Russian Federation and, as a Western European reference, Finland, contrasting two periods, 1988–89 and 1998–99, found improvements in life expectancy across all educational groups in Finland and the Czech Republic, with only a slight widening of educational inequalities. However, Estonia and Russia exhibited a huge widening of the educational gap with a decrease in life expectancy in those with low and middle education (Shkolnikov et al, 2006).

Research investigating the causes of the post-socialist mortality crisis suggests that the rapid economic changes of privatisation and deindustrialisation, which (unlike in Germany) occurred in the absence of sufficient public policy support, drove an increase in poverty, psychosocial stress, excess alcohol consumption and, ultimately, rising mortality (King et al, 2022). For example, Stuckler and colleagues (2009) found an association between mass privatisation and higher working-age male mortality in all post-socialist economies. The rapidity of the economic reforms was also a factor in the increased death rates between 1989–94 (Brainerd, 1998). Deindustrialisation also contributed to increases in male mortality. For example, an analysis by Scheiring and colleagues (2023), of Russia and Hungary between 1991 and 1999 found a significant increase in stress-related hazardous drinking after deindustrialisation. The effects on mortality were much less pronounced in Hungary than they were in Russia – potentially a result of differences in social security levels in the two countries (relatively generous in Hungary and practically non-existent in Russia) (Scheiring et al, 2023). This further suggests a protective effect of poverty relief in cushioning the negative health effects of unemployment.

## Conclusion

Post-reunification Germany provides an important example of how a long-term approach to improving the economy and living standards can improve health and reduce health inequalities. As we have seen, in 1990, the life expectancy gap between the former East and the former West of Germany was almost three years for women and three and a half years for men. Despite rapid deindustrialisation in the East, this gap rapidly narrowed in the following decades so that by 2020 life expectancy for women in the East was higher than women in the West, and for men the gap has decreased to around 18 months. East Germany now has better health and living standards than many UK and other European regions (Centre for Cities, 2021). This unprecedented health improvement was achieved through improving living standards in the East via higher productivity, better wages, pensions and access to better quality food and consumer goods; and modernising hospitals and healthcare equipment in the East and increasing nursing care, public health and pharmaceuticals. East Germany was also democratised. These wide ranging economic, social, political and healthcare reforms were the result of the deep and sustained political decision to reunify Germany as fully as possible so that, in the words of Helmut Kohl (West German Chancellor from 1982 to 1998), 'what belongs together will grow together'. German reunification was funded by a special Solidarity Surcharge. This was levied across the whole of Germany at a rate of up to 5.5 per cent on income taxes owed (for example, a tax bill of €5000 attracts a solidarity surcharge €275) (Centre for Cities, 2021). Around £70 billion a year for 25 years has been invested in 'levelling up' East Germany, funded by this solidarity surcharge (Centre for Cities, 2021).

The German case study therefore has clear lessons for tackling health inequalities in other countries: even very large health gaps can be significantly reduced; it can be done in an epidemiologically short time frame; and the tools to do this are largely economic and social. The latter are though – perhaps crucially – within the control of politics and politicians. Ultimately, the German experience shows that if there is a sufficient political desire to reduce health inequalities, it can be done. This is something we reflect on further in Chapter 6.

# 5

# Things can only get better: England's Health Inequalities Strategy

This chapter examines the positive impact of England's National Health Inequalities Strategy, which was enacted between 2000 and 2010. In contrast to the US, Brazilian and German case studies, the English example involved a specific policy drive to reduce health inequalities. The Health Inequalities Strategy focused on supporting families, engaging communities in tackling deprivation, improving prevention, increasing access to healthcare and tackling the underlying social determinants of health, including poverty reduction. This chapter provides an overview of the social determinants of health and trends in health inequalities in England and the UK prior to the strategy. It then outlines the details of the policy reforms enacted and summarises the reductions in inequalities in life expectancy, infant mortality, old age mortality and mortality amenable to healthcare that occurred during the strategy period. It concludes by reflecting on what this means for the importance of politics and policies in promoting better health for all.

## Shock therapy: Thatcherism and health inequalities, 1979 to 1997

As noted in Chapter 1, after the Second World War (1945) there was a 'golden age' of welfare state capitalism, the '*Trente Glorieuses*', during which a mainstream political consensus favoured a generous, redistributive welfare state – even in the UK. This 'golden age' ended with the responses to the economic crisis of the 1970s, which were characterised by the emergence – and later hegemony – of neoliberal economics. The political consensus of the early post-war years broke down as governments started to dismantle and restructure the welfare state. The 'reforms' (which in the UK largely occurred in the 1980s and 1990s) included the privatisation and marketisation of welfare services; an increased emphasis on an active rather than a passive welfare system (with benefit entitlement restrictions and increased qualifying conditions, and a shift towards targeting and means testing; cuts or limited increases to the actual cash values of benefits); radically modified public funding arrangements (with a shift away from business taxation); deregulation of the economy with the promotion of labour market flexibility, supply-side economics and a desire to minimise public social expenditure; and the subordination of social policy to the demands of the market (Jessop, 1991).[1] This was all accompanied by an implicit ideology of individualism – exemplified by Thatcher's (in)famous comment that 'there is no such thing as society, only individuals and their families' (cited in Ward and England, 2007, p 7). In this chapter we examine this policy turn and its impact on health in more detail, through an examination of the UK.

## Thatcherism and neoliberalism in the UK

Neoliberal ideology has the following key suppositions: that markets are the normal, natural and preferable way of organising most if not all forms of human interaction; that the primary function of the state is to ensure the efficient functioning of markets; and that institutions or policies that lead to outcomes different from those that would be expected from a market functioning as markets are supposed to in economics textbooks require justification (for a more detailed overview, see Schrecker and Bambra, 2015; 2025). In the UK, neoliberalism was implemented rapidly – as a 'shock doctrine' (Collins and McCartney, 2011) – by the consecutive Conservative governments of Margaret Thatcher (1979–90) and John Major (1990–97). Thatcher's critique of UK social democracy during the 1970s and her adoption of key neoliberal strategies, such as financial deregulation, trade liberalisation and the privatisation of public goods and services, were popularly labelled 'Thatcherism'. Thatcherism was as an ideological project that set out to radically recast the relationship between labour and capital and between the state, society and the individual (Gamble, 1994). Thatcherism and the New Right provided a narrative which explained the crisis of British capitalism in the 1970s as a crisis of the welfare state, high wages and low productivity; and of the 'undemocratic' power of what in 1984 she called 'the enemy within' – the trade unions (Hall and Jacques, 1983). Thatcherism set out to dismantle the structures of the post-war Keynesian consensus through the aggressive promotion of the free market alongside the 'hollowing out' of the state (Moran, 1999).

These changes all led to a fundamental rebalancing of British economic and social life. The growing economic equality promoted by the UK's Golden Age social reforms was reversed, with income inequality increasing significantly. For example, the richest 0.01 per cent had 28 times the mean national average income in 1978 but this increased under Thatcher's tenure to 70 times in 1990 (Dorling, 2012). Additionally, because of welfare state retrenchment, high unemployment, falling wages and lower job security for many workers (due to the decreased bargaining power of trade unions), there was a near doubling of poverty rates in the UK in a decade from 6.7 per cent in 1975 to 12.0 per cent in 1985 (Ginsburg, 1992). By the 1990s and 2000s, these new higher levels of poverty became normalised.

Social mobility gains were also stalled via changes to the education system as well as the 'lost generation' of young people who left school and went straight onto 'the dole' in the early 1980s. From 1980, the number of unemployment claimants rose from around 1 million to around 3 million in 1983; a further peak was seen in the early 1990s. Meanwhile, there was also a steady rise in the number of claimants of long-term sickness (disability) benefits (Bambra, 2011). A writer who grew up in Grimshaw in the North of England provides a sense of the lived experience of this transition:

> [M]y whole family kind of plopped ... after the miners' strike of 1984–85. Before that, we felt that we were a part of something, a community, a great nation, with a great history. After that, we knew that we were redundant, rubbish, nothing. Years of idleness and indolence followed. More and more people were thrown on the dole, our communities crumbled, people lost hope and felt betrayed. (Hare, 2006)

In the new economy that emerged in the 1980s, manufacturing and extraction industries, public utilities and collective housing provision were displaced by finance and banking industries, low-wage services, privatised utilities and rampant property speculation. The 1986 deregulation of the City of London unleashed new forms of financial speculation. 'Giving power back to the people' through privatisation, in fact, led to the radical de-democratisation of the power industry – now largely externally owned – and other utilities. And the ambition to create 'a nation of home owners' by selling off public housing units produced mushrooming homelessness due to a chronic shortage of affordable social housing. It also underpinned a new culture of speculation and chronic indebtedness on which a new breed of amoral 'entrepreneurs' in banking and finance would be able to prey. All of this sharply increased inequalities of income and wealth across the UK, and a dramatic increase in poverty. It also put in place most of the prerequisites for the great banking and finance crisis of 2008 (Gamble, 2009). In this way Thatcher's governments engineered an economic catastrophe across large parts of the UK and kick started the dismantling of the welfare state and the privatisation of the National Health Service (NHS) in England (Davis and Tallis, 2013).

## Thatcherism and the determinants of health

The impact of these changes on the key social determinants of health was dramatic. Inequalities in both educational outcomes and access to healthcare, for example, increased following policies implemented under Thatcher's leadership (Scott-Samuel et al, 2014). In housing, Thatcher's 'right to buy' initiative gave council tenants the right to purchase the homes they occupied, often at greatly discounted rates. This policy was popular among many of those it helped move onto the housing ladder. However, it contributed to growing wealth inequalities and sowed the seeds of the housing market crash in 1989, which left many homeowners trapped by 'negative equity' (Dorling, 2014). Meanwhile, as better-quality houses were sold off, local councils were left with responsibility for a far smaller and increasingly poor-quality housing stock, contributing to growing levels of homelessness (Loveland, 1993).

Thatcher avoided any wholesale reform of the NHS, allegedly fearful of an adverse public reaction. Her government did, however, introduce several policy initiatives which set the NHS on a course from which it has not deviated since. The most significant NHS development under her premiership was the introduction of a quasi-market in healthcare centred around competition and choice (Hunter, 2008). Among the most controversial changes Thatcher introduced was the policy of contracting out or outsourcing, introduced in 1983, whereby health authorities were required to set up competitive tendering arrangements for their cleaning, catering and laundry services. Other non-clinical services were later added to the list. This established the principle that the core responsibility of health authorities was no longer to directly provide non-clinical services but merely to ensure that they were in place at least cost. It marked a substantial break with the past and opened the NHS up to market forces.

During the 1980s and 1990s the number of standard full-time, permanent jobs declined, while flexible or precarious employment on temporary contracts or no contracts, with limited or no employment or welfare rights, increased.[2] This partly reflected a decline in manufacturing employment (deindustrialisation) and the rise of the service sector. It also reflected the anti-trade union laws introduced starting in 1979 (the UK now has some of the most restrictive trade union rights of any wealthy democracy). In this new economy, skills, working hours, contracts, conditions, pay and location are all more flexible and precarious. The once-standard full time, permanent contract with benefits has been superseded by several atypical forms of employment characterised by lower levels of security and poorer working conditions (Benach et al, 2002). Rather than being a transitory stage in an individual's employment history, atypical forms of labour are becoming the norm for many workers in the labour force of high-income countries (Virtanen et al, 2002).

Permanent or structural unemployment has also increased in the UK. Until the late 1970s, governments of both major parties in the UK were commitment to the pursuit of full employment (unemployment rates of <3 per cent or employment rates of >80 per cent). There were, of course, periods of higher unemployment during the early post-war years, but these were cyclical, following the boom and bust of patterns of the economy (for example, the early 1960s in the UK). The commitment to full employment was abandoned under Thatcher and subsequent UK governments, which accepted high unemployment and its social consequences as collateral damage in pursuit of the neoliberal goal of controlling inflation. Indeed, Norman Lamont, the Conservative UK Chancellor of the Exchequer stated in 1991 that 'rising unemployment and the recession have been the price that we have had to pay to get inflation down. That price is well worth paying' (Lamont, 1991). This was echoed in 1998 by Eddie George, the Governor of the Bank of England, who stated that 'northern unemployment is an acceptable price to pay for curbing southern inflation' (BBC News, 1998).

Even as unemployment grew, the support provided to people when they are out of work was reduced. For example, in the UK the percentage of an average worker's wage that would be replaced by unemployment benefits (the unemployment replacement rate) for one earner supporting a partner and two children declined from 69 per cent in 1971 to 36 per cent in 1990 (Eikemo and Bambra, 2008). For a single worker with no dependents, the decline was even more dramatic, from 54 per cent in 1971 to 20 per cent or less after 1990 (Scruggs et al, 2014). These figures apply only to those workers who are eligible for benefits; a further neoliberal 'reform' was restricting eligibility for any compensation at all. The savings here were used to give significant tax reductions for businesses and top earners. All this contributed to a steep rise in income and wealth inequalities during the 1980s and 1990s. The share of UK wealth held by the top 1 per cent and top 0.1 per cent of the population increased by more than 50 per cent between 1977 and 1997 (Piketty, 2014).

## Thatcherism and health inequalites

The effects of Thatcherism's neoliberal economic and social policies on health inequalities have been stark (or of 'epidemic' proportions, to use Schrecker and Bambra's term, 2015); those at the bottom of the social hierarchy have fallen even further behind. During the 1980s the social determinants of health became more stratified with the poorest areas and poorest people faring worse in relative terms than they had at any point since the Second World War (Dorling, 2012). As a result – and unsurprisingly given what we know about the importance of the social determinants of health (Chapter 1) – health inequalities increased during the 1980s and 1990s. Mortality rates in the UK, as across Western and Central Europe, had been improving for around 150 years (Bambra, 2016). This long-run improvement continued throughout the period of the Thatcher government, with all-cause mortality rates declining at a similar rate to those in other countries and compared to the time periods before and after. However, despite the overall improvement in mortality rates, some specific causes of mortality increased markedly during the period of the Thatcher government or immediately afterwards. For example, alcohol-related mortality (a so-called 'death of despair' [Case and Deaton, 2015]) increased dramatically during the late 1980s and early 1990s in the UK, in stark contrast to the improving trends in other parts of Europe (WHO, 2012). Increases were also seen in other 'deaths of despair' in the UK: drug-related mortality, suicide, and violence (WHO, 2012). Further, within the UK, mortality rates improved much more slowly in northern and inner-city areas than in more affluent southern England (Hacking et al, 2011). In some particularly deprived local areas mortality rates actually worsened (Norman, 2011). And for young adults in Scotland, there has been no improvement in mortality over the course of the last 40 years (Whyte et al, 2012).

The gap in mortality between the least and most deprived areas in Scotland increased rapidly between 1981 and 2001, leaving Scotland with the highest inequalities in Western and Central Europe (Leyland, 2004; Mackenbach et al, 2008). The rise in inequalities in health during the 1980s was also reflected in a rapid rise in mortality inequalities by occupational social class in England and Wales. In England and Wales, life expectancy increased for all social class groups among males and females over time, but the increase was more rapid among higher social classes than in lower ones, such that inequalities increased (Scott-Samuel et al, 2014). The rises in cause-specific mortalities such as alcohol- and drug-related deaths, suicide and violence, and the widening health inequalities, occurred during the same period in which unemployment, poverty and income inequality all rose.

## Tough on the causes? New Labour and health inequalities 1997–2010

In the 1997 general election, after 18 years in opposition, the Labour Party was re-elected to office with a landslide victory and a manifesto that promised to tackle the 'root causes' of ill health, such as poor housing and unemployment. The new government was keen to emphasise the previous Conservative governments' failure to address health inequalities. The Labour government initially criticised the Conservatives for placing an 'excessive emphasis on lifestyle issues' and for putting the responsibility for ill-health onto individuals rather than the economic and social structures of society and the places where people live (Department of Health, 1997). In addition, and as promised in their manifesto, the Labour government's Public Health minister Tessa Jowell (the nation's first ever minister dedicated to that portfolio) commissioned an independent inquiry into health inequalities, which came to be known as the Acheson Inquiry.

The inquiry echoed the last Labour government's actions (1974–79) when, in 1977, the Chief Scientist, Sir Douglas Black, had been appointed to lead a working group of experts to investigate health inequalities and make policy recommendations for the government (Berridge and Blume, 2003). The resulting 'Black Report' (1980) argued that poverty played a large role in explaining health inequalities and, therefore, that policymakers ought to prioritise the reduction of differences in the economic circumstances between socio-economic groups and between deprived and affluent areas. The report was published in 1980 (on a Bank Holiday Monday in August to minimise publicity and with only 260 copies produced), by which time the commissioning left-wing Labour government had been replaced by the first Thatcher-led Conservative, right-wing government (1979–83). The Black Report's recommendations, which included increasing welfare benefits and decreasing child poverty, were wholeheartedly rejected by the new government. In an infamous report foreword, Patrick Jenkins, the then Secretary of State for Social Services, claimed the report was 'wildly unrealistic' and 'seriously flawed'. This set the tone for the next 17 years as, under the Conservative governments of 1979–97 (1979–83, 1983–87, 1987–92, 1992–97), health inequalities were not on the official policy agenda (Berridge and Blume, 2003). Even the term 'health inequalities' was discarded and health differences between socio-economic groups and places were instead referred to using the less emotive term 'health variations' – which implied that health differences could be 'natural', individual and therefore not something for which politicians and policymakers were responsible.

In stark contrast to the chilly reception faced by the Black Report, on publication in 1998, the Acheson Inquiry Report and its recommendations were officially welcomed by the Labour government, and then used as the basis of a new national Health Inequalities Strategy for England (while the newly devolved administrations in Scotland, Northern Ireland and Wales pursued their own approaches to tackling health inequalities health – see Smith et al, 2009). In broad terms many of the resulting Acheson Report's 39 recommendations reflected the conclusions of the earlier Black Report: both highlighted the need to have a multifaceted approach to health inequalities and both advocated a reduction in income inequalities, with a particular focus on child poverty as a way to reduce health inequalities (Bambra et al, 2011). The Acheson Report's recommendations also included policies to: reduce income inequalities and improve the living standards of households in receipt of social security benefits; increase benefits in cash or in kind to reduce poverty in women of childbearing age, expectant mothers, young children and older people; and many other recommendations that called for action to reduce the poor health effects of unemployment and deprivation among ethnic minority groups, the elderly and disabled people, and families with children (Black et al, 1999). Other recommendations were concerned with meeting material needs in schools, housing, the environment, transport, and diet as well as improving NHS funding, especially in the most deprived areas (Black et al, 1999).

The key difference between the Black and Acheson Reports was that the latter was released in a far more favourable political climate than its predecessor and might, therefore, be expected to have had more of an impact on policy – and on health inequalities. However, Labour had also stipulated that the Inquiry's recommendations should recognise the government's fiscal promises made during the election campaign, which included an agreement not to increase public spending above the levels of the previous government for two years. This restriction made it difficult to attempt to tackle the fundamental economic and political determinants of health in any of the emerging policy initiatives linked to the report (Smith et al, 1998). Despite this constraint, the UK became the first European country in which policymakers systematically and explicitly attempted to reduce inequalities in health (Mackenbach, 2011).

A wealth of policy statements referring directly to the report were produced, indicating that policy decisions had, as promised, been directly informed – or at least influenced – by the recommendations of the report. Health policy across the UK reflected some of the ideas set out in the Acheson report, including a consistent rhetorical emphasis on the need to tackle the social and economic determinants of health inequalities. Fundamental to the Health Inequalities Strategy was the inclusion of targets against which the government would measure its success. In 2000, the Department of Health made its first commitment to setting a national target for reducing health inequalities in England (Department of Health, 2000). The first iteration of these targets appeared in 2001:

- Starting with children under one year, by 2010 we will reduce by at least 10 per cent the gap in infant mortality between manual groups and the population as a whole.
- Starting with Health Authorities, by 2010 we will reduce by at least 10 per cent the gap between the fifth of areas with the lowest life expectancy at birth and the population as a whole.

In this initial wording, the target for infant mortality focused on a difference between socio-economic groups (assessed via occupation), while the target for life expectancy was area-based. However, during the following year, the two targets were amended several times, before being combined into a single area-based target in the *Spending Review 2004 Public Service Agreements 2005–2008* (HM Treasury, 2004): Starting with Local Authorities, by 2010 to reduce by at least 10% the gap between the fifth of areas with the worst health and deprivation indicators and the population as a whole.

The indicators on which this target was to be assessed included measures of life expectancy and infant mortality, reflecting the focus of the two original targets. In effect, possibly because of the greater availability of geographical data, the whole health inequalities target became area-based. This is the target that remained in place until 2010 and it is this version of the target that most subsequent analysis has used to assess performance.

Two years later, the Treasury – which played a key role in negotiating targets with other government departments (Hood, 2006) – added health and deprivation indicators to existing population-level, disease specific targets, effectively creating two additional health inequalities targets for England (HM Treasury, 2004):

- Substantially reduce mortality rates by 2010 from heart disease and stroke and related diseases by at least 40% in people under 75, with a 40% reduction in the inequalities gap between the fifth of areas with the worst health and deprivation indicators and the population as a whole;
- Substantially reduce mortality rates by 2010 from cancer by at least 20% in people under 75, with a reduction in the inequalities gap of at least 6% between the fifth of areas with the worst health and deprivation indicators and the population as a whole.

In sum, a complex array of targets for reducing health inequalities in England was introduced. Further, various policy documents made it clear that the government expected a range of other national targets and related policies to contribute to reductions in health inequalities in England. These included targets focusing on material and environmental factors, such as the Neighbourhood Renewal targets to narrow the 'gap' in employment rates, education, crime, housing and liveability as well as health (Social Exclusion Unit, 2001); the Department of Transport's target to reduce the number of people killed in road accidents and the number of children killed and seriously injured in road accidents (for which there was a steep social gradient); the Department for Education and Skills target to narrow the gap in the educational attainment of disadvantaged children compared to the population as a whole; and the target of improving access to affordable healthy food (Department of Health, 2002). Additionally, the UK's aim of halving child poverty by 2010 and eradicating it by 2020 was mentioned in several policy statements as a key target expected to help achieve reductions in health inequalities (for example, Secretary of State for Health 2004).

Indeed, there was a commitment to employing cross-cutting government policies – that went beyond the Department of Health and the NHS – to tackle health inequalities and meet the targets (Smith et al, 2009). The NHS was awarded above historical average budget increases. For example, the NHS in England has had an average budgetary increase of 3.7 per cent per annum since it was established in 1948, but between 1997 and 2010, it grew by 5.7 per cent a year (Appleby and Gainsbury, 2022; The Kings Fund, 2022). Alongside an overall increase in the NHS budget, funds were also channelled to the most deprived areas by including a weighting for health inequalities in the formula used to allocate NHS funding to local areas (thus ensuring that the poorest areas with highest health needs got more resources). There were also significant and wide-ranging changes across other areas of government policy between 1997 and 2010. These included large increases in levels of public spending on a range of social programmes, the introduction of the national minimum wage, a child poverty strategy, an increase in pension rates, as well as area-based interventions such as Health Action Zones and the New Deal for Communities (Whitehead and Popay, 2010). These policies led to reductions in social inequalities in the key social determinants of health – including unemployment, child poverty, housing quality, access to healthcare and educational attainment (Bambra, 2016). Some of the larger reforms enacted by the Labour government between 1997 and 2010 are described in Table 5.1.

Table 5.1: Main health inequalities policies and interventions in England, 1997–2010

| Intervention name | Intervention description |
| --- | --- |
| Sure Start | Sure Start was an early years intervention programme which provided parents with an outreach worker within three months of birth and provided a range of easily accessible services (e.g. childcare, primary healthcare, early education, play and support). At its peak in 2010, 3,663 Sure Start Children's Centres were open in England, providing support to 2.9 million children under five, at a cost of £1.5 billion (based on 2019–20 prices) (Britton et al, 2019). |
| Tax Credits | The Working Family Tax Credit was introduced in 1999. It was a significant shift as it changed the administration of benefits from a traditional income-related cash benefit to a tax credit paid directly through a person's wage packet. Generosity of support also increased, with state expenditure increased by £2 billion per year to £5 billion (Dilnot and McCrae, 1999). Later reforms in 2003 replaced it with Child Tax Credit and Working Tax Credit. The latter reforms merged different components of the tax and benefit system, as well as increasing support available to those in-work and on a low income, regardless of whether they had children (Brewer, 2006). The Tax Credits significantly reduced child poverty in the period. |
| Minimum Income Guarantee for Pensions | The Minimum Income Guarantee for Pensions, later renamed as Pension Credit, introduced a means-tested payment to the basic pension. It boosted the income of the poorest older person from £69 a week in 1997 to above £130 a week (minimum) in 2010. This significantly reduced pensioner poverty in the period. |
| Health Action Zones | Health Action Zones were multi-agency partnerships located in 26 deprived areas of England, with the intention of reducing health inequalities. They involved an investment of £4–£5 million (at 2004 prices) per year, per zone. Local communities were asked to develop plans for how to allocate this investment (so which initiatives to support) to improve health and reduce inequalities over a seven-year period. |

(continued)

**Table 5.1:** Main health inequalities policies and interventions in England, 1997–2010 (continued)

| Intervention name | Intervention description |
| --- | --- |
| New Deal for Communities | The New Deal for Communities was another area-based initiative that formed part of the wider National Strategy for Renewal, which was based on the principle that no-one should be disadvantaged by where they live. It specifically targeted the poorest neighbourhoods in England, aiming to bridge the gap with the wealthiest areas. Core aspects of the programme included dedicated neighbourhood agencies, community engagement, partnership working, and learning and innovation. Some 39 partnerships were established, each receiving approximately £50 million over 10 years, totalling £2.9 billion between 1999 and 2008 (in 2010 prices) for neighbourhood renewal activities (Fordham, 2010). |
| The NHS Plan 2000 | The NHS Plan 2000 led to the introduction of a health inequality weighting into the NHS budget allocation formula. Alongside a wider package of reforms, that included increased investment and new waiting time targets, the NHS Plan also amended how the NHS funding formula was devised so that resources were targeted more at the most deprived areas – where health needs were highest. The local NHS commissioning organisations in these areas were free to use these additional resources to purchase primary or secondary healthcare or public health services, to better meet the needs of their populations and improve the quality of care they received (Barr et al, 2014). The allocation of NHS resources increased in real terms in the most deprived areas: from £1074/head in 2001 to £1938/head in 2011, representing an 81% increase. In more affluent areas allocations still increased but to a lesser extent: from £881/head in 2001 to £1502/head in 2011: an increase of 70% (Barr et al, 2014). |
| Tobacco control measures | Specifically with the intent of helping reduce health inequalities, England invested significant resources in smoking cessation, targeted so that more resource was invested in poorer areas. Additionally, the 1997–2010 Labour governments banned tobacco advertising and introduced a ban on smoking in indoor public places, under legislation designed to improve workplace safety. The UK Government also actively supported negotiations for the Framework Convention on Tobacco Control (FCTC), and was one of the first signatories of this international agreement. The FCTC includes a clause (Article 5.3) to protect health policy development from tobacco industry interference. |

The 1997–2010 Labour governments also introduced a series of measures to reduce tobacco consumption (which was, and remains, higher in more disadvantaged groups). Repeated investments were made in programmes to support smoking cessation (Bauld et al, 2007). The services were initially piloted in Health Action Zones (see Table 5.1) and then rolled out more broadly but retaining a focus on more disadvantaged areas and low-income smokers. In addition, Labour introduced a series of policies to restrict the influence of the tobacco industry. These included a comprehensive ban on tobacco advertising (2003); ratification of the United Nations Framework Convention on Tobacco Control, including an article protecting health policy from tobacco industry influence (2004) and a ban on indoor smoking (2007).

## Was the English Health Inequalities Strategy successful?

In England, the performance assessment approach to governance meant that progress against key targets was regularly updated and considered in some depth. In 2007, for example, the Department of Health published a review of the health inequalities infant mortality target. This review suggested that there had been a series of implementation failures associated with the target, leading to low local recognition of the infant mortality target compared to other targets, and a lack of understanding of how the target could be achieved. The report also noted that the focus of the target on occupational groups was potentially limiting, in light of data suggesting that a more useful focus might be on particular ethnic groups (for example, Pakistani and Caribbean communities, both of which experienced substantially higher rates of infant mortality than other ethnic groups) and particular categories of mothers with higher infant mortality rates (single mothers, younger mothers and older mothers). This kind of report provided an opportunity to address some of these issues by raising awareness of the target and focusing on identifying actions deemed likely to help achieve the target.

Towards the end of the targets period in England, a 2009 House of Commons report on health inequalities considered the broader approach to tackling health inequalities. Their report noted that available indicators suggested the English national health inequalities target was not on track to be achieved (House of Commons, 2009). In reflecting on this, the report notes:

> We heard that in having a target which explicitly aims to reduce inequalities rather than simply improving the health of the poor, *England has one of the toughest targets in the world*. It was suggested that a better approach to improving health might be a focus on improving the health of the most disadvantaged groups rather than on narrowing differences. (House of Commons, 2009, p 59 [our emphasis])

The report also notes that this was in line with senior advice provided to the government:

> One should focus on the absolute level of ill-health of the poor. One of the pieces of advice I gave the Government a very long time ago was that setting a target in health inequalities is almost certainly a mistake, because almost certainly you will miss it – and, indeed, that is exactly what has happened. (Professor Julian Le Grand, then Chair of Health England, quoted in House of Commons, 2009, p 60)

In other words, the decision to commit to a target for reducing health inequalities in England looked, by 2009, bold, 'difficult and possibly unrealistic' (House of Commons, 2009, p 59).

In sum, it seems clear that the government had been advised they would be safer to focus on improving the health of disadvantaged communities rather than reducing inequalities *per se*. External experts and advisors quoted in the 2009 House of Commons report seemed uniformly pessimistic about the possibility of meeting the English health inequalities targets by the 2010 deadline. The only voices defending the targets were those of the Healthcare Commission, which suggested the target played a valuable role in raising the profile of health inequalities (regardless of whether it was eventually reached), and the then Secretary of State for Health, Alan Johnson, who argued that 'it would be depressingly unambitious just to say, "Let's target the poor and forget about the inequality gap"' (House of Commons, 2009, p 60).

When asked to assess the likelihood of achieving the national health inequalities target, the Secretary of State for Health was one of the only optimistic voices in the House of Commons report. In the end, this optimism proved well placed. Although some earlier analyses of the English Health Inequalities Strategy were pessimistic (for example, Mackenbach, 2011 wrote an article on why the English strategy had failed), more recent analyses using more accurate long-term data and more appropriate measures have found that the English health inequalities targets were largely achieved, with notable reductions in (geographical) health inequalities between 2000 and 2010 (Barr et al, 2014; 2017; Robinson et al, 2019; Holdroyd et al, 2022; Albani et al, 2022; Bennett et al, 2024).

Barr and colleagues (2017) analysed trends in geographical inequalities in life expectancy and found that the national target to reduce the gap between Spearhead areas (the 20 per cent most deprived local authorities in England) and the English national average by at least 10 per cent was achieved for male life expectancy, though not for female life expectancy: inequalities in life expectancy were just over a year smaller among men during the English Health Inequalities Strategy period of 2000 to 2010 and around six months smaller among women than they would have been if the trends in inequalities before the strategy had continued (Barr et al, 2017). Before the strategy in the 1980s and 1990s (and, as we will see in Chapter 6, after

**Figure 5.1:** Inequalities in infant mortality rates by English local authority, 1983–2017

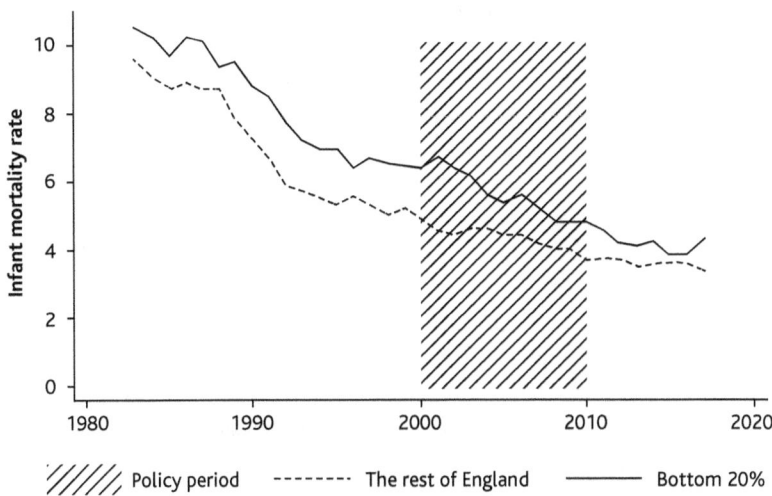

the strategy post-2010), the gap in life expectancy between the 20 per cent most deprived areas and the national average had increased.

Similarly, Robinson and colleagues (2019) analysis found that inequalities in the infant mortality rate (IMR) between the 20 per cent most deprived local authorities in England and the national average also shrank during the strategy period, with the gap in IMR narrowing by 12 deaths per 100,000 births per year across the period (Figure 5.1). This also reversed pre-strategy trends (and again – as will be outlined in Chapter 6 – trends after the end of the strategy) of increasing inequalities in IMR (Figure 5.1). This reduction in inequalities in IMR was likely related to the reduction in child poverty achieved between 1997 and 2010 as well as to related child/family policies such as Sure Start (Robinson et al, 2019; Taylor-Robinson et al, 2019).

Inequalities in mortality amenable to health care between the most deprived and least deprived local authorities also fell by 35 deaths per 100,000 for men and 16 deaths per 100,000 for women.[3] Each additional £10 million of resources allocated to deprived areas was associated with a reduction in four male deaths per 100,000 and two female deaths per 100,000 (Barr et al, 2014). This success was likely directly linked to the policy of increasing the proportion of NHS resources allocated to deprived areas as compared to more affluent areas (Barr et al, 2014).

A study by Bennett and colleagues (2024) examined the impact of the strategy on inequalities in mortality among those aged over 65 years. They found a similar pattern, with absolute inequalities between the 20 per cent most deprived areas and the rest of England decreasing from 657 per 100,000 in 2000, to 519 in 2010. Absolute inequality then began to increase again after the end of the strategy in 2010, from 566 per 100,000 in 2011 to 585 in 2019. Another study examined the impact of Labour's pension improvements on inequalities in mental health among pensioners (Albani et al, 2022). It found no change in mental well-being for women but an improvement for men overall and especially for men living in the most deprived areas.

A full systematic review examining trends in health inequalities (both mortality and morbidity) in England between 2000 and 2010 (Holdroyd et al, 2022) found that: 'absolute and relative inequalities had decreased throughout the strategy period for both [target] measures', that inequalities in all-cause mortality narrowed, and that absolute inequalities in mortality due to cancer and cardiovascular disease decreased. However, the review did also find 'there was a lack of change, or widening of inequalities in mental health, self-reported health, health related quality of life and long-term conditions'.

Nonetheless, taken together, these studies demonstrate convincingly that the Health Inequalities Strategy was broadly successful and that its targets – which were widely criticised at the time for being unachievable and over ambitious – were, in fact, largely achieved. Examining evaluations of the health inequalities effects of specific policies can help to unpack how the strategy was successful. There were multiple different policies and interventions implemented in this period (some of which are described in Table 5.1). While not all of these have been evaluated in terms of their health effects, many have; positive impacts on health inequalities have been noted for Sure Start, Tax Credits, the Minimum Income Guarantee for Pensioners, New Deal for Communities and the addition of an inequality weighting into the NHS budget allocation formula (Holdroyd et al, 2022).

Insights on Sure Start's health impacts are likely to continue emerging over time (just as findings from the High/Scope Perry Pre-School programme in the USA found significant benefits from the programme when participants were aged 40 [Buchanan, 2006]). Early analysis showed positive effects of Sure Start on early childhood development, such as better social development, more positive social behaviour and greater independence (Melhuish, 2008). More recent analysis has shown that Sure Start had a significant effect on rates of hospitalisation: For younger children, the probability of an externally caused hospitalisation fell by 10 per cent or more with greater access to Sure Start. For preventable health conditions, greater access to Sure Start was associated with a 20 per cent reduction (from baseline levels) in hospitalisations by age 11 (Cattan et al, 2021). Qualitative assessments of Sure Start have focused on the benefits that parents experienced, such as having a place to go for respite, building community connections and accessing employment training opportunities (Avis et al, 2007). For example, one participant reported that:

> I've got somewhere to go when the kids are ... when you're fed up, isn't it? When the kids are doing your head in. Just somewhere to go. Somewhere friendly. I was depressed and [Sure Start] really helped me. I felt isolated and I've got nobody and so they really helped me. I think I would have cracked up. It got me out the house, which has also helped. (Participant cited in Avis et al, 2007, p 206)

Qualitative studies suggest the Sure Start intervention had a positive impact on the mental health and well-being of parents who engaged with local Sure Start centres, though they also identify eligible parents who did not engage for a host of reasons.

Tax credits, too, led to improvement in mental health (anxiety and depression symptoms) among lone mothers (Gregg et al, 2009). Other effects of the introduction of tax credits included significant improvements in life satisfaction among mothers and in adolescent self-esteem and happiness, particularly for adolescent boys (Gregg et al, 2009). Wickham et al (2017) argue that these improvements in mental health among families living in poverty were due to the impact of higher incomes.

The Minimum Income Guarantee for Pensions, later called Pension Credit, was associated with an increase in mental well-being for men living in the most deprived areas, with a 2.43 point reduction on a 12-point mental health scale, the General Health Questionnaire [GHQ-12]. There was not an observed change in mental well-being for women, but this may have been due to this group receiving a smaller, 22 per cent increase in their income, compared to 31 per cent for men (Albani et al, 2022).

Health Action Zones and the New Deal for Communities were both area-based initiatives that aimed to reduce geographical health inequalities through investments in areas with poorer health outcomes. Partly because there was an emphasis on involving communities in shaping the activities involved and partly because of contextual differences (for example, rural versus urban areas), evaluating this aspect of the Health Inequalities Strategy in England was challenging (Judge and Bauld, 2006). An early evaluation of Health Action Zones suggested that it was hard to identify significant positive outcomes within the short time-scale elapsed, and reflected that the scale of ambition in some areas (and among some policymakers) perhaps outstripped the level of resource that was invested (Judge and Bauld, 2006). However, a later evaluation of the New Deal for Communities was more positive, finding that the incidence of poor health declined faster in New Deal areas between 2002 and 2008; and that there were also improvements in smoking, mental health, educational attainment and employment rates in the areas during the period. Within-area inequalities also reduced, with the most disadvantaged respondents experiencing greater improvements in mental health and life satisfaction than similarly disadvantaged groups in comparator areas (Popay et al, 2015). While the variation in the precise configuration of each New Deal for Communities area made evaluating the impacts challenging, it also allowed researchers to cluster different approaches and compare some of the variants. These comparisons showed that people in New Deal areas that encouraged more local control of the design reported more positive experiences, across a range of outcomes (Popay et al, 2015). This suggests that greater public policy engagement can itself play an important role in people's well-being (there are echoes, here, of some of the findings within Chapters 2 and 3, though the efforts to engage local communities in policymaking were on a much smaller scale in England compared to Brazil, and less focused than in the US on electoral participation).

Labour's approach to tobacco, a commercial determinant of health which, in England, has highly unequal health impacts, also appears to have contributed to decreasing health inequalities. Health promotion campaigns often unintentionally increase health inequalities as more advantaged groups tend to be more responsive to information-based interventions. However, evaluations of the targeted smoking cessation support in England suggest that this approach had some success, concluding that these measures made a small but significant contribution to reducing health inequalities in England (Bauld et al, 2007; Hiscock et al, 2013).

The introduction of a health inequality weighting into the NHS budget allocation formula has been found to have contributed to 85 per cent of the total reduction of absolute inequality in mortality amenable to healthcare (Barr et al, 2014). More specifically (as noted earlier), it accounted for a reduction in the gap between deprived and affluent areas by 35 deaths per 100,000 for the male population, and 16 deaths per 100,000 for the female population (Barr et al, 2014). Each additional £10 million of resources allocated to deprived areas was associated with a reduction of 4 deaths per 100,000 for males and 1.8 deaths per 100,000 for females. In affluent areas, the same association between absolute increases in NHS resources and improvements in mortality amenable to healthcare was not significant.

## Conclusion: Could more have been done?

So, despite contemporary concerns that the government's targets to reduce health inequalities were too ambitious, the strategy was successful with decreases in inequalities in life expectancy, IMR, mortality amenable to healthcare and mortality at age 65. Evidence reviewed here also shows the specific success of certain policies in improving the health of the poorest such as Sure Start, Tax Credits, the Minimum Income Guarantee for Pensioners, New Deal for Communities, and the addition of an inequality weighting into the NHS budget allocation formula as well as targeted smoking cessation (combined with wider action to reduce the influence of the tobacco industry). However, was this success enough? Could even more have been done?

One criticism of the strategy is that while it started off focusing on the social determinants of health, it later suffered from 'lifestyle drift' whereby policy went from thinking about the wider economic and social context to focusing almost exclusively on trying to change individual health behaviours (Whitehead and Popay, 2010). A more sustained focus on the social determinants of health may have led to even greater gains in health equity. While there were policies enacted under the 1997–2010 New Labour governments that focused on the more fundamental determinants (for example, the implementation of a national minimum wage, the minimum pension, and tax credits for working parents, and a reduction in child and pensioner poverty) as well as significant investment in the NHS, there was, however, little redistribution of income between rich and poor people or areas. Nor was there much by way of a regional policy to rebalance the country (for example, between north and south) with further declines in manufacturing and the private sector outside of London – albeit offset by increases in public sector employment (Toynbee and Walker, 2011). And Labour's policy decisions around alcohol increased availability and failed to curb the influence of the alcohol industry (Nicholls, 2012). The deregulation approach to business prompted scathing assessments of the 1997–2010 Labour governments' record on workplace safety (Tombs and Whyte, 2010) and environmental health (Barry and Paterson, 2003), despite the ban on smoking in indoor public improving air quality in key employment sectors.

There were also policies which negatively targeted the poorest (for example, cutting benefit entitlements for lone parents and people with disabilities) (Bambra and Smith, 2010; Gibson et al, 2018). Income inequalities continued to rise. Indeed, a senior Labour government minister claimed at the time that he was 'seriously relaxed' about people getting rich. This is demonstrated in Figure 5.2, which shows that income inequalities (measure as the income share of the wealthiest 1 per cent of the population) in the UK continued to rise during the 2000s. Analysts have calculated that the social policy measures enacted by the 1997 to 2010 Labour governments only slowed (rather than stopping or reversing) the general rate of increase in income inequalities (Toynbee and Walker, 2011). This is because in wider economic policy, the New Labour governments continued the neoliberal approach of Thatcherism – including, for example, continuing a narrative of individualism; further marketisation

**Figure 5.2:** Income inequality in the UK from 1910 to 2010, income share of the wealthiest 1 per cent

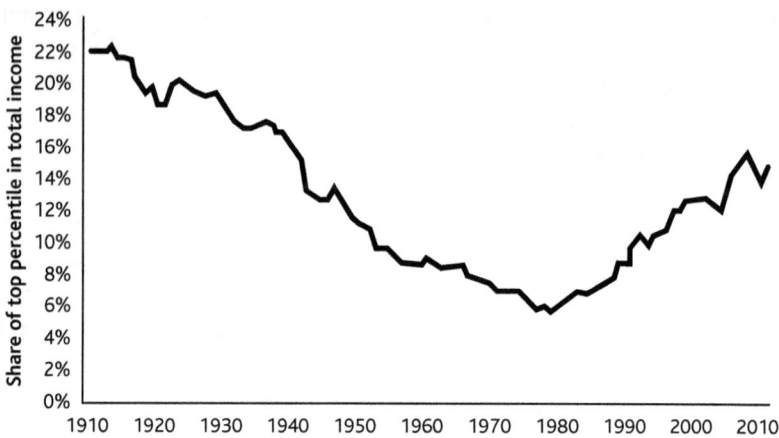

and privatisation of the NHS; keeping tax rates low (the tax-GDP ratio never went above 36 per cent); substantially reducing capital gains tax rates (to the benefit of the wealthiest individuals and companies); further deregulating business rules and the finance sector; and never articulating the case for redistribution (Toynbee and Walker, 2011). The latter arguably made the reversal of most of Labour's changes easier post-2010 – as there had been no persuasion of the public that better services required higher taxation (discussed in Chapter 6).

Health inequalities policy was therefore overshadowed by the far more powerful, fundamental, and politically driven trends in economic and social policy both domestically and internationally as a result of the dominance of neoliberal ideology. As described earlier in this chapter, the effects of these neoliberal economic and social policies on health inequalities have been stark (or of 'epidemic' proportions) and have meant that those at the bottom have fallen even further behind (Schrecker and Bambra, 2015; 2025). In the face of such substantial (and largely unchallenged by the Social Democratic Labour Party) neoliberal structural changes to the fundamental determinants of health, the specialist area of 'health inequalities policy' (as outlined in this chapter) was unable to substantially turn the tide on such longstanding health divides. It was therefore a case of 'too little, too late' – a lot of rhetoric and good intentions but little in the end by way of strong action on social inequality (Bambra, 2016). The earlier post-war experience – in which smaller health inequalities were achieved through a more extensive welfare state and a different spatial and socio-economic distribution of national wealth (Bambra, 2024), and the recommendations of the Black and Acheson policy reviews examined earlier in this chapter, do though provide clear guidance as to what is actually needed to fundamentally 'turn the tide' on health inequalities. The likelihood of such substantial change happening became even less though with the election of Conservative-led governments from 2010 on a platform of neoliberal inspired austerity. What happened to health inequalities in England from 2010 onwards is examined in Chapter 6.

# 6

# Waxing and waning: the four levellers of health inequalities

This chapter discusses the waxing and waning of efforts to reduce health inequalities. The first section looks across the four case studies to identify four mechanisms for reducing health inequalities that are common to the cases during the periods in which health inequalities reduced ('waxing'): welfare state expansion; growing economic equality; improved access to timely, high-quality healthcare; and enhanced political incorporation. In the second part of the chapter, we examine what happens when the converse, 'waning', situation occurs: when social safety nets are dismantled; labour markets produce poverty and precarity for many; access to healthcare is unequal; and large groups of people become (or start to feel) politically excluded. While the waxing of efforts to reduce health inequalities occurred in our cases when combatting inequality more broadly was high on the political agenda, the waning, as we shall see, is prompted by the victory of neoliberal economic and social policy ideas and by persistent structural inequalities, power struggles and the erosion of democratic gains.

## Waxing social and political incorporation contribute to reducing health inequalities

In this section, we reflect across the four case studies included in this book to consider the policy changes that are associated with reductions in health inequalities. We begin by summarising the changes highlighted in each country case study, before considering these changes comparatively. This analysis helps draw out levelling mechanisms that seem important for reducing health inequalities but also suggests that there may not be a single, 'best' approach to reducing health inequalities. Rather, the multiple social, economic and commercial determinants that shape health inequalities require effective action across multiple policy areas.

### The United States of America

The Great Society in the US was an ambitious package of policies explicitly designed to reduce socio-economic and ethnic inequalities across a vast swathe of the economy, society, welfare state and the polity. It expanded income guarantees for the poor, especially those who were elderly or disabled, and substantially reduced poverty; introduced significant new programmes that broke down financial and racist barriers to accessing medical care; provided access to healthier foods for women and children; and effectively desegregated public primary and secondary education in the south. Desegregation of the labour market allowed many Black men and women to enter sectors previously off limits to them, leading to a reduction in earnings inequalities. Chapter 2 summarised compelling evidence that the latter three developments, in particular, contributed to a reduction in the Black–White infant mortality gap in the US for cohorts affected by the policies in their infancy, and to longer-term well-being into adulthood. The Civil Rights Act of 1964 and the Voting Rights Act of 1965 led to an end of Jim Crow segregation in the South, while programmes sponsored by the Office of Economic Opportunity harnessed civic activism in poor communities nationwide, resulting in political enfranchisement and engagement. Some health scholars see the democratisation of American life as a fundamental cause of the reduction in health inequalities in the US for the generations who lived through the Great Society. In sum, both expansion of the welfare state and a commitment to democratising the economy and the polity appear to have been key pathways linking changes in the distribution of the political, economic and social determinants of health to reductions in health inequalities.

## *Brazil*

Much analysis of health inequalities in the post-1985 Brazilian era has focused on the impacts of the ambitious healthcare reforms. These reforms built on a 1988 constitutional commitment to people's right to health and led to the creation of the largest tax-funded healthcare system in the world. This development was complemented by Brazil's global advocacy to improve pharmaceuticals access. There were also, however, major policy changes relating to income inequalities, including pro-poor transfers (variously conditional on children's school attendance, vaccinations and health checkups) and minimum wage increases. There were multiple efforts to enfranchise the Brazilian population, including embedding participatory governance mechanisms (for example, participatory budgeting) and support for civil society groups and trade unions. Reflecting the stronger union voice in policy and the trade union background of President Lula, Brazil also strengthened labour market regulations, which contributed to improved workplace conditions, and introduced changes that encouraged people to move into the formal economic sector (meaning more people were covered by these regulations and subject to the minimum wage). Brazil also took action to limit the negative health impacts of key commercial determinants of health, especially tobacco, introducing multiple regulations and strengthening these via the International Framework Convention on Tobacco Control, in which Brazil had a leading role. Researchers have tended to focus on the impacts that each of these policies had on proximal outcomes (for example, considering how healthcare reforms impacted on health, and how cash transfers impacted on poverty and income inequalities), but since poverty and income are interconnected, and many policies were implemented simultaneously, it is challenging (if not impossible) to identify policy-specific causal pathways. What is clear is that this combination of policies occurred alongside a much sought-after combination of substantial reductions in health inequalities and simultaneous population-wide health improvements. Given the multiple pathways connecting democratisation to policies that seem plausibly connected to reductions in health inequalities, we argue that there are good reasons to believe democratisation played a fundamental role.

### Germany

Chapter 4's example of East–West unification in Germany demonstrates that large health gaps can be significantly reduced in a relatively short time frame, and suggests that the key policy 'levers' are economic and social. By the fall of the GDR in 1990, the health gap between West–East Germany was around three years (2.8 years for women and 3.4 for men). By as early as 1999, the West–East health divide for women was only around six months and by 2017, female life expectancy in the East exceeded that in the West by around six months (West: 82.8 years; East: 83.4 years). Although the story for men is less impressive, the health gap also reduced over the same rapid time period. Chapter 4 argues that a key explanation for this improvement was the transition from living in an authoritarian, totalitarian regime, to living in a democratic, conservative welfare state. Another clear policy benefit of reunification for East Germans was that their wages improved significantly, and rapidly, following a currency union whereby the (much more internationally valuable) West German Deutsche Mark replaced the East German Ostmark as the official currency – a mark for a mark. This meant that salaries and savings in the East were protected while, as early as 1996, wages in the East rose very rapidly to around 75 per cent of Western levels (from less than 40 per cent in 1990). There were also improvements in social security measures, notably higher benefits (especially for pensioners), and in housing, diet and the wider living environment (a silver lining of the collapse of East Germany companies was the rapid reduction in pollution). Hence, even though unemployment rates rose in East Germany following unification due to rapid deindustrialisation, the combination of measures to protect the value of people's savings and to provide social security appears to have protected people from some of the health consequences of unemployment. Accordingly, the German population did not experience the downward spiral of increased poverty, psychosocial stress and excess alcohol consumption that many other former Eastern Bloc countries displayed in this period (King et al, 2022). This highlights the crucial role that public policy support can play in buffering the health impacts of negative economic changes.

## England

The English strategy for reducing health inequalities, a decade-long push to equalise health outcomes, set ambitious targets for improvements in health outcomes between deprived areas and the rest of England. To achieve these targets, the government harnessed policies across multiple areas: It allocated new resources not only to the health system but also to pensions and to families with children; introduced a national minimum wage; and engaged in multi-sectoral, area-based initiatives such as the New Deal for Communities and Health Action Zones. As Chapter 5 outlines, these area-based policies were intentionally designed to promote local community engagement with local policy design and implementation so there was also a conscious, albeit limited, attempt to do more to engage people living in disadvantaged areas. While the initial assessments of the English strategy were sceptical, subsequent research has shown that it led to notable reductions in geographical inequalities in health and mortality between 2000 and 2010. Because geographical inequalities overlap to a considerable degree with socio-economic inequalities, these improvements also left a mark on the social inequalities in health that have long characterised English society.

The important gains in health equity resulting from the English strategy occurred despite the New Labour government's continuation of neoliberal economic policies introduced to the UK by former Prime Minister Margaret Thatcher. Had the incoming Labour government been willing to increase overall social and public spending above the levels set by their predecessor, intervene more forcefully to limit the harms caused by commercial determinants, redistribute access to core social determinants of health such as earnings from work or promote the political participation of excluded communities, it is possible that they might have achieved even greater gains in health equity. However, the Labour government did not attempt to persuade the public of the necessity of these more fundamental changes. As we shall see, one result was that the gains achieved under the Health Inequalities Strategy of 2000–10 were easy to unravel when a new Conservative-led coalition came to office.

## Levelling mechanisms

The four case studies summarised previously offer four different perspectives on how significant reductions in health inequalities can be achieved – at least temporarily. Each case study tells a slightly different story, in part because the geographical and temporal contexts differ. To give just one example, the Great Society in the US came too early in the epidemiological transition away from widespread smoking to really improve health equity through its regulation of tobacco: In 1965, over 40 per cent of US adults smoked cigarettes, with similar rates for those in different education brackets, and for Black and White Americans (US Centers for Disease Control and Prevention, 2018). Information about the health dangers of cigarette smoking was most readily taken up by people with higher levels of education, with the result that socio-economic and racial differences in smoking behaviour increased over time (Hill, 2014). In contrast, by the time of the UK Labour government's smoking cessation efforts in the first decade of the 21st century, smoking rates were twice as high among manual workers as among professionals, so there were greater potential gains in health equity to be made by interventions, especially those that targeted people with lower incomes and education (Brown et al, 2014). Yet there are commonalities to these four countries' experience that can help us understand what really can help reduce health inequalities. In particular, we see four potential levelling mechanisms at work in these cases. Since these contexts are diverse historically, socially and in geo-political terms, there are good reasons to think that these levellers may also help reduce health inequalities in other contexts.

First, significantly expanding social protection and the welfare state can lead to substantial reductions in health inequalities. As noted in Chapter 4, previous research has shown that countries with larger, more encompassing welfare states generally enjoy smaller health inequalities. All four case studies expanded social protection, either by adding new programmes, extending coverage to new groups, or simply spending more to ensure that everyone has access to health-promoting social determinants of health, such as decent nutrition, safe housing, education and an income sufficient to secure basic needs. It is not necessary to do all of these things simultaneously to have an impact on health equity. But to have the best chance at reducing health inequalities, making efforts across multiple domains is likely to be important, both because it is not always obvious what will have an effect, and because there may be unexpected complementarities and amplification effects when pursuing improvements across multiple sectors. The converse of this proposition is that when the ideological or economic environment curtails welfare state expansion – as under neoliberalism or the late Soviet-era economic collapse – it may prove impossible to use this mechanism to achieve reductions in health inequalities (Lynch 2020).

Reducing economic inequality is a similarly promising, but similarly constrained, lever for reducing health inequalities. Economic inequality is often associated with high levels of poverty, which is a critical determinant of poor health. Inequalities in wages and income may themselves contribute to poor health by way of psychosocial mechanisms. And inequalities in opportunities to engage in safe and well-remunerated work have their own pathways to health inequity. For these reasons, when governments have intervened to introduce minimum wages, empower labour movements, regulate the safety of working conditions, and redistribute resources through progressive taxation, health inequalities have become smaller. There is no question that a strong economic tailwind can make such labour market reforms easier. The 1950s to mid-1960s in the US, and the 1990s to mid-2000s in Western Europe and Brazil, were periods of sustained economic growth, and contributed to the ability of the governments to regulate, reform and redistribute work and incomes in ways that did not invoke immediate political rebuke. Even so, growth alone is not enough. As the US experience of the fast-growing 1950s and the so-called Brazilian 'economic miracle' of the 1960s–70s both show, if governments do not regulate the labour market to foster economic equality during periods of economic growth, health equality will not follow.

When inability to pay, discrimination, or insufficient supply or quality of healthcare services limit opportunities for health, expanded access to healthcare can be important for reducing health inequalities. When access to basic medicines and healthcare services have been denied, as in poor and rural areas of Brazil during the military dictatorship, or when the capacity of the health system to provide high-quality care has broken down, as happened in East Germany prior to reunification and in deprived areas of England after the Thatcher-era funding cuts, shoring up the healthcare system can lead to reductions in health inequalities by preventing disease and death that is amenable to medical intervention. Expanded access to health insurance in the US during the Great Society has not been shown to have had an independent effect on health outcomes, likely in part because medical care in the 1960s did not lead to long extensions of life for those made newly eligible under Medicare or Medicaid. Providing access to high quality, affordable healthcare is a precondition for reducing inequalities in health stemming from causes that are amenable to medical intervention. However, without simultaneous efforts to reduce inequalities in the distribution of the social, economic and political determinants of health, overall health inequalities are not likely to be reduced significantly by healthcare measures alone. Expanded access to healthcare is thus a potential levelling mechanism, but one that must be used in concert with others if significant health inequality reductions are to be achieved.

The final levelling mechanism emerging from our four case studies – political incorporation – is possibly the most important to acknowledge during our current period of political upheaval. Our case studies clearly show that when governments have acted to exclude certain groups from political and civic participation – as in the US under Jim Crow (voting rights), East Germany under the socialist regime (voting rights, free speech), England under Thatcher (union rights), Brazil under authoritarianism (voting rights, protest) – health inequalities have followed. Conversely, when governments act to include marginalised groups in the polity, as members with full voice and voting rights, health inequalities are reduced. This is partly because the right to be heard and to have a political voice is itself beneficial for health (Bambra et al, 2005; Hirono, 2023). It is also because political participation allows people to take control of the policy agenda and, through that control, enact the kinds of reforms that benefit health equity by acting on multiple determinants of health. Even under the most controlled and regulated forms of capitalism, economic activity results in inequalities. Political systems that offer, and that truly guarantee, 'one person, one vote' are the most effective way to counteract the inequalities created by economic activity. Universal political participation is what allows us to hear the voices of those who are most likely to be in poor health: the poor and otherwise marginalised. In this sense, political incorporation is truly a 'fundamental cause' of health equity (Link and Phelan, 1995; McCartney et al, 2021).

## Waning welfare and political exclusion contribute to increases in health inequalities

In this section, we examine what happens during the 'waning' of our four mechanisms: when social safety nets are dismantled; labour markets produce poverty and precarity for many; access to healthcare is unequal; and large groups of people become (or start to feel) politically excluded. The waning, across all our case study countries, happened with power struggles, a political shift towards neoliberal economic and social policy and resurgent structural inequalities, and the erosion of democratic gains.

### *The United States: sunset over the Great Society*

The most significant programmes of the Great Society were passed in 1964 and 1965. By 1967 President Johnson's majority in Congress had dwindled, weakening the group of liberal legislators who had supported the Great Society, and strengthening the hand of the conservative coalition of Republicans and southern Democrats. By 1968, the growing expense of the US's war in Vietnam was draining the country's gold reserves, setting off an economic crisis and making it necessary for Johnson to raise taxes and curtail domestic and military spending. In this environment, only the assassination of the Black civil rights leader Reverend Martin Luther King Jr would give a reprieve to the contraction of the Great Society, opening a brief window in 1968 to pass the (tepidly enforced) Fair Housing Act.

Fiscal issues were not the only problem that the Great Society faced at the dawn of the 1970s. As we saw in Chapter 2, an essential element of the Great Society, and particularly of programmes enacted under the Economic Opportunity Act of 1964, was the mandate for 'maximum feasible participation of the poor'. The desegregation of public institutions and enforcement of voting rights largely affected the US South, but the empowerment of largely minority communities in northern cities through War on Poverty programmes (many of which intentionally bypassed state and local officeholders by providing direct funding to community groups) threatened the interests of a broader swath of White America.

As inner-city minority residents became increasingly politically active, including in a series of demonstrations in large cities that were met with police violence, White America moved to shut down the programmes seen as abetting Black militancy. To some extent, then, the Great Society was a victim of its own success. As one contemporary observer put it,

> the War on Poverty profoundly upset a large enough body of Americans to provide the impetus for eventual destruction or dilution of most of the programmes through outright termination, inadequate funding, or pressure to change some programmes to the point that they no longer filled the purposes for which they had been established. (James, 1972, p 315)

By 1967, two thirds of the Office of Economic Opportunity's (OEO) funding had been earmarked for politically palatable programmes such as Head Start, rather than for Community Action programmes aimed at empowering local actors. In 1973, President Nixon abolished the OEO altogether (Quadagno, 1994).

In the early 1970s, new tax cuts for low-income earners and an expansion of social security benefits for the elderly, survivors and disabled people led to continued successes of the War on Poverty. President Nixon actually spent more on social programmes than Johnson did, and he proposed a number of new universal benefits that would have blunted the impact of racism on the developing welfare state (Quadagno, 1994). These programmes were not implemented, however, and, as the economy worsened with the 1970s oil crisis, public appetite for pro-poor spending waned.

Ronald Reagan's election as president in 1980 ushered in a new era of deregulation, regressive economic policies and retrenchment of the already comparatively limited US welfare state. The Reagan administration cut Aid for Families with Dependent Children (AFDC – 'welfare' in the American parlance) and disability rolls and raised taxes on the poor. It also sponsored a new vilification of Black women as 'welfare queens', leading to public pressure to retrench welfare benefits for poor people who were not working (Gilens, 1999; Nadasen, 2007). A new, neoliberal approach to social policy continued throughout the 1990s and into the 2000s, under both Democratic and Republican leadership (Berman, 2022). In the early 1990s Earned Income Tax Credits (EITC) for low-income working families were expanded, providing significant relief from risk of poverty. But in 1996, the Clinton administration carried out its campaign pledge to 'end welfare as we know it', cutting Food Stamps and replacing the few unconditional entitlements to cash benefits with time limits and work requirements (Weaver, 2000). The combination of changes to tax policies and hostility to the efforts of labour unions in the 1980s and 1990s contributed to rapidly growing earnings inequality in the US, which was notable both for the increase in very high incomes and for the hollowing out of incomes at the bottom of the distribution (Hopkin and Lynch, 2016).

The net result of the end of the War on Poverty was a flattening of the steep decline in poverty observed during the Great Society years. Accounting for the impact of taxes and transfers, and adjusting for the bias in price indexes, one study found that, while the poverty rate fell by a total of 26.4 percentage points in the half century 1960 and 2010, only 8.5 percentage points of that occurred after 1980 (Meyer and Sullivan, 2012). This flattening of poverty reduction after the end of the Great Society is shown in Figure 6.1. In other words, the vast majority of the poverty reduction took place during the Great Society, while much of the remaining effect was due to EITC increases and to the booming economy of the 1990s.

Great Society-era housing and education policies suffered similar setbacks beginning in the 1970s. Housing policy had never been the Great Society's strongest suit, although it did succeed in promoting new housing construction and attracting private financing to the housing sector, both of which mainly benefited White homebuyers. However, despite major

**Figure 6.1:** Official and alternative US income poverty rates, 1963–2010

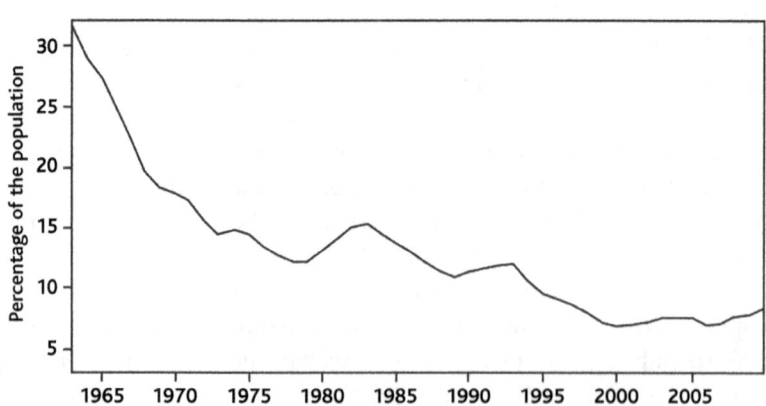

protests over poor living conditions in urban centres in 1965 through 1969, federal government investment in low-income urban neighbourhoods, never massive, was curtailed beginning in the early 1970s. In 1973 the Nixon administration imposed a moratorium on Department of Housing and Urban Development (HUD) subsidies for new public housing construction and funding for community development programmes (Downs, 1974). The construction of new affordable rental units gave way to vouchers to be spent on private housing, and during the Reagan administration, some public housing units were privatised. Funding to urban areas prioritised the creation of public-private Enterprise Zones over neighbourhood rehabilitation. HUD has come under repeated scrutiny for failing to enforce fair housing rules (Hahn et al, 2018), and privatisation and deregulation of the mortgage industry beginning in 1968 has resulted in continuing discrimination against non-White prospective homebuyers (Abramovitz and Smith, 2021). The failure to close the gap between White and non-White home ownership after 1970 (Haurin et al, 2007) contributed to continuing neighbourhood segregation and to racial disparities in wealth as well as housing quality.

Great Society programmes in education did succeed in closing Black–White gaps in cognitive test scores, college attendance and annual earnings. These gaps, which evidence shows are related to improved conditions in infancy and the pre-school years, narrowed significantly for cohorts born during the Great Society (1963–71). However, the waning of the Great Society after 1971 meant no further improvements in educational equity were gained among later cohorts (Chay et al, 2014). Moreover, after some success with desegregation of schools in the south after 1964, efforts to equalise opportunities stalled. In fact, as one study reports:

> In recent decades, the Executive Branch of the federal government, and in particular, the US Department of Education and its Office of Civil Rights, have increasingly limited their efforts in promoting school desegregation, thus slowing the potential contributions of desegregation to the health and well-being of many racial/ethnic minority students. (Hahn et al, 2018, p 21)

Healthcare programmes enacted during the Great Society were not dismantled, and coverage was even expanded in various ways throughout the 1970s through 2000s. However, the promise of providing public insurance that could cover the costs of equitable medical care for rich and poor alike was never achieved. Plans to expand Medicare coverage to mothers, children and older workers went by the wayside as budgetary pressures stemming from the war in Vietnam demanded a growing share of federal spending (Quadagno, 2022, p 378). Medicaid was subjected to federal cost-cutting efforts in the 1970s and 1980s, and federal block grants to states allowed for a wide variety of coverage exclusions – most recently, in the form of requirements encouraged by the first Trump administration that beneficiaries show proof of gainful employment or education (Coleman and Federman, 2024). Despite surviving a 1980s threat, the resources allocated to CHCs have not kept pace with either inflation or the number of patients served (currently around 30 million) (Brill, 2023). One major expansion to the healthcare social safety net came under President Obama in 2008 with the passage of the Patient Protection and Affordable Care Act (ACA). The ACA provided subsidised health insurance to most of the almost 45 million previously uninsured Americans and provided federal support for expanding Medicaid to more low-income people, although many states in the south and west declined to do so – and there is 'evidence that current opposition to Medicaid expansion is driven by assumptions about whether or to what extent racial and ethnic minority groups or "foreigners" will benefit from expansion' (Yearby et al, 2022, p 189; see also Béland et al, 2016). In healthcare, as in education and housing policy, the influence of structural racism meant that improvements stemming from even big policy innovations such as the ACA have left non-White Americans significantly behind (Gornick, 2008; Yearby, 2018; Yearby et al, 2022).

Even the political rights gained during the Great Society were not immune to rollback in the ensuing decades. Enforcement of the Voting Rights Act and the empowerment of a new generation of urban activists resulted in movement towards equalisation of voting rates and of representation between Black and White Americans between the late 1960s and the 2010s. However, Americans from lower socio-economic backgrounds still vote at much lower rates than do wealthier Americans, and there are vanishingly few national-level elected officials from working-class backgrounds in the US (Carnes, 2012; Leighley and Nagler, 2014). In general, US politicians of all stripes were reluctant to *openly* oppose voting rights in the decades following the Great Society. However, conservative legislators in both parties had already begun to chip away at voting rights through low-visibility administrative changes before the US Supreme Court overturned critical sections of the Voting Rights Act in 2013 (Rhodes, 2017). State- and local-level provisions introduced in recent decades have also made voting significantly more difficult for people of colour: banning convicted felons from voting even after their sentences have been served, introducing requirements to show official identification at the ballot box, failing to provide adequate facilities for voting in poor and minority areas, and preventing volunteers from delivering water to voters waiting in long lines are just a few examples of legal voter suppression techniques that are likely to have an indirect impact on health inequalities (Hing, 2020).

Despite significant expansions of access to healthcare during and after the Great Society, the progress in reducing health inequalities made during the Great Society years waned as support faded for programmes that reduced inequalities in the social and political determinants of health. As we saw in Chapter 2, one of the most important impacts of the Great Society on health equity was the reduction in Black–White mortality gaps, particularly among infants. However, this gain in health equity was quickly reversed: starting in 1972, the Black–White infant mortality gap began to grow once again and, by the early 1990s, had surpassed the level of inequity in place before the gains of the Great Society. By 2000, the size of the Black–White gap in infant mortality was double that in 1960 (80 versus 40 infant deaths per 1000 live births) (Singh et al, 2017). Racial inequalities in overall mortality began to decline again after 1990 but, at the same time, stark urban–rural mortalities emerged, with mortality decreasing faster in urban than in rural areas from the mid-1990s onwards (James and Cossman, 2017). As is to be expected in a country where the social and political determinants of health have become more unequally distributed since the early 1970s, infant mortality, life expectancy and all major causes of death affecting Americans show sharp gradients by race, income and education, and urbanicity (Singh et al, 2017). Further, the US has fallen down the global health rankings in this period: for example, it fell from being ranked 15th globally in terms of life expectancy in 1980 to 53rd globally by 2020 (Hiam et al, 2023).

*Brazil: democratic fragility in the shadows of military dictatorship*

In recent years, Brazil has experienced a widening of health inequalities between more and less deprived groups. Analysis of Brazil's 27 federated units found that, between 2013 and 2019, inequalities in life expectancy and healthy expectancy at 60 years widened between the poorest and wealthiest areas (Szwarcwald et al, 2022). Brazil was subsequently badly hit by COVID-19, with mortality, morbidity and economic impacts all falling unequally across the population, exacerbating health inequalities further (Castro et al, 2021). Over the same (2013+) period, Brazil has experienced a new wave of social protests, an economic crisis and a populist, right-wing President, Jair Bolsonaro, who espoused the merits of the country's military dictatorship, focused more on enforcing order than tackling inequalities, and openly disparaged many of Brazil's more marginalised groups. Bolsonaro's success was linked to a wider far-right movement that is capable of mobilising massive political support, including among groups who benefitted from the progressive policies introduced several years earlier. Lula has recently been re-elected as president, returning Brazil to a more progressive politics focused on reducing inequalities. Yet the rapid rise of Bolsonaro continues to cause concern about the precarity of Brazil's young democracy (Junge et al, 2021). In this section we consider how and why, despite Brazil's success in reducing health and economic inequalities (set out in Chapter 3), there has been a decade of 'waning', during which health inequalities have once again begun to widen. We identify five factors: a rapid series of economic, political and health crises; multiple implementation failings of key pro-poor policies (we cite five key examples); the perpetuation of state violence against marginalised communities, which escalated in the run up to hosting two global sporting events; and deliberately manufactured moral panics that incited a backlash against efforts to recognise state harms during the military dictatorship and carefully curated cultural nostalgia for Brazil's military past. Each of these factors has reinforced social division and despair, laying the foundations for the rise of a populist, right-wing president with authoritarian inclinations.

Given that Brazil's achievements in the 2003–10 period, which included 30 million people exiting poverty (Junge et al, 2021), were internationally celebrated, retrenchment has come as a surprise to many commentators. Early signs that the dominant political party, the Workers' Party (PT), might be in trouble came with an explosion of popular protests in summer 2013 (Junge et al, 2021). Brazil subsequently experienced a series of economic, political and health crises. By 2014, Brazil was experiencing a severe economic crisis, which informed discussions of 'fiscal constriction' during the government of President Rousseff (2011–16) (Pinho, 2021). By 2015, these ideas solidified into a unified austerity programme, *Uma Ponte para o Futuro* (A Bridge to the Future) (Pinho, 2021). At the same time, a series of corruption scandals was engulfing senior figures in the Workers' Party, including former President Lula and incumbent President Rousseff. This led, ultimately, to President Rousseff's impeachment in 2016. The austerity programme was, subsequently, rapidly implemented by the governments of President Michel Temer and his successor Jair Bolsonaro (Pinho, 2021). Alongside this, in 2015–16, a Zika virus outbreak resulted in a surge of babies born with congenital anomalies, causing panic and tragedy in affected communities, and placing significant pressure on Brazil's healthcare system. While Brazil's response to the Zika virus was internationally lauded, four years later, Brazil struggled to contain the COVID-19 pandemic (Malta et al, 2020). Each of these crises, as well as the retrenchment of welfare and public services through austerity measures, likely fed into the rising sense of hopelessness and distrust in politicians that researchers identify (De Almeida, 2020; Junge et al, 2021).

A collection of ethnographic studies exploring this shift within different segments of the Brazilian population (Junge et al, 2021) argues that persistent inequalities, implementation gaps and elite power grabs all contributed to the widespread social pessimism and disillusionment that underpinned the sudden change in the popular mood. Other evaluations also point to some major implementation failings in Brazil and suggest they played a role in the declining public support for the PT and a surge in the number of voters feeling angry, mistrustful and politically apathetic (Kopper, 2021; Rojas et al, 2021). Five examples of implementation failures stand out. First, local landowners hijacked the roll-out of policies intended to support people living in poverty in Amazonia to purchase the land on which they lived and, in many cases, made a living. The target community for these policies described local elites using them to increase their own land ownership while creating the impression that they (not national politicians) were the only ones who could offer poorer local community members practical support (Rojas et al, 2021). In effect, while the PT succeeded in 'the technocratic task of investing billions in pro-poor programmes', implementation challenges meant they failed in 'the essential affective task of eliciting hopes in collective politics' among Brazil's poorer, rural populations (Rojas et al, 2021).

The second example relates to reports that some local politicians are interfering with the distribution of *Bolsa Família* payments in order to garner political support. For example, a 2013 *Guardian* article reported that, in Maranhão, many people said they were not receiving their full entitlement, noting (unverified) claims among some of these recipients that *Bolsa Família* was becoming 'another tool for regional politicians to wield patronage because it is local officials who register people for payments' (Watts, 2013).

The third example relates to education, where implementation issues arose at state and local levels. Although the 1988 Brazilian Constitution required state and county governments to spend 25 per cent of their revenues on public education, there were significant variations in the distribution of investment in early years, primary, secondary, and university (tertiary) education levels, and in the allocation of spending across buildings, infrastructure and teachers' pay (Arends-Kuenning, 2009). In Hunter and Sugiyama's (2009) assessment, some state-level and local investment decisions have exacerbated educational inequalities, allowing Brazilians who were already socially advantaged to experience greater benefits from education investments in secondary and tertiary education.

The fourth example relates to workplace safety where, despite progress in the 1985–2000 era, poor practices continued. The *Petrobrás* scandal was a high-profile example of the tragic consequences of limitations to the implementation of workplace safety measures, even in the formal sector. In March 2001, the P-36 oil platform, which was owned by *Petrobrás* (a Brazilian oil company), experienced two explosions and sank, killing 11 emergency responders. Subsequent investigations revealed multiple examples of poor practices and negligence within *Petrobrás* (Siqueira and Haiama-Neuhohr, 2006).

The fifth example of implementation failings relates to Brazil's efforts to improve housing, where policies and programmes appear to have been both poorly conceived and under-resourced. For example, a 2010 report by the Brazilian Ministry of Cities underlined the need to improve living conditions for poorer communities, framing informal settlements as manifestations of inequality that could be remedied by *urbanização de favelas* (slum upgrading) (Ministério das Cidades, 2010). The reality of this policy involved the forced resettlement of favela residents to new neighbourhoods with new but poor quality, state-built social housing, which left residents feeling betrayed by the state and experiencing the 'territorial stigma' (Wacquant, 2007) of being labelled by new neighbours as former favela occupants (Kolling, 2019). Kopper's (2021) analysis of Brazil's *Minha Casa Minha Vida* housing programme (part of President Lula's broader Growth Acceleration Programme), charts how promises to improve urban housing through public–private investments resulted in social pessimism and disillusionment. Kopper (2021) identifies the 'erratic conditions' of the programme's implementation, which brought local, private disputes to the fore, contributing to an affective shift from collectivism and hope to individualism and despair.

A third factor that researchers have identified as important in explaining the increasingly polarised politics of Brazil relates to state violence. In this case, the issue appears to be more one of limited action than poor implementation. Although many changes occurred during Brazil's democratic transition, including governance changes designed to enfranchise poorer and marginalised populations, many people holding senior positions in the military and the police remained in post. Hence, while the political administration governing Brazil underwent transformative changes, there was much more continuity in the infrastructure of 'hard' power (Harr, 2020). This contributed to the persistence of violent policing, often targeted at more marginalised communities:

> This dismal record of violence against mostly innocent and unarmed civilians includes the massacre of indigenous populations, peasants, rural leaders (like Chico Mendes), street children, adolescents in poor urban neighbourhoods, and prisoners (as in São Paulo's Casa de Detenção, where military police killed 111 unarmed prisoners in a 1992 prison rebellion). Police violence has reached unprecedented levels, and the forces of law and order are themselves one of the main agents of violence in many cities. Various police forces are plagued by corruption, entangled with organized crime, and accustomed to violent and illegal methods of action. (Caldeira and Holston, 1999, p 695)

As highlighted in the extract, the consequences of violence and crime in Brazil are not evenly felt; rather, multiple studies find that it is Brazil's poorer and more marginalised populations (including Indigenous communities, Black populations, people living in Favelas, women and children, and those incarcerated in prison) that too often bear the brunt (Caldeira and Holston, 1999; Smith, 2018; Snider, 2018). Preparations for Brazil to host the 2014 Football World Cup and the 2016 Olympic Games led to an increase in the scale and intensity of this state violence and attracted significant media attention, as more than 2000 members of the special forces invaded Rio's favelas, using military helicopters and armoured troop vehicles, in a bid to improve security and reassure potential investors (Rojas et al, 2021). This high-profile example of state violence and criminalisation was watched on TV screens and mobile phones across Brazil, further undermining the trust of poorer communities in politicians and authority figures (Rojas et al, 2021). State-led violence targeting marginalised groups likely enabled the further perpetration of far-right violence, which was used to silence progressive social movements. One of the most high-profile examples was the assassination of Afro-Caribbean, bisexual, socialist council woman, Marielle Franco (Junge et al, 2021).

Such violent acts were justified by a manufactured 'moral panic' (a term developed by Stanley Cohen (2002 [1972]) to describe a mass movement based on the false or exaggerated perception that particular cultures, behaviours or social groups are dangerously deviant and poses a threat to society's values and interests). This was fuelled by mass media coverage, to which Bolsonaro and other ultra right-wing politicians were active contributors (Da Silva Pereira, 2023). There were multiple strands, statements and rumours involved in Brazil's moral panic, each targeting different marginal population groups. For example, Da Silva Pereira (2023) charts the rapid spread of the 'alarming notion' that Brazilian children and adolescents were 'in great danger and need to be legally protected against moral corruption, unnatural sexualities, and indoctrination into "gender ideology"' (Da Silva Pereira, 2023, p iii). The rise of social media helped ensure that these false rumours spread rapidly (Junge et al, 2021). There was also a backlash against Brazil's efforts to establish a truth commission and to create some accountability for the mass torture and killing undertaken during Brazil's military dictatorship. This focused more on denigrating those who had suffered under the military dictatorship, including those with left-wing political views, Black and Indigenous populations, and women. Once again, Bolsonaro played a key role; having openly declared in 1993 that he favoured dictatorship, he repeatedly indicated (and sometimes explicitly stated) that he approved of state torture and killing (Schneider, 2020). In short, Bolsonaro, other ultra right-wing politicians, religious leaders and aligned community members collaborated to manufacture a multi-layered sense of 'moral panic' in Brazil. This enabled Bolsonaro, who has a military background, to promote a sense of 'cultural nostalgia' for Brazil's 1964–85 era of military dictatorship as a necessary response, framing life then as 'more moral, more prosperous and safe' (Junge et al, 2021, p 5). The military dictatorship was reconfigured as a symbol of order, patriotism and traditional family values and old fascist slogans, such as 'God, Nation, and Family' resurfaced.

Taken together, these five factors help explain the 'waning' of Brazil's efforts to reduce inequalities from 2013 onwards. This not only led to a widening, once again, of health and other social inequalities but also to concerns that Brazil's period of democratisation may be short-lived: 'It seems that democracy itself has been rendered precarious in Brazil by the politics that emerge from hopelessness, disenchantment and anger' (Junge et al, 2021, p 8).

While the recent re-election of President Lula may signal a new period of 'waxing', in which policy efforts to reduce the socio-economic inequalities that underlie health inequalities come to the fore once more, the shadow of authoritarian dictatorship and unequal politics continues to loom large in Brazil.

## *Germany: a new East–West divide and the resurgence of the far right*

In recent years, Germany has, much like the other case studies, experienced a widening of health inequalities between more and less deprived groups. Analysis of district level data in Germany from 2003 to 2021 found that the gap in life expectancy increased between the most and least deprived quintiles of districts for men and women (Tetzlaff et al, 2024). During this period, Germany pursued a series of austerity measures. This included, for example, reforming means tested unemployment benefits in 2005, so that they became substantially less generous. A quasi-experimental study found that unemployed individuals directly affected by the reform experienced a substantial rise in the prevalence of poor self-rated health relative to similar but unaffected controls and that this persisted over time (Shahidi et al, 2020). Since unemployment rates remain higher in the East, the impact of these reductions was unequal across the old East–West divide. The COVID-19 pandemic expedited this increase, with unequal patterns of mortality and morbidity exacerbating existing health inequalities (Tetzlaff et al, 2024).

Against this backdrop of rising inequalities, political support for the parties responsible for the health-promoting changes described in Chapter 4 is fragmenting, and far-right parties are on the rise. In 2013 a new political party called *Alternative für Deutschland* (Alternative for Germany, AfD) was formed by an economist, Bernd Lucke, initially in opposition to the Eurozone. The AfD has subsequently developed an increasingly xenophobic, Islamophobic, anti-migrant and anti-LGBT+ rhetoric; has promulgated the idea that human-induced climate change is a myth; and has promoted 'welfare chauvinism', the idea that welfare benefits should be tightly restricted to specific groups who are considered worthy of support. While far-right parties espousing similar ideas are currently emerging in several other European countries, the AfD stands out for the way it mobilises violence against minority groups (Hockenos, 2023). It has been classified as a 'suspected extremist' party by the German judiciary (Brady, 2024), and as 'extreme right' by Germany's domestic security agency, which placed the party under observation on the basis that they perceived it to be a threat to democratic order (Hockenos, 2023). Support for the AfD is strongly regionally patterned, with much higher support in areas that were once part of East Germany (Weisskircher, 2020). The rest of this section considers why, despite success with reducing inequalities in the years immediately following reunification, large numbers of people living in former East German areas now seem so dissatisfied with traditional political parties that they are seeking such radical alternatives.

This question has prompted a wealth of empirical research and critical reflection, from which three central arguments emerge. First, despite substantial progress in reducing inequalities immediately after reunification, structural inequalities have persisted, with some economic inequalities even widening in the past decade. Indeed, researchers analysing recent increases in area-based health inequalities in Germany conclude that efforts to reduce health inequalities need to focus on improving the living conditions of more socio-economically disadvantaged communities (Hoebel et al, 2024). Examples of East–West structural inequalities that persist include differences in income, pensions, tax revenues, wealth and housing quality (Reiser and Reitner, 2022). Post-unification policy decisions around housing have also contributed to a high level of vacant properties in East German areas, which, it has been argued, is a contributory barrier to regional economic growth (Reiser and Reitner, 2022). Broader indicators of economic performance also lag behind in East German areas, with lower manufacturing outputs and higher rates of unemployment (Aumann and Scheufele, 2010). Researchers argue that these inequalities are informing growing dissatisfaction with political leaders and a sense of unfairness among socio-economically disadvantaged communities, more of whom live in the former East (Reiser and Reiter, 2022).

The second argument focuses more on East–West differences across values, culture and identity. Key contributors argue that the cultural dominance of West Germany within post-reunification Germany informed a sense among many East Germans that they are treated as 'second class citizens' within Germany (Reister and Reiter, 2022). Miethe (2019) proposes that the marginalisation of East Germans in elite positions and within media outlets are illustrations of the 'dominance culture' of West Germany. After unification, there was a 'Westernisation' of elites in Eastern areas (Boyer, 2001), with mass media and elite leadership positions quickly becoming dominated by West

Germans; in effect, West German 'experts' were exported to East Germany since they were considered to have required 'know how' that professionals in East Germany lacked (Boyer, 2001). The consequent under-representation of East Germans in leadership positions, and a lack of East German led media companies, contributed to a belief among East Germans that they were being marginalised (Miethe, 2019; Reiser and Reiter, 2022); indeed, critics have sometimes referred to 'colonialism' by the west (Weisskircher, 2020). In short, initial expectations of (and progress towards) equality were gradually eroded through people's unequal experiences in which cultural norms, values and discourses were predominantly set by West Germans. This, in turn, informed perceptions of under-representation in politics (Reister and Reitter, 2022).

Third, some authors have noted that there are historical dimensions to the rise of the far right within former East Germany, noting that far-right activists in West Germany deliberately sought to inculcate support in East German areas following unification, moving into East German properties with the aim of developing local networks of support (Weisskircher, 2020). Even before unification, there were strong far-right youth movements in East Germany despite government restrictions (Weisskircher, 2020). The closed borders of the GDR era had also created a society that was relatively culturally homogenous and not accustomed to welcoming migrants.

These three factors are intertwined, with persistent inequalities feeding a sense of marginalisation and unfairness, which new political parties can exploit by presenting themselves as alternatives to dominant ways of thinking. All of this has solidified support for more radical and extreme political parties in Eastern Germany while, at the same time, traditional (often long-standing) voter support for mainstream political parties has begun to fragment in Western Germany (Reister and Reitter, 2022). Hence, having been celebrated as an example of how to reduce health and economic inequalities and reunify populations, a new, potentially disruptive East–West political divide is emerging in Germany. Although East–West health inequalities are not yet as wide as they once were, these health gaps are widening once again (Hoebel et al, 2024; Tetzlaff et al, 2024). Health inequalities researchers in Germany are now calling for action to reduce the socio-economic inequalities that underlie these health gaps (for example, see Hoebel et al, 2024), but the fragmentation of traditional political alliances may make this hard to achieve in the near future.

### *All in it together? Austerity and health inequalities in England since 2010*

In Chapter 5, we examined the national Health Inequalities Strategy in England which ran from 2000 to 2010. We concluded that it was associated with reductions in geographical health inequalities. This section examines what happened next to heath inequalities in England – after 2010.

The Global Financial Crisis of 2007–08 was a result of a downturn in the US housing market, which led to a massive collapse in financial markets across the world (largely driven by financial investments in securities backed by sub-prime mortgages). Banks increasingly required state bailouts (for example, in the UK, the retail bank Northern Rock was nationalised while, in the US, Lehmann Brothers investment bank filed for bankruptcy and mortgage companies Freddie Mac and Fannie Mae were given major government bailouts) (Gamble, 2009). Stock markets posted massive losses and, in the 'real' economy, the crisis led to peak unemployment rates of over 8 per cent in the UK, and over 10 per cent in the USA and the Eurozone. In 2009, the IMF announced that the global economy was experiencing its worst period in the past 60 years (Gamble, 2009). The global economic recession continued throughout 2009 and 2010.

The Global Financial Crisis was accompanied in many European countries (including the UK, but most notably in Greece, Portugal and Spain) by austerity-led public expenditure cuts. Austerity involves reducing budget deficits in economic downturns by decreasing public expenditure and/or increasing taxes (Akhter et al, 2018). The UK, while not as affected as the Eurozone by the financial crisis and subsequent recession, still embarked on a programme of austerity. Indeed, no time was wasted in 'making the most of a crisis'. When a Coalition government of Conservatives and Liberal Democrats replaced Labour in 2010 (followed by successive Conservative majority governments – elected in 2015, 2017 and 2019), they enacted large scale cuts to local government budgets, underfunded the National Health Service (NHS) and made steep reductions in welfare services and benefits. They ended most of the schemes that, as shown in Chapter 5, had started to reduce health inequalities during the 1997–2010 Labour governments, such as Sure Start and Child and Working Tax Credits. In the rest of this section, we summarise the changes introduced under austerity and examine the impact on health inequalities.

Starting in 2010, the NHS was awarded below historical average budget increases. For example, the NHS in England received around 1.4 per cent increases per annum between 2009–19 compared to a historical average rise of 3.7 per cent since it was established in 1948 (The Kings Fund, 2022). When adjusting for demographic change (that is, a larger proportion of older people) and inflation, the NHS budget in England grew at 2 per cent per capita per year from 1979 to 1997 and at 5.7 per cent a year from 1997 to 2010; but shrunk by 0.07 per cent from 2010 to 2015 and fell by a further 0.03 per cent from 2015 to 2021 (Appleby and Gainsbury, 2022).

Public expenditure on social care was also reduced between 2010 and 2019, particularly in England, as part of local government budget reductions. The impact on social care is noted in a recent Nuffield Trust report into social care during COVID-19: 'A decade of sustained cuts to local authority budgets had put downward pressure on the fees paid to providers, which meant many were already struggling, and had low reserves, as they went into the Covid-19 crisis' (Nuffield Trust, 2023, p 21). Local authority social care budgets were simultaneously challenged by growth in demand (for example, a result of the ageing population) (National Audit Office, 2018). These disproportionately impacted the most deprived local authorities and resulted in substantial service reductions.

Across England, local authority spending power fell by 28.6 per cent in real terms from 2010–11 to 2017–18 (National Audit Office, 2018). However, there were inequalities in where these spending reductions fell. For example, in England the most deprived 20 per cent of local authorities had to make cuts to adult social care of 17 per cent per person, compared to only 3 per cent per person for councils in the least deprived fifth of areas (Institute for Fiscal Studies, 2018). These inequalities in local government funding also led to other differential reductions in a wide range of local government services including housing, highways and transport, environment and regulatory and planning and development services (Alexiou et al, 2021; Jenkins et al, 2022).

Additionally, the local government public health grant for English local authorities was reduced by 24 per cent in real terms per capita since 2015/16 (equivalent to a reduction of £1 billion) (The Health Foundation, 2021).[1] The reductions fell more heavily on those living in the most deprived areas. For example, in Blackpool, ranked as the most deprived local authority in England, the per capita cut to the grant was one of the largest, at £43 per person per year. This compares to a reduction of just over £9 per head in Surrey, one of the most affluent areas in the country (The Health Foundation, 2021).

Austerity across the UK was also characterised by significant changes in welfare services and benefits. The 2012 Welfare Reform Act (HM Government, 2012) led to the introduction of Universal Credit,[2] the household benefit cap,[3] and the under-occupancy penalty (colloquially referred to as the bedroom tax);[4] the abolition of Child and Working Tax credits;[5] and freezing child benefit rates (as well as abolishing it for higher rate taxpayers).[6] The subsequent Welfare Reform and Work Act (HM Government, 2016) included a further reduction in the household benefit cap; freezing the value of all working-age social security benefits for four years; and introduction of a two-child limit for Child Benefit and Universal Credit.[7]

These changes to the welfare system reduced the local income of deprived areas. Research based on Treasury data has suggested that the financial impacts of welfare reforms varied greatly across the country (Beatty and Fothergill, 2016). The older industrial areas (including parts of North West and North East England, such as Blackpool and Middlesbrough) as well as less prosperous coastal areas (for example, Blackpool and Great Yarmouth) experienced the largest reductions. In contrast, the most prosperous areas across the UK (for example, Guildford, Richmond upon Thames in the South East of England) experienced the smallest reductions. Early calculations by Beatty and Fothergill (2013) using HM Treasury's own data estimated that the financial losses arising from welfare reform up to 2014/5 were largest in the North East and North West regions of England (£560 per working age adult per year) and the lowest losses were in the South East region of England at £370 per working age adult per year. The higher receipt of benefits and tax credits among people living in more deprived areas across the UK explains why the reforms had a greater financial impact in more deprived parts of the country.

Austerity-era welfare changes also disproportionately impacted low-income households of working age, women, minority ethnic communities, and those with children (Beatty and Fothergill, 2016). Post-2010, child poverty rates increased substantially in England – particularly in the most affected parts of the country. Using the relative measure of poverty – living in a household at less than 60 per cent of the national median income (calculated for each devolved country respectively) –, child poverty after housing costs was 28 per cent in England in 2014–15 but rose to 30 per cent by 2019/20 (Stone, 2022). Once again, this was geographically patterned: child poverty increased from 26 per cent to 37 per cent in North East England, from 30 per cent to 35 per cent in the West Midlands, and from 28 per cent to 33 per cent in Yorkshire and Humber (Stone, 2022).

Correspondingly, since 2010, health inequalities in England have increased (Office for National Statistics, 2021a). In 2011, the gap in life expectancy at birth between men living in the most and least deprived 10 per cent of neighbourhoods in England was 9 years. The gap in healthy life expectancy was 18.6 years.[8] For women, the deprivation gap in in life expectancy in 2011 was 6.9 years and for healthy life expectancy it was 19.1 years. By 2019, this had *risen* among men to a 9.4 year gap in life expectancy and a 19.0 year gap in healthy life expectancy between those living in the most and least deprived areas. It also rose among women to a 7.6 year life expectancy gap and a 19.3 year healthy life expectancy gap. Indeed, life expectancy actually started an unprecedented (outside of famines or wars) decline in some areas: male life expectancy in County Durham in the North East of England fell by 6 months between 2015–17 and 2018–20; and female life expectancy in Darlington in the North East of England also fell by over a year in the same period (Office for National Statistics, 2021b). Nationally, life expectancy among men in the most deprived areas only rose slightly between 2011 and 2019 from 73.9 years to 74.1 years, while for women in the most deprived areas it fell from 79.0 years to 78.7 years (Office for National Statistics, 2021a).

Relatedly, regional inequalities in health in England also increased since 2010 as average life expectancy for men and women across all levels of deprivation rose in London but fell in most regions outside of London. For example, in the North East, life expectancy did not increase for men living in the poorest areas, and it fell for the poorest women (Marmot, 2020). The health outcomes associated with deprivation appear to have become amplified since 2010 in North East England (Bambra et al, 2023).

In addition to increasing inequalities in life expectancy, there is evidence that other health inequality measures also increased during austerity. For example, the gap in mental health and well-being between deprived and affluent areas in England increased, with people living in more deprived areas bearing the brunt of rising rates of mental ill health (Barr et al, 2015). Reflecting this, there were greater rates of increases in suicide in the North than the South: by 2012 they were 12.4 per 100,000 in the North West compared to 8.7 per 100,000 in London. Similarly, people living in the local authorities most adversely economically impacted by the financial crisis and austerity had the highest epidemiologic risk of beginning a new course of antidepressants (Cherrie et al, 2021). Socio-economically and spatially concentrated increases in unemployment since 2007–08 were also associated with increasing inequalities in morbidity and mortality (Moeller, 2013). Mortality rates among women in the most deprived areas of England also increased between 2010/2012 and 2017/2019 (Walsh et al, 2022).

These widespread and large scale austerity-induced cuts in public spending, and the regressive nature of the cuts, arguably led to increases in health inequalities by negatively impacting the social determinants of health (such as increasing rates of child poverty or limiting access to social care or affordable housing) (Bambra and Marmot, 2023). Looking more specifically, a study of Universal Credit (the flagship welfare reform) found that there were adverse impacts on the mental health of unemployed people who were transitioned onto Universal Credit from 2013 to 2018 (Wickham et al, 2020). Further, as child poverty rates increased in England from 2010 to 2020, inequalities in infant mortality rates also increased (Robinson et al, 2019; Taylor-Robinson et al, 2019). There is also evidence that the areas of England which experienced the greatest cuts in local government expenditure had the largest adverse effects on life expectancy (Alexiou et al, 2021). It has also been shown that austerity has had a disproportionate impact on the health of vulnerable groups, especially individuals and families, including children, with the lowest incomes or in receipt of welfare benefits (MacLeavy, 2011).

Further evidence for the likely role of austerity in driving England's resurgent health inequalities is found in the international literature. A large body of public health research has found that austerity was accompanied by adverse health changes in many countries. For example, those countries (such as Iceland) that responded to the financial crisis of 2007–08 with an economic stimulus fared much better in health terms (particularly in terms of mental health and suicides) than those countries (for example, Greece, Portugal, Spain, UK) that responded with austerity (Stuckler and Basu, 2013).

A study of mortality trends in 37 high-income countries between 2000 and 2019 found that there were slower improvements, or actual deteriorations, in life expectancy and mortality trends in most countries that implemented austerity after the financial crisis of 2007–08 (McCartney et al, 2022). Trends were generally worse for women than men. The study concluded that 'austerity is likely to be a cause of stalled mortality trends'. In the UK, it was estimated that the additional pressures placed on key social and healthcare services during austerity were associated with up to 10,000 additional deaths in 2018 compared to previous years (Dorling, 2018).

England therefore entered the COVID-19 pandemic in 2020 with 'stalling life expectancy, increased regional and deprivation-based health inequalities, and worsening health for the poorest in society' (Bambra and Marmot, 2023, p 22). Perhaps unsurprisingly, there were significant inequalities in the impacts of the pandemic (Bambra et al, 2021), likely exacerbated by austerity (Bambra and Marmot, 2023).

## Conclusion

This chapter has summarised four levelling mechanisms that the governments in the US, Germany, Brazil and England put to work to reduce health inequalities: welfare state expansion, economic equalisation, healthcare access and political incorporation. All four of these mechanisms led to improved health equity during the 'waxing' periods in these countries, and when these mechanisms began to wane, so too did health equity.

Examining cases studies allows us to capture a holistic, longitudinal picture of how health equity comes about in a way that would not be possible if we relied solely on evidence drawn from experimental or quasi-experimental assessments of individual policies. In each case, levelling mechanisms took slightly different forms. To take just one example, in the US during the Great Society, antidiscrimination and civil rights legislation was a core part of welfare state expansion, while this element was mostly absent in the other cases. No one mechanism, used alone, would likely have caused the reductions in health inequalities that were observed when multiple levellers are used together. And not all levelling mechanisms are equally possible to activate in all contexts. But taken together, they show how governments in the past have achieved important gains in health equity – and how quickly the gains can be reversed when different politics take over. In the final chapter, we will consider the antecedents of 'waxing' and 'waning' periods and reflect on what this means for those committed to reducing health inequalities, who may want to elongate a period of 'waxing' or help achieve a shift from 'waning' to 'waxing'.

# 7

# Conclusion: The politics of health inequalities

We began this book by noting that health inequalities between social groups are virtually ubiquitous and that the groups with worse health outcomes are almost always groups who are socially or economically disadvantaged in some way. Since social and economic disadvantages (and advantages) are often embedded within the structures of society, it is no surprise that health inequalities are often also visible geographically. There are many axes of inequality, including socio-economic position, ethnicity and gender. And while researchers often seek to understand specific types of inequality, the reality of people's lives is that inequalities intersect in ways that are not always simply additive; this interaction is central to the concept of intersectionality (as detailed in Chapter 1). Applying an intersectional lens to health inequalities research and policy can be challenging, but the fundamental principle of health revealing the 'biological embodiment of social disadvantage' (Vineis et al, 2020, p 1) remains. It is, therefore, hard to imagine a society in which health inequalities might not exist.

Yet, as all four country case studies featured in this book illustrate, the scale of health inequalities *can* be reduced. And in fact, with the right combination of policies it is possible to achieve quite substantial reductions in relatively short periods of time. There are good reasons, therefore, to push for the kinds of policies and programmes that seem likely to reduce health inequalities.

For those seeking more equitable health outcomes, however, identifying precisely which policies and programmes hold the most promise is a formidable task. Much of the research on this topic to date has been led by researchers trained to be guided by a 'hierarchy of evidence' inherited from medical research, even though its suitability for public health and social policy can be questionable (Parkhurst and Abeysinghe, 2016). This hierarchy, which places meta-analyses and systematic reviews of experimental research at the top, and case studies and expert opinion at the bottom, does an excellent job of identifying negative and positive health outcomes of medical and pharmaceutical interventions. However, there has been limited success with efforts to employ this kind of methodological approach to identify the most promising policies, programmes and interventions for reducing health inequalities. Systematic reviews of evidence on this topic (some of which we have been involved in) are almost always disappointing, as Box 7.1 illustrates.

> **Box 7.1: The disappointingly limited insights of systematic reviews for identifying which policies are effective in reducing health inequalities**
>
> Generally, the effects of interventions on health inequalities were unclear. (Bambra et al, 2010, p 284)
>
> Studies about the effectiveness of interventions on equity in maternal or child health are limited. (Yuan et al, 2014, p 634)
>
> The review does tentatively suggest interventions that policy makers might use to reduce health inequalities, although whether the programmes are transferable between high-income countries remains unclear. (Thomson et al, 2018, p 869)
>
> [W]e found tentative evidence that the provision of housing/home modifications, improving the public realm, parks and playgrounds, supermarkets, transport, cycle lanes, walking routes, and outdoor gyms – can all have positive impacts on health outcomes – particularly physical activity. However, ... the effect of these interventions on health inequalities remains unclear. (McGowan et al, 2021, p 1888)

Faced with such unenlightening conclusions, authors of systematic reviews frequently propose further research, or identify new data sources, arguing that the absence of such data is 'impeding progress on identifying interventions that are effective in reducing health inequalities' (McGowan et al, 2021). Yet while more and better data are always welcome, and may lead to new insights, we should perhaps concede that we are unlikely to ever have *quite* the breadth or quality of data that researchers would like.

Indeed, in the four country examples within this book, the types of evidence available varies enormously. For a variety of reasons, the available evidence and data that can lead to strong causal claims are more plentiful for the US and the English case studies than for Germany or Brazil. In the US, even the Great Society policies that were meant to apply across the board were sometimes implemented more fully in some states or localities than others, creating natural experiments in which researchers can compare 'intervention' groups (who received a full 'dose' of the policy/programme) with 'control' groups (who did not). In England, the New Labour government's decision to set explicit, quantified national targets to reduce health inequalities meant there was a need for policymakers to invest in data collection to track health inequalities and to commission research to inform decisions with a view to increasing the chances of achieving the targets. Meanwhile, in contrast to the US, many of the most important policy changes in Germany and Brazil, such as democratisation, population wide healthcare systems and, in the German case, monetary unification, affected the whole population at the same time, making it impossible to identify a 'control' group for quasi-experimental analysis. Moreover, in contrast to the UK, the policies implemented in Germany and Brazil were designed to achieve a range of social and economic outcomes; they were not, primarily, designed to reduce health inequalities. There was, therefore, no equivalent motivation to invest in data to track health inequalities, or evidence to unpack the way particular changes were impacting on health inequalities.

The fact that the evidence base underpinning the US and English examples is better suited to a certain kind of analysis does not, however, mean that these countries are necessarily 'better' examples of reducing health inequalities. Indeed, the scale of the policy reforms undertaken in Germany and Brazil was far more ambitious, and the reductions in health inequalities that occurred shortly afterwards are impressive. So there are good reasons to try to understand how combinations of policy reforms appear to impact on health inequalities, even if causal evidence is thin on the ground (Kelly-Irving et al, 2022). This book takes a more methodologically inclusive approach than many, by exploring the insights that emerge when we look across four very different case studies of countries that have seen progress in reducing health inequalities.

This holistic, case-based analysis leads us to conclude (as laid out in Chapter 6) that *combinations* of policy change that address disadvantage are likely to be required if significant reductions of health inequalities are to be achieved. In short, single policy changes are unlikely to get the job done, and given the unique historical and contextual specifics of every country, there may not even be a 'magic' combination of policies. However, we were able to identify what we call four health inequality 'levellers'; types of policy change that were evident in all four case studies of success, where there exists either evidence that helps identify causal links or scholarship that establishes plausible causal pathways. In each instance, the waxing of these efforts – involving expansion of the welfare state, reduction of economic inequality, eliminating barriers to access high-quality healthcare, and enhancing the political integration of previously marginalised groups – has led to increases in health equity. And the waning of these efforts has led to stalled progress and the emergence of new health inequalities.

## Health inequality leveller 1: welfare state expansion

In Chapter 5, we saw that the expansion of social welfare under the (1997–2010) English Health Inequalities Strategy was accompanied by reductions in heath inequalities. In Chapter 6, we saw that subsequent reductions in welfare and public services during austerity have been accompanied by increases in health inequalities in England. Similarly, Chapter 5 showed that health inequalities increased under the Thatcher-led governments (1979–1990), where there was also a large-scale dismantling of the welfare state. Looking across all three policy periods (Thatcherism 1979–97; strategy 2000–10; and austerity 2010–24), we can see a large role for the 'waxing and waning' of the welfare state in terms of driving patterns of health inequalities (Bambra, 2022).

This 'levelling up' health inequalities mechanism is also evident in our case study of the USA (Chapter 2), where racial and income inequalities in premature mortality (deaths under age 75) and infant mortality rates (deaths before age 1) declined between 1966 and 1980 – during a period of welfare and healthcare expansion (the 'War on Poverty' and the enactment of civil rights legislation). These inequalities then increased between 1980 and 2002, during the Reagan–Bush period of neoliberalism, when public welfare services and healthcare insurance coverage were cut (Krieger et al, 2008). Later periods of rebuilding – for example, with pandemic-era income supports and housing protections – led once again to decreasing health inequalities (Berkowitz and Basu, 2021; Leifheit et al 2021).

Likewise, in Brazil and Germany, an expansion of social welfare measures was associated with reductions in health inequalities. In Germany, which rapidly reduced the East–West differences in life expectancy, welfare expansion occurred quickly, as the social welfare available to residents of West Germany was extended to people living in East Germany, following unification. In Brazil, which achieved remarkable reductions in inequalities in life expectancy and infant mortality, the expansion of social welfare measures took place over a longer period, centring on an evolving programme of cash-transfers linked to children's school attendance and family engagement with public health measures. Yet, as with the other case studies, the 'waxing' of the welfare state was time limited. In both cases, a subsequent 'waning' of social welfare has been associated with increases in health inequalities. Both Germany and Brazil, like England, implemented austerity policies in subsequent periods, leading to reductions in welfare support. In Germany, this included a 2005 reform which substantially reduced the means-tested benefits available to people experiencing unemployment. Much like England, this appears to have contributed to worsening health outcomes for directly affected groups (Shahidi et al, 2020). In Brazil, austerity measures were implemented slightly later, from 2015 onwards, and health inequalities also began widening.

Our case study findings about the effects of welfare state waxing and waning on health inequalities are mirrored in other studies of welfare state expansion and retraction. For example, studies of welfare state changes in New Zealand (Shaw et al, 2005; Pearce and Dorling, 2006; Pearce et al,

2006; Blakely et al, 2008) found that socio-economic inequalities in all-cause mortality among men, women and children increased in the 1980s and the 1990s, a period in which New Zealand underwent major structural reform (including introducing: a less redistributive tax system, more restricted (targeted) social benefits, regressive taxes on consumption, the privatisation of major utilities and public housing, user charges for welfare services and the deregulation of the labour market). Data suggest a subsequent stabilisation of health inequalities in the early 2000s, a period in which there were some improvements in public service provision (for example, better access to social housing, more generous social assistance, and a decrease in healthcare costs). Indeed, it appears to be a dose-response relationship at the macro level – more expansive and supportive welfare states lead to lower poverty rates and smaller health inequalities; conversely, contractions to the welfare state are associated with increased health inequalities (Simpson et al, 2021).

## Health inequality leveller 2: improved healthcare access

In all four cases, there was an expansion of access to healthcare in the 'waxing' periods studied in Chapters 2 to 5. The scale of the change was perhaps most ambitious in Brazil, which established the *Sistema Único de Saúde* in 1990, which is the world's largest tax-funded, government-run healthcare system. While it was created as a public healthcare system, available to all, this made a bigger difference to those for whom healthcare was otherwise unaffordable (that is, poorer communities). In Germany, the expansion focused primarily on the former East Germany area, where people who had been living with a crumbling, state-run health system were rapidly integrated into West Germany's relatively high performing social health insurance system. In the 1960s US, the desegregation of healthcare, combined with the creation of the Medicaid and Medicare systems, increased access to healthcare for a wide range of marginalised groups, including African Americans, poorer, elderly people, people with disabilities, and children who lacked parental support. In England, which already had a tax-funded, government run healthcare system, a combination of investment in the NHS and organisational reforms led to performance improvements, with more care being delivered more quickly in more deprived areas (Thorlby and Maybin, 2010).

In subsequent periods, the waning of healthcare access in these four case studies has not typically involved profound or sudden changes. In the US, Medicare and Medicaid both enjoy relatively strong political support, particularly as compared to other social programmes aimed at poorer communities. And while there are some new efforts at the state level to restrict access to Medicare, federal-level policies have worked to dramatically expand access to health insurance during the 2000s. In England, the NHS has been maintained so healthcare access remains free at the point of delivery. However, austerity cuts have reduced the performance of the NHS across multiple measures and there are now long waiting times, difficulties accessing healthcare, and low confidence in government policies to improve NHS performance (Powell et al, 2019; Thorlby et al, 2019; Cameron et al, 2024). Similarly, in Brazil, fiscal restrictions, combined with a series of public health emergencies (the large-scale Zika virus outbreak and the COVID-19 pandemic), have contributed to declining healthcare performance across a range of measures (Massuda et al, 2018; de Oliveira Andrade, 2020; OECD, 2021). In both cases, there are concerns that reduced healthcare performance is exacerbating health inequalities (Fisher et al, 2022; Coube et al, 2023). In contrast, Germany is something of an outlier; its social insurance-based healthcare system means investments are less dependent on government funding, so healthcare has not been as affected by austerity measures and healthcare performance remains strong, even though some inequities persist (Blümel et al, 2022).

Unpacking the precise role that healthcare plays in health inequalities is challenging, including within the four case studies in this book, since changes to healthcare systems often happen at a national scale (meaning we often lack control groups) and often occur alongside broader welfare reforms. For the US, Brazil, Germany and England, the expansion of healthcare access described earlier were just one part of much larger scale policy changes. The best data come from the US case study, since both Medicaid and Community Health Centres were rolled out in ways that allowed comparisons to control groups. This research, summarised in Chapter 2, concludes that expanded access to healthcare (notably via the Medicaid programme and federally funded Community Health Centres) probably did help narrow income-related and ethnic health inequalities, albeit in a limited way. There are multiple studies in Brazil which claim that the expansion of healthcare access via the creation of the *Sistema Único de Saúde* and the Family Health Programme, which uses Community Health Workers, helped reduce the infant mortality rate (Macinko et al, 2006; Aquino et al, 2009; Ceccon et al, 2014; Roman, 2023). However, what these studies show is an association between healthcare access and reduced infant mortality. Since these studies did not consider how the other policy changes set out in Chapter 3 might have impacted on infant mortality rates, it is hard to be confident about the precise role of healthcare versus other policy changes in this substantial health improvement. Longitudinal ecological analysis by Guanais (2013) suggests that it was a combination of the expanded healthcare access and the *Bolsa Família* social welfare programme that led to Brazil's infant mortality reductions. This leads us to agree with Graham Watt, a Scottish doctor who has long campaigned for policies to address the 'inverse care law':[1]

> The principal causes of inequalities in health lie outside the health service, which is why policies to prevent health inequalities must address

the wider social determinants of health, starting in childhood. However, it is insufficient to focus on the prevention of future inequalities in health. It is also necessary to reduce existing inequalities in health, and to prevent them getting wider. (Watt, 2013, p 494)

In other words, while healthcare may not have as much impact on health inequalities as social welfare, income sufficiency and political voice, ensuring healthcare access is a necessary component of policy efforts to address health inequalities and appears to have played a role in the ability of England, Brazil, Germany and the US to reduce health inequalities. An analysis of data from 17 European countries (including England, but not Germany) supports this conclusion by showing that 'higher healthcare expenditure was associated with lower mortality from amenable causes' (Mackenbach et al, 2017, p 1110). This leads the study authors to conclude that, at least in Europe, 'more generous healthcare funding provides some protection against inequalities in amenable mortality' (Mackenbach et al, 2017).

## Health inequality leveller 3: reduced income inequalities

The third health inequalities 'leveller' that is evident across our four country case studies is a reduction in poverty and in income inequalities. The waxing and waning of income inequality is, of course, related to changes in welfare state generosity. Larger welfare states tend to invest more in 'pre-distributive' social policies such as high quality childcare and education, as well as in redistributive policies that generate a greater equality of incomes, after accounting for taxes and social transfers. However, welfare state waxing and waning is only one contributor to the waxing and waning of economic inequality more broadly. Tax policies and labour market interventions, such as minimum wages and support for labour unions, set the basic shape of the earnings and wealth distributions in society. The shape of these distributions is in turn related to health inequalities (Pickett and Wilkinson, 2015).

In most rich democracies, the distribution of economic resources has grown more unequal since the mid-1970s. The Great Society in the US was a waxing period for equality of earnings. And as the Great Society waned, income and wealth inequalities grew at an alarming pace. The reunification of East and West Germany was a rare instance in the late 20th century of a large-scale reduction of economic inequality within a rich democracy, created by the rapid merger of two previously distinct economies, and a large transfer of resources from the West to the East. Despite this, some material inequalities persisted and a period of austerity subsequently contributed to widening inequalities in the disposable income of households (Blömer et al, 2023), albeit not in ways that were strongly patterned by region (Frieden et al, 2023). The waning of efforts to reduce economic inequality reinforced the waning of welfare state expansion in both the US and German cases, ensuring the (re)growth of health inequalities.

In England, New Labour's (1997–2010) strategy to reduce health inequalities did not seriously attempt to reduce market-generated inequalities, and instead focused on pre-distribution and redistribution through the welfare state as a means to address poverty. The subsequent period of austerity has not substantially worsened income inequalities in England, but this is not especially good news since income inequalities were already very high, having increased dramatically in the 1980s (Brewer and Wernham, 2022; see also Figure 5.2 in Chapter 5). In Brazil, as we saw in Chapter 3, pro-poor cash transfers, employment policies that incentivised transitions from the informal to the formal economy, and minimum wage increases all helped reduce income inequalities. However, this was in the context of Brazil being one of the most unequal countries in the world and, despite some improvements, very high income inequalities persist in Brazil. Indeed, more recent analysis, which incorporates income tax data suggests that the reduction in income inequalities in the 2000s may not have been as substantial as earlier analyses suggested (Medeiros, 2016). The English and Brazilian stories are, therefore, ones of persistently high income inequalities throughout the periods of waxing and waning health inequalities, over the past three decades, with only limited reductions during the 'waxing' periods, as a result of social welfare, employment and economic policies.

The wider academic literature exploring the role of income inequalities on health inequalities is mixed. While some analyses find no relationship between income inequalities and health outcomes (Hoffmann et al, 2016; Deaton, 1999), a causal review by Pickett and Wilkinson (2015, p 316) concludes that, 'evidence strongly suggests that income inequality affects population health and wellbeing'. While there is more agreement within international research literature about poverty (rather than income inequalities) being bad for health (Gupta et al, 2007; Habibov et al, 2019), we have focused on income inequalities because our four case studies all, in different ways, underline the importance of power struggles and of people's sense of how fairly they are being treated, relative to others. Both Brazil and Germany illustrate well how persistent material inequalities can contribute to situations in which people begin to feel hopeless and in despair. And high income and wealth inequalities, as the case of rural land reform in Brazil illustrates well, can contribute to inequalities in power that people can exert to adapt policy change to their advantage; in short, those with wealth can sometimes use their resources to take advantage of policies, even where these are intended to improve the circumstances of people who are less well off.

We close this section by noting that, while we have proposed 'reducing income inequalities' as a 'leveller', 'reducing wealth inequalities' may be a greater leveller. Our focus on income inequalities simply reflects the available research and data (both for our four case studies and more broadly). However, the pathways via which existing research suggests that income inequalities impact on health inequalities apply equally to inequalities in wealth: by contributing to relative poverty, by negatively impacting on poorer people's sense of status relative to others, and by reducing social cohesion within societies. Moreover, the distribution of wealth is often much more unequal than the distribution of income. This leads health inequalities researcher, Fran Baum, to conclude that public health researchers should shift their focus towards efforts to analyse the impacts of wealth, and wealth inequalities, on health (Baum, 2005).

## Health inequality leveller 4: enhanced democratic participation

We have already, in Chapter 4, reviewed the impact of democracy on health, in the context of the German case study. As we saw, the population of East Germany was suddenly integrated into a democratic welfare state, gaining new freedoms and voting rights, which an extensive body of research has shown to be beneficial for population health. Two other case studies, Brazil and the US, also involved substantial democratisation. In Brazil, the whole country transitioned from an authoritarian military dictatorship to a democracy and, during the leadership of President Lula (2003–11), there were extensive efforts to embed democratic governance systems, including by bringing trade unions and civil society organisations into policymaking processes, as well as via experiments with participatory budgeting. And in the US, the success of the civil society movement led to the Voting Rights Act of 1965, which sought to secure the right to vote for racialised minorities, extending democratic engagement to many communities in the US that had been persistently discriminated against. The reverse situation is also touched on in Chapter 6, which notes the rise of anti-democratic politics in the US, and a rise in support for far-right, authoritarian politics in both Germany and Brazil occurring as efforts to reduce health inequalities 'waned'. In Germany, state authorities have sought to limit the influence of far-right political parties by closely monitoring their activities and by publicly categorising them as extremist organisations that pose a threat to democracy. In Brazil, the election of Jair Bolsonaro as President was viewed by many as an illustration of how fragile and precarious democracy can be, in light of his repeated explicit statements about the benefits of authoritarian rule (for example, Junge et al, 2021). However, the more recent re-election of President Lula has assuaged some of these fears. Nonetheless, these examples suggest that the waxing and waning of reductions of health inequalities has some association with the state of democracy.

Unpacking how democratic engagement impacts on health inequalities is no easy task. However, the wider international literature supports our assertion that democratisation is an important leveller of health inequalities. A European analysis of survey data from 28 European countries finds that exposure to democracy reduces health inequalities (Costa-Font and Knust, 2023). There is also a much broader body of evidence that finds links between democracy and population health, including a historically focused evidence review that concludes 'democracy is a (frequently forgotten) determinant of health' (Wise and Sainsbury, 2007, p 177) and a comparative analysis of countries categorised as having autocratic, incoherent and democratic polities that concludes that democracy has a positive influence on population health (Safaei, 2006).

In previous chapters, we have proposed at least three pathways through which democratisation plausibly impacts health inequalities: (1) substantive: democratically elected administrations, who depended on popular support for electoral success, introducing policy changes that better reflect population needs and interests and are, therefore, more likely to favour the masses; (2) social: democratisation builds social solidarity and social support and helps foster a sense of social connectivity that facilitates and enables policies that reflect population interests (as opposed to policies that reflect elite interests, at the cost of others); and (3) psychosocial: democratisation can provide people with a sense of hope, fostering a belief that change is possible and that people can effect change in positive ways. Taken together, these mechanisms help explain the observed connection between political incorporation and a reduction in health inequalities in our studies, as well as globally.

## What can we conclude about the policies required to reduce health inequalities?

By looking across the four case studies in this book, and situating our reflections in the wider, international evidence base, we are confident that the four levellers described previously can play an important role in reducing health inequalities. However, as Chapter 6 illustrates, it is also important to acknowledge that, while each of our four case studies achieved some reduction in health inequalities, the precise policy mixes differed and none of the four case studies of success in reducing health inequalities managed to fully address all four levellers. This suggest that reducing health inequalities is likely to require a mixture of policies to address a combination of the levellers we have identified. However, given the contrasting historical circumstances of each country, there is unlikely to be a 'magic' ('best practice') mix. It also seems likely that some of these levellers are dose dependent; for social welfare, for example, we conclude that more expansive and supportive welfare states lead to lower poverty rates and narrower health inequalities; while contractions to the welfare state are associated with increased health inequalities.

It is also important to note additional potential levellers that were evident in only some of the case studies. For example, in Brazil we saw substantial state investments in efforts to improve housing (especially in large, urban areas) and to support poorer communities in rural areas to purchase the land on which they lived. As the implementation of these ambitious policies proved challenging and chaotic, and as none of the other case studies featured substantial improvements in these areas, we were not able to conclude (based on the evidence within *this* book) that addressing inequalities in housing or land ownership is necessarily a key 'leveller' for health inequalities. However, there is a wealth of broader evidence that suggests housing is a crucial health determinant and that inequalities in housing play an important role in health inequalities (Gibson et al, 2011).

Other additional policy levers were attempted more successfully in some cases than in others. These included actions on the commercial determinants of health, where Brazil and England took action to address the influence of tobacco (and tobacco companies) on health, while US efforts were ineffective and, in Germany, were not apparent; in environmental policy, where health improvements in East Germany followed the closure of poorly regulated businesses, but early, tentative environmental regulations in the US had little immediate impact on health; and in workplace safety, where both Brazil and Germany introduced a range of measures during the periods in which health inequalities reduced, but this was not a core element of either the US or English cases.

The pursuit of policies to reduce health inequalities should not, therefore, be restricted to the four levellers we identify in this book. However, at a minimum it seems unlikely that health inequalities can be substantially reduced if all four levellers are moving in the wrong direction. Since our case studies also show that policy efforts to reduce inequalities are rarely sustained, the next section considers what our case studies reveal about how this waxing and waning of efforts to reduce health inequalities occurs.

## What precedes periods of waxing and waning?

Most of us would accept that welfare state and healthcare expansion are not processes that can be sustained infinitely: While the level of provision that society deems adequate may evolve over time to encompass new needs and new social groups, there are nevertheless likely to be limits on how much social spending a society is willing to support. Increases in economic equality, too, are likely to be related to broader economic trends that may be cyclical (or even dialectical). But since the end of the Second World War, the waxing of political incorporation, without risk of a future waning, has been largely taken for granted in the West. Once political rights are granted, once democracy is established, it is unlikely to be taken away. Indeed, one influential late 20th-century public intellectual even asserted that, with the fall of the Soviet Union, all potential ideological competitors had failed, and we had arrived at the 'end of history' (Fukuyama 2006 [1992]).

The early 21st century has shown us that a waning of democracy in the West is not only possible but already occurring. The rise of populist far-right ideologies and parties in the US, Germany and Brazil, and the growth of nationalist politics in the UK (as reflected in Brexit), all show that liberal democracy is not like toothpaste: it can, in fact, be put back in the tube. The effects on health inequalities of the waxing of democratic inclusion have been nothing short of transformational. The waning of democracy should concern us, not only because it is likely to contribute to the waning of the other three levellers but also because it imposes new health threats, ranging from police violence to a rising likelihood of civil and international conflicts.

If we look across our four case studies, we see three common antecedents to periods of waxing, in which governments take successful action to reduce health inequalities. The first is a surge in social movements pushing for the kinds of progressive policies that help reduce health inequalities. The types of organisations involved vary but can include civil rights movements, non-governmental organisations, trade unions and people coming together to protest specific policies or issues. It is important to note that none of these social movements coalesced around campaigns to reduce health inequalities. Rather, all were variously focused on improving people's living and working conditions. Where different social movements come together, as we saw in Brazil and Germany, this can inform a sense of collectivism and a push for policies that work to benefit society (rather than particular individuals or groups, at the cost of others). A second factor that can spark the onset of a 'waxing' period, which was especially evident in Brazil but also present (albeit to a lesser degree) in England and the US, is the presence of ambitious political leaders and/or parties, with a clear agenda for progressive social reform, and widespread popular support. Third, when we consider the more qualitative insights within each case study, we see evidence of a high degree of hope and optimism within the electorate.

By contrast, if we focus on the stories that emerge in Chapter 6, we can identify four common antecedents to periods of waning. First, we see evidence of persistent structural and material inequalities, despite governments that had indicated these inequalities would be addressed. There are many reasons why this occurs: these can include a lack of policies to address the issue, as with state violence in Brazil; implementation failures, as with housing in the US and Brazil; or the existence of policies that counter the impacts of progressive efforts, such as combinations of economic policies that result in increases in inequalities in wealth even where social welfare is seeking to reduce poverty, as in England. In all cases, the result appears to be an increasingly disaffected electorate.

Second, we see evidence of discourses and ideologies that actively advocate inequalities (these were particularly apparent in the discussions of the US, Brazil, and Germany, in Chapter 6). Macro-ideologies, such as neoliberal proposals for a small state, free markets, and trickle-down economics (ideas that have been especially influential in England and the US), can provide the ideational basis for anti-equality sentiments. These can also be inculcated by those who create 'moral panics' (Cohen, 2002 [1972]) and other deliberate attempts to inculcate social division, as is typically evident in far-right politics.

Third, persistent material and structural inequalities and discourses advancing inequality can combine to inform power struggles between social groups. These sometimes erupt into violent social protests aimed at denigrating or disavowing particular social groups, usually those who are already marginalised and disempowered, such as minority ethnic communities, unemployed people, women, migrants and/or LGBT+ communities. This can prompt backlash against health levellers from conservative elements in society, who come to view the levelling policies themselves as sources of social unrest that need to be undone in order to regain a sense of security (Bambra and Lynch, 2020).

## If we want to reduce health inequalities, what can we do?

The scale of change required to reduce health inequalities can seem intimidating, and the factors that seem to precede periods of waxing and waning can seem beyond our control. Yet, in each of the four examples in which health inequalities were successfully reduced, social movements (and sometimes researchers) played a role. Reflecting on this, we close the book by proposing six actions that we can all take to help reduce health inequalities, each of which requires some adaptation, depending on the waxing and waning context.

First, work to develop, or contribute to, coalitions of actors who are working to make the case for reducing health inequalities or the broader social and economic inequalities that underlie health inequalities. Research and data can play an important role in helping demonstrate that different advocacy groups share an interest in addressing social determinants of health. For example, since non-communicable diseases are shaped by social determinants, major charities that advocate for action to address particular diseases all have a potential interest in addressing major social determinants. There will also be other organisations advocating to address these determinants (for example, poverty, low incomes or housing) and yet others who are advocating the rights and needs of particular communities (for example, charities that focus on people experiencing homelessness, or refugees, or trade unions). The benefit of the breadth of social determinants is that there are a wealth of different organisations working to influence policy who have an interest in improving social determinants, even if most of these organisations are not primarily concerned with health inequalities.

Second, it is important to share the message that it is possible to reduce health (and other) inequalities. It is here, we hope, that this book makes an important contribution. If politicians and publics do not believe that reducing inequalities is possible, it is hard to envision how the political and public support necessary for large-scale, progressive policy reform can be achieved. While this may feel both more important and more of a challenge in periods of waning, it remains imperative in periods of waxing, to help push back on premature conclusions that policy efforts are failing when the reality is simply that they may take time to achieve their goals.

Third, when periods of waxing occur, it can help to institutionalise some of the major social goals that have widespread popular and political support. Brazil's decision to include a right to health within its constitution is a good example as this commitment helped the government make the case for a tax funded healthcare system, navigate complicated trade agreements to achieve access to much-needed pharmaceuticals, and prevent the easy dismantling of the healthcare system when the political winds changed. Explicit legal commitments to civil and political rights, as undertaken during the US Great Society, are also likely harder to undo than simple budgetary increases for individual social policies – as in England. While no legal or policy change is immune from reversal, those that create powerful constituencies and allies are generally much harder to undo (Pierson, 1993).

Fourth, the account of Brazil's waning period in Chapter 6, in particular, highlights the importance of mass media and social media for spreading information and ideas. Indeed, the media have been identified by some researchers as an important determinant of health (Even et al, 2024). This suggests there is a need to think strategically about how to influence and use media in work to reduce inequalities. It also suggests it is important to promote a free press and to push back on situations in which media outlets are dominated by a small number of vested interests.

Fifth, when it comes to proposing policy change, our case studies (and the example of housing in particular) suggest it is crucial to carefully plan for what happens after a policy is passed, in order to avoid policy failures at the implementation stage. Promising policies can easily be dashed by chaotic or poorly conceived implementation and this then informs public disappointment and mistrust.

Finally, the extent to which periods of waning appear to be preceded by popular anger, disaffection and despair underlines the importance of engaging with people – not simply promoting evidence-based policies to improve their lives from the outside, but listening, reflecting and adapting. This is crucial because political and public will rests not only on what works but on what people believe and how they feel.

Reducing health inequalities is demonstrably feasible. Policies that aggressively target the social, economic and political determinants of health can have an equalising impact. But it requires political will and popular support to enact and sustain these policies over the long term. When we enter periods of waxing, research on what is effective in reducing health inequalities has the potential to play an important, potentially direct, role in policy. When we are faced with periods of waning, as is the case for many countries at the moment, we may have more impact by focusing our efforts on (re)building the political and popular will to support the case for tackling inequalities. In this case, we may be more influential if we focus on engaging with others who are making a case for progressive policy reform, and who are working to counter ideas and interests that advocate policies that are likely to increase health inequalities.

# Notes

## Chapter 1
1. Source: Bambra (2024) reproduced with permission under Creative Commons licence.

## Chapter 3
1. The Gini coefficient runs from 0 to 1 where 0 reflects perfect equality, where everyone in the population has exactly the same income or wealth, and a Gini coefficient of 1 reflects maximum inequality where one person has everything and everyone else has nothing.
2. Brazil has around 5600 municipalities with an average population of 37,728 people each.

## Chapter 4
1. Relative poverty is when a household has an income that is less than 60 per cent of the median household income.
2. The funding of the healthcare system in the East also changed to match that of the West – shifting from a centralised state funded system to a social insurance one.

## Chapter 5
1. Supply-side economics argues that lower taxes and limited business regulation, free trade, is the most effective way of producing economic growth (Schrecker and Bambra, 2015; 2025).
2. Flexible labour allows for the easy hiring and firing of workers, use of temporary contracts with no job security and few rights (for example, to sickness pay).
3. Mortality from causes for which there is evidence that they can be prevented given timely, appropriate access to high quality care (Nolte and McKee, 2011).

## Chapter 6
1. The public health grant is paid to local authorities from the central UK government. It is used to provide preventative services including smoking cessation, drug and alcohol services, children's health services and sexual health services.
2. Universal Credit turned six previous working-age benefits and tax credits into a single monthly payment, employed a 'digital by default' claims process, applied job-seeking conditions to receipt and added a five-week waiting-period before the first payment.
3. The benefit cap was introduced in 2013. It limits the maximum amount in benefits a working-age household can receive. As of April 2024, the cap in London is £25,323 a year for a family and £16,967 a year for a single person. Outside of London it is £22,020 a year for a family, and £14,753 a year for a single person (House of Commons Library, 2024).
4. The Under Occupancy Charge (or bedroom tax) was introduced in 2013 and is a reduction in Housing Benefit for working-age people (16–64 years) living in social housing if the government decide that you have one or more spare rooms: one spare room results in a decrease in Housing Benefit of 14 per cent; for two or more spare rooms then the reduction is 25 per cent.
5. Working Tax Credit was a means tested benefit paid to people in low-income employment. It was introduced in 2003 and was phased out from 2010. In addition, means tested Child Tax Credit was paid to households with children.
6. Child Benefit was a universal benefit (paid to all families regardless of income and with additional payments for each child) since its introduction, but from 2013, it became means tested (so that higher earners would have a reduced benefit or would receive nothing at all).

7 The two-child limit of 2017 means that Child Benefit and Universal Credit is only paid for the first two children in a family, with nothing for the third or additional children. This measure alone is estimated to have put 250,000 children into poverty (End Child Poverty, 2024).

8 Healthy Life Expectancy is the average number of years that a person can expect to live in full health, not impeded by disabling illnesses or injuries or poor health. It is a self-reported measure so may include mental health.

## Chapter 7

1 The inverse care law was originally put forward by Julian Tudor Hart, a Welsh doctor, stating that the availability of good medical care tends to vary inversely with the need for it in the population served (Hart, 1971).

# References

Abramovitz, M. and Smith, R.J. (2021) 'The persistence of residential segregation by race, 1940 to 2010: The role of federal housing policy', *Families in Society*, 102, pp 5–32.

Acevedo-Garcia, D. and Osypuk, T.L. (2006) 'Racial disparities in housing and health', in C. Hartman (ed) *Poverty and race in America: The emerging agendas*. Washington: Lexington Books, pp 130–6.

Acheson, D. (1998) *Independent inquiry into inequalities in health: Report*. London: Stationery Office.

Akhter, N., Bambra, C., Mattheys, K., Warren, J. and Kasim, A. (2018) 'Inequalities in mental health and well-being in a time of austerity: Follow up findings from the Stockton-on-Tees cohort study', *SSM – Population Health*, 6, pp 75–84.

Albani, V., Brown, H., Vera-Toscano, E., Kingston, A., Eikemo, T.A. and Bambra, C. (2022) 'Investigating the impact of on mental wellbeing of an increase in pensions: A longitudinal analysis by area-level deprivation in England, 1998–2002', *Social Science & Medicine*, 311, p 115316.

Aldridge, R.W., Story, A., Hwang, S.W., Nordentoft, M., Luchenski, S.A., Hartwell, G., et al (2018) 'Morbidity and mortality in homeless individuals, prisoners, sex workers, and individuals with substance use disorders in high-income countries: A systematic review and meta-analysis', *The Lancet*, 391(10117), pp 241–50.

Alexiou, A., Fahy, K., Mason, K., Bennett, D., Brown, H., Bambra, C., et al (2021) 'Local government funding and life expectancies in England: A longitudinal ecological study', *The Lancet Public Health*, 6(9), pp e641–7.

Almond, D., Chay, K.Y. and Greenstone, M. (2006) *Civil rights, the War on Poverty, and Black–White convergence in infant mortality in the rural South and Mississippi*. MIT Department of Economics Working Paper No. 07–04. Available at: https://doi.org/10.2139/ssrn.961021 [Accessed: 4 December 2023].

Almond, D., Hoynes, H.W. and Schanzenbach, D.W. (2011) 'Inside the War on Poverty: The impact of Food Stamps on birth outcomes', *The Review of Economics and Statistics*, 93(2), pp 387–403.

Amaral De Sampaio, M.R. (1994) 'Community organization, housing improvements and income generation: A case study of "Favelas" in São Paulo, Brazil', *Habitat International*, 18(4), pp 81–97.

Anderson, D.M., Charles, K.K. and Rees, D.I. (2020) *Imposing policy on reluctant actors: The hospital desegregation campaign and Black postneonatal mortality in the Deep South*. NBER Working Paper No. 27970. Available at: https://doi.org/10.3386/w27970 [Accessed: 4 December 2023].

Aneja, A.P. and Avenancio-Leon, C.F. (2019) *The effect of political power on labour market inequality: Evidence from the 1965 Voting Rights Act*. Washington Centre for Equitable Growth Working paper series. Available at: https://equitablegrowth.org/working-papers/the-effect-of-political-power-on-labour-market-inequality-evidence-from-the-1965-voting-rights-act/ [Accessed: 4 December 2023].

Appleby, J. and Gainsbury, S. (2022) *The past, present and future of government spending on the NHS*. The Nuffield Trust. Available at: https://www.nuffieldtrust.org.uk/news-item/the-past-present-and-future-of-government-spending-on-the-nhs [Accessed: 1 November 2023].

Aquino, R., de Oliveira, N.F. and Barreto, M.L. (2009) 'Impact of the family health programme on infant mortality in Brazilian municipalities', *American Journal of Public Health*, 99, 87–93.

Arends-Kuenning, M. (2009) 'A report card for Lula: Progress in education', in J.L. Love and W. Baer (eds) *Brazil under Lula*. New York: Palgrave Macmillan, pp 205–20.

Arntzen, A. and Nybo Andersen, A. (2004) 'Social determinants for infant mortality in the Nordic countries, 1980–2001', *Scandinavian Journal of Public Health*, 32(5), pp 381–9.

Arretche, M. (2016) 'Federalism, social policy and reductions in territorial inequality in contemporary Brazil', in B.R. Schneider (ed) *New order and progress: Development and democracy in Brazil*. New York: Oxford University Press, pp 162–84.

Ault, J.E. (2015) *Saving nature in socialism: East Germany's official and independent environmentalism, 1968–1990*. PhD thesis. University of North Carolina. Available at: https://doi.org/10.17615/pm7w-ke54 [Accessed: 4 December 2023].

Aumann, B. and Scheufele, R. (2010) 'Is East Germany catching up? A time series perspective', *Post-Communist Economies*, 22(2), pp 177–92.

Avis, M., Bulman, D. and Leighton, P. (2007) 'Factors affecting participation in Sure Start programmes: A qualitative investigation of parents' views', *Health & Social Care in the Community*, 15, pp 203–11.

Avritzer, L. (2009) *Participatory institutions in democratic Brazil*. Baltimore, MD: John Hopkins University Press.

Ayers, J., Garcia, M., Guillén, D.A. and Kehoe, P.J. (2019) *The monetary and fiscal history of Brazil, 1960–2016*. National Bureau of Economic Research Working Paper 25421. Cambridge, MA: NBER. Available at: http://www.nber.org/papers/w25421 [Accessed: 4 December 2023].

Bailey, M.J. and Goodman-Bacon, A. (2015) 'The War on Poverty's experiment in public medicine: Community Health Centres and the mortality of older Americans', *American Economic Review*, 105(3), pp 1067–104.

# References

Bailey, M.J., DiNardo, J. and Stuart, B.A. (2021a) 'The economic impact of a high national minimum wage: Evidence from the 1966 Fair Labour Standards Act', *Journal of Labour Economics*, 39(S2), pp S329–67.

Bailey, M.J., Sun, S. and Timpe, B. (2021b) 'Prep school for poor kids: The long-run impacts of head start on human capital and economic self-sufficiency', *American Economic Review*, 111(12), pp 3963–4001.

Bambra, C. (2011) *Work, worklessness and the political economy of health*. Oxford: Oxford University Press.

Bambra, C. (2012) 'Social inequalities in health: The Nordic welfare state in a comparative context', in J. Kvist, J. Fritzell, B. Hvinden and O. Kangas (eds) *Changing social equality: The Nordic welfare model in the 21st century*. Bristol: Policy Press, pp 143–64.

Bambra, C. (2016) *Health divides: Where you live can kill you*. Bristol: Policy Press.

Bambra, C. (2022a) 'Levelling up: Global examples of reducing health inequalities', *Scandinavian Journal of Public Health*, 50(7), pp 908–13.

Bambra, C. (2024) 'The u-shaped curve of health inequalities over the 20th and 21st centuries', *International Journal of Social Determinants of Health and Health Services*, 54(3), pp 199–205.

Bambra, C. and Lynch, J. (2020) 'Welfare chauvinism, populist radical right parties and health inequalities', *International Journal of Health Policy and Management*, 10(0), pp 581–4.

Bambra, C. and Marmot, M. (2023) *Expert report for the UK COVID-19 public inquiry. Module 1: Health inequalities*. Available at: https://covid19.publicinquiry.uk/wpcontent/uploads/2023/06/16183457/INQ000195843.pdf [Accessed: 30 November 2023].

Bambra, C. and Smith, K. (2010) 'No longer deserving? Sickness benefit reform and the politics of (ill) health', *Critical Public Health*, 20, pp 71–83.

Bambra, C., Barr, B. and Milne, E. (2014) 'North and South: Addressing the English health divide', *Journal of Public Health*, 36(2), pp 183–6.

Bambra, C., Fox, D. and Scott-Samuel, A. (2005) 'Towards a politics of health', *Health Promotion International*, 20, pp 187–93.

Bambra, C., Lynch, J. and Smith, K.E. (2021a) *Unequal pandemic: COVID-19 and health inequalities*. Bristol: Policy Press.

Bambra, C., Munford, L., Bennett, N. and Khavandi, S. (2023) *Northern Exposure: COVID-19 and regional inequalities in health and wealth*. Bristol: Policy Press.

Bambra, C., Riordan, R., Ford, J. and Matthews, F. (2020) 'The COVID-19 pandemic and health inequalities', *J Epidemiol Community Health*, 74(11), pp 964–8.

Bambra, C., Smith, K.E., Garthwaite, K., Joyce, K. and Hunter, D. (2011) 'A labour of Sisyphus? Public policy and health inequalities in the UK from the Black Report and the Acheson Inquiry to the Marmot Review', *Journal of Epidemiology and Community Health*, 65(5), pp 399–406.

Bambra, C., Gibson, M., Sowden, A., Wright, K., Whitehead, M. and Petticrew, M. (2010) Tackling the wider social determinants of health and health inequalities: Evidence from systematic reviews, *Journal of Epidemiology & Community Health*, 64, pp 284–91.

Bandi, P., Chang, V.W., Sherman, S.E. and Silver, D. (2020) '24-year trends in educational inequalities in adult smoking prevalence in the context of a national tobacco control programme: The case of Brazil', *Preventive Medicine*, 131, p 105957.

Barbosa de Melo, F.L. (2015) 'The minimum wage campaign in Brazil and the fight against inequality', *Global Labour Journal*, 6(3), pp 283–301.

Barr, B., Bambra, C. and Whitehead, M. (2014) 'The impact of NHS resource allocation policy on health inequalities in England 2001–11: Longitudinal ecological study', *British Medical Journal*, 348.

Barr, B., Kinderman, P. and Whitehead, M. (2015) 'Trends in mental health inequalities in England during a period of recession, austerity and welfare reform 2004 to 2013', *Social Science & Medicine*, 147, pp 324–31.

Barr, B., Higgerson, J. and Whitehead, M. (2017) 'Investigating the impact of the English Health Inequalities Strategy: time trend analysis', *British Medical Journal*, 358.

Barry, J. and Paterson, M. (2003) The British state and the environment: New Labour's ecological modernisation strategy, *International Journal of Environment and Sustainable Development*, 2(3), pp 237–49.

Barth, J. (2006) 'Public policy management councils in Brazil: How far does institutionalised participation reach?', *Public Administration and Development*, 26, pp 253–263.

Bartles, L.M. (2004) 'Partisan politics and the US income distribution', Department of Politics and Woodrow Wilson School of Public and International Affairs, Princeton University. Unpublished paper. Available at: https://web.archive.org/web/20070627125108/http://www.princeton.edu/~bartels/income.pdf [Accessed: 23 December 2023].

Bartley, M. (2017) *Health inequality: An introduction to theories, concepts and methods*. Cambridge: Polity Press.

Bauld, L., Judge, K. and Platt, S. (2007) Assessing the impact of smoking cessation services on reducing health inequalities in England: Observational study. *Tobacco Control*, 16(6), pp 400–4. http://www.jstor.org/stable/20748228

Baum, F. (2005) 'Wealth and health: The need for more strategic public health research', *J Epidemiol Community Health*, 59, pp 542–5.

BBC News (1998) 'Business: The Economy Governor tries to douse north's fire', 22 June. Available at: http://news.bbc.co.uk/1/hi/business/197995.stm [Accessed: 4 November 2023].

Beardsley, E.H. (1986) 'Good-bye to Jim Crow: The desegregation of southern hospitals, 1945–70', *Bulletin of the History of Medicine*, 60(3), pp 367–86.

Beatty, C. and Fothergill, S. (2013) *The impact of welfare reform on Northern Ireland: A research paper*. Northern Ireland Council for Voluntary Action. Available at: https://www.nicva.org/sites/default/files/d7content/atta chments-resources/the_impact_of_welfare_reform_in_ni_2013.pdf [Accessed: 21 November 2023].

Beatty, C. and Fothergill, S. (2016) *The uneven impact of welfare reform: The financial losses to places and people*. Sheffield: Joseph Rowntree Foundation, Oxfam GB and Sheffield Hallam University Centre for Regional Economic and Social Research. 10.21201/2016.604630. Available at: https://pol icy-practice.oxfam.org/resources/the-uneven-impact-of-welfare-ref orm-the-financial-losses-to-places-and-people-604630/ [Accessed: 4 November 2023].

Beckfield, J. and Bambra, C. (2016) 'Shorter lives in stingier states: Social policy shortcomings help explain the US mortality disadvantage', *Social Science & Medicine*, 170, pp 30–8.

Beckfield, J., Bambra, C., Eikemo, T.A., McNamara, C., Huijts, T., and Wendt, C. (2015) 'Towards an institutional theory of welfare state effects on the distribution of population health', *Social Theory and Health*, 13, pp 227–44.

Beckfield, J. and Krieger, N. (2009) 'Epi+ demos+ cracy: linking political systems and priorities to the magnitude of health inequities—evidence, gaps, and a research agenda', *Epidemiologic Reviews*, 31(1), 152–77.

Béland, D., Rocco, P. and Waddan, A. (2016) *Obamacare wars: Federalism, state politics, and the Affordable Care Act*. Lawrence, KS: University Press of Kansas.

Bellos, A. (2002) 'Lula promises poverty relief and stability', *The Guardian*, Tue 29 October 2002. URL: https://www.theguardian.com/world/2002/ oct/29/brazil.alexbellos [Accessed: 17 January 2024].

Benach, J., Amable, M., Muntaner, C. and Benavides, F.G. (2002) 'The consequences of flexible work for health: Are we looking at the right place?' *Journal of Epidemiology and Community Health*, 56(6), pp 405–6.

Bennett, N., Norman, P.N., Albani, V., Kingston, A. and Bambra, C. (2024) 'The impact of the English national Health Inequalities Strategy on geographical inequalities in mortality at age 65: A time-trend analysis', *European Journal of Public Health*, 34(4), pp 660–5.

Berg, J. (2010) 'Laws or luck? Understanding rising formality in Brazil in the 2000s', Série Trabalho Decente no Brasil, Documento de Trabalho 5. Organização Internacional do Trabalho. URL: https://www.wiego.org/ sites/default/files/publications/files/Berg_Brazil_Labour_Market_Reg.pdf [Accessed: 12 February 2024].

Inserted Berkowitz, S.A. and Basu, S. (2021) 'Unmet social needs and worse mental health after expiration of COVID-19 federal pandemic unemployment compensation', *Health Affairs*, 40(3), pp 426–34.

Berman, E.P. (2022) *Thinking like an economist: How efficiency replaced equality in US public policy*. Princeton, NJ: Princeton University Press.

Bernini, A., Facchini, G., Tabellini, M. and Testa, C. (2023) *Black empowerment and White mobilization: The effects of the Voting Rights Act*. National Bureau of Economic Research Working Paper No. 31425. Cambridge, MA: NBER. Available at: https://doi.org/10.3386/w31425 [Accessed: 4 June 2024].

Berridge, V. and Blume, S. (2003) *Poor health: Social inequality before and after the Black Report*. London: Frank Cass.

Besley, T. and Kudamatsu, M. (2006) 'Health and democracy', *American Economic Review*, 96(2), pp 313–18.

Bess, K.D., Miller, A.L. and Mehdipanah, R. (2023) 'The effects of housing insecurity on children's health: A scoping review', *Health Promotion International*, 38(3), p daac006.

Bessudnov, A., McKee, M. and Stuckler, D. (2012) 'Inequalities in male mortality by occupational class, perceived status and education in Russia, 1994–2006', *Eur Journal of Public Health*, 22(3), pp 332–7.

Bhattacharya, J., Currie, J. and Haider, S. (2004) 'Poverty, food insecurity, and nutritional outcomes in children and adults', *Journal of Health Economics*, 23(4), pp 839–62.

Bitler, M.P. and Karoly, L.A. (2015) 'Intended and unintended effects of the War on Poverty: What research tells us and implications for policy', *Journal of Policy Analysis and Management*, 34(3), pp 639–96.

Black, D. (1980) *Inequalities in health: Report of a research working group*. London: DHSS.

Black, D., Morris, J.N., Smith, C. and Townsend, P. (1999) 'Better benefits for health: Plan to implement the central recommendation of the Acheson report', *British Medical Journal*, 318(7185), pp 724–7.

Blakely, T., Tobias, M. and Atkinson, J. (2008) 'Inequalities in mortality during and after restructuring of the New Zealand economy: Repeated cohort studies', *British Medical Journal*, 336(7640), pp 371–5.

Blömer, M., Lay, M., Peichl, A., Rathje, A.-C., Ritter, T., Schüle, P. and Steuernagel, A. (2023) *Inequality in Germany: 1983–2019*. London: Institute for Fiscal Studies. Available at: https://ifs.org.uk/inequality/wp-content/uploads/2023/11/Inequality-in-Germany.pdf [Accessed: 27 June 2024].

Bloomfield, K., Grittner, U. and Kramer, S. (2005) Developments in alcohol consumption in reunited Germany. *Addiction*, 100, pp 1770–8.

Blümel, M., Hengel, P., Achstetter, M., Schwarzbach, M. and Busse, R. (2022) 'Health system performance assessment: Does Germany provide good access to healthcare?', *European Journal of Public Health*, 32, pp iii459.

Boing, A.F., Subramanian, S.V. and Boing, A.C. (2019) 'Reducing socioeconomic inequalities in life expectancy among municipalities: The Brazilian experience', *International Journal of Public Health*, 64, pp 713–20.

Borman, G.D. and D'Agostino, J.V. (1996) 'Title I and student achievement: A meta-analysis of federal evaluation results', *Educational Evaluation and Policy Analysis*, 18(4), pp 309–26.

Boudreaux, M.H., Golberstein, E. and McAlpine, D.D. (2016) 'The long-term impacts of Medicaid exposure in early childhood: Evidence from the programme's origin', *Journal of Health Economics*, 45, pp 161–75.

Boyer, D. (2001) 'The impact and embodiment of Western expertise in the restructuring of the Eastern German Media after 1990', *Anthropology of East Europe Review*, 19(1), pp 77–84.

Brady, K. (2024) 'Far-right German party may threaten democracy, can be spied on, court rules', *The Washington Post*, 13 May. Available at: https://washingtonpost.com/world/2024/05/13/germany-afd-extremist-party-court/ [Accessed: 27 June 2024].

Brainerd, E. (1998) 'Market reform and mortality in transition economies', *World Development*, 26(11), pp 2013–27.

Brewer, M. (2006) *Tax credits: Fixed or beyond repair?* London: Institute for Fiscal Studies. Available at: https://ifs.org.uk/sites/default/files/2022-08/06chap7.pdf [Accessed: 4 November 2023].

Brewer, M. and Wernham, T. (2022) *Income and wealth inequality explained in 5 charts*. London: Institute for Fiscal Studies. Available at: https://ifs.org.uk/articles/income-and-wealth-inequality-explained-5-charts [Accessed: 27 June 2024].

Brill, A. (2023) *The overlooked decline in community health centre funding*. Washington, DC: Matrix Global Advisors. Available at: https://www.nachc.org/wp-content/uploads/2023/07/Overlooked-Decline-Community-Health-Centre-Funding_2023_Full-report.pdf [Accessed: 22 June 2023]

Britton, J., Farquharson, C. and Sibieta, L. (2019) *2019 annual report on education spending in England*. London: Institute for Fiscal Studies. Available at: https://ifs.org.uk/publications/2019-annual-report-education-spending-england [Accessed: 23 November 2023].

Brown, T., Platt, S. and Amos, A. (2014) 'Equity impact of European individual-level smoking cessation interventions to reduce smoking in adults: A systematic review', *European Journal of Public Health*, 24(4), p cku065.

Buarque, C. (2001) *Bolsa-Escola: An education and poverty reduction programme*. UNCTAD – United Nations Conference on Trade and Development. Available at: https://unesdoc.unesco.org/ark:/48223/pf0000136425 [Accessed: 20 June 2024].

Buchanan, A. (2006) 'Children aged 0–13 at risk of social exclusion: Impact of government policy in England and Wales', *Children and Youth Services Review*, 28(10), pp 1135–51.

Bueno, N.S., Nunes, F. and Zucco, C. Jr. (2018) *Do Governments Make Dreams Come True? An Analysis of the Minha Casa Minha Vida Housing Program*. Working Paper. URL: https://repositorio.fgv.br/server/api/core/bitstreams/36c530b7-673f-4252-81c8-121ecf20a36c/content [Accessed: 29 January 2024].

Burda, M.C. and Hunt, J. (2001) 'From reunification to economic integration: Productivity and the labour market in Eastern Germany', *Brookings Papers on Economic Activity*, 32(2), pp 1–92.

Burgard, S.A. and Treiman, D.J. (2006) 'Trends and racial differences in infant mortality in South Africa', *Social Science & Medicine*, 62(5), pp 1126–37.

Burstrom, B. (2003) 'Social differentials in the decline of infant mortality in Sweden in the 20th century: The impact of politics and policy', *International Journal of Health Services*, 33(4), pp 723–41.

Burstrom, B. and Bernhardt, E. (2001) 'Social differentials in the decline of child mortality in nineteenth century Stockholm', *European Journal of Public Health*, 11, pp 29–34.

Caldeira, T.P.R. and Holston, J. (1999) 'Democracy and violence in Brazil', *Comparative Studies in Society and History*, 41(4), pp 691–729.

Cameron, G., Buzelli, L., Duxbury, K., Sinclair, R., Jefferson, A. and Gardner, T. (2024) *The public's views on the future of the NHS in England: Findings from deliberative research and polling with the public and what it means for the next government*. London: The Health Foundation. Available at: https://www.health.org.uk/publications/reports/public-views-on-the-future-of-the-nhs-in-england [Accessed: 27 June 2024].

Cameron, N. (2003) 'Physical growth in a transitional economy: The aftermath of South African apartheid', *Economics & Human Biology*, 1, pp 29–42.

Card, D. and Krueger, A.B. (1992) 'Does school quality matter? Returns to education and the characteristics of public schools in the United States', *Journal of Political Economy*, 100, pp 1–40.

Card, D. and Krueger, A.B. (1993) 'Trends in relative Black–White earnings revisited', *The American Economic Review*, 83(2), pp 85–91.

Cardoso, J.C. (2007) *De volta para o futuro? As fontes de recuperação do emprego formal no Brasil e as condições para sua sustentabilidade temporal*. Brasília: IPEA. Available at: https://portalantigo.ipea.gov.br/agencia/index.php?option=com_content&view=article&id=4550 [Accessed: 27 June 2024].

Carlin, W. (1992) 'Privatization in East Germany, 1990–92', *German History*, 10(3), p 335.

Carnes, N. (2012) 'Does the numerical underrepresentation of the working class in congress matter?', *Legislative Studies Quarterly*, 37(1), pp 5–34.

Cascio, E. and Reber, S. (2013) 'The K-12 education battle', in M.J. Bailey and S. Danziger (eds) *Legacies of the War on Poverty*. New York: Russell Sage Foundation, pp 66–92.

Cascio, E.U., Gordon, N. and Reber, S. (2013) 'Local responses to federal grants: Evidence from the introduction of Title I in the South', *American Economic Journal: Economic Policy*, 5(3), pp 126–59.

Case, A. and Deaton, A. (2015) 'Rising morbidity and mortality in midlife among White non-Hispanic Americans in the 21st century', *Proceedings of the National Academy of Sciences*, 112(49), pp 15078–83.

Case, A. and Deaton, A. (2020) *Deaths of despair and the future of capitalism*. Princeton, NJ: Princeton University Press.

Case, A. and Deaton, A. (2021) 'Life expectancy in adulthood is falling for those without a BA degree, but as educational gaps have widened, racial gaps have narrowed', *Proceedings of the National Academy of Sciences*, 118(11), p e2024777118.

Castro, M.C., Gurzenda, S., Turra, C.M., Kim, S., Andrasfay, T. and Goldman, N. (2021) 'Reduction in life expectancy in Brazil after COVID-19', *Nature Medicine*, 27, pp 1629–35.

Cattan, S., Conti, G., Farquharson, C. and Ginja, R. (2021) *The health impacts of Sure Start*. London, UK: Institute for Fiscal Studies. https://ifs.org.uk/publications/health-impacts-sure-start [Accessed: 4 November 2023].

Ceccon, R.F., Bueno, A.L.M., Hesler, L.Z., Kirsten, K.S., Portes, V.D.M. and Viecili, P.R.N. (2014) 'Mortalidade infantil e Saúde da Família nas unidades da Federação brasileira, 1998–2008', *Cadernos Saúde Coletiva*, 22.

Centres for Disease Control and Prevention (2018) *Health of Black or African American non-Hispanic population*. Available at: https://www.cdc.gov/nchs/fastats/black-health.htm [Accessed: 6 November 2023].

Centre for Cities (2021) What can German reunification teach the UK about levelling up? Available at: https://www.centreforcities.org/blog/what-can-german-reunification-teach-the-uk-about-levelling-up/ [Accessed: 6 November 2023].

Chapa, J. (2015) 'Chapter 4 expansion and contraction in LBJ's voting rights legacy', in R.H. Wilson, N.J. Glickman and L.E. Lynn (eds) *LBJ's neglected legacy: How Lyndon Johnson reshaped domestic policy and government*. New York: University of Texas Press, pp 98–123. Available at: https://doi.org/10.7560/300541-007 [Accessed: 27 June 2024].

Chay, K.Y. and Greenstone, M. (2000) 'The convergence in Black–White Infant mortality rates during the 1960's', *The American Economic Review*, 90(2), pp 326–32.

Chay, K.Y., Guryan, J. and Mazumder, B. (2014) 'Early life environment and racial inequality in education and earnings in the United States', National Bureau of Economic Research Working Paper No. 20539. Cambridge, MA: NBER. Available at: https://doi.org/10.3386/w20539 [Accessed: 27 June 2024].

Cherrie, M., Curtis, S., Baranyi, G., Cunningham, N., Dibben, C., Bambra, C. and Pearce, J. (2021) 'A data linkage study of the effects of the Great Recession and austerity on antidepressant prescription usage', *European Journal of Public Health*, 31(2), pp 297–303.

Chiro, M. (2018) *Politics in uniform: Military officers and dictatorship in Brazil, 1960–1980*. Pittsburgh, PA: University of Pittsburgh Press.

Charlton, T.L., Myers, L.E. and Sharples, R. (eds) (2008) *Thinking about oral history: Theories and applications*. Lanham, MD: AltaMira Press.

Chowkwanyun, M. (2018) 'The War on Poverty's health legacy: What it was and why it matters', *Health Affairs*, 37, pp 47–53.

Chung, H. and Muntaner, C. (2007) 'Welfare state matters: A typological multilevel analysis of wealthy countries', *Health Policy*, 80(2), pp 328–39.

CIA (2003) *CIA world factbook 1990*. Available at: https://www.cia.gov/readingroom/docs/THE%20WORLD%20FACTBOOK%201990%5B15815916%5D.pdf [Accessed: 6 November 2023].

Coburn, D. (2004) 'Beyond the income inequality hypothesis: Class, neoliberalism, and health inequalities', *Social Science & Medicine*, 58, pp 41–56.

Cohen, R.A., Makuc, D.M., Bernstein, A.B., Bilheimer, L.T. and Powell-Griner, E. (2009) *Health insurance coverage trends, 1959–2007: Estimates from the national health interview survey*. National health statistics reports; No. 17. Hyattsville, MD: National Centre for Health Statistics.

Cohen, S. (2002 [1972]) *Folk devils and moral panics*. Adbingdon, Oxon, UK: Routledge [first published by MacGibbon and Kee Ltd in 1972].

InsCoelho, V.S.P. and Dias, M. (2019) 'Health and inequalities', in M. Arretche (ed) *Paths of inequality in Brazil*. Cham: Springer.

Coleman, A. and Federman, S. (2024) *Work requirements for Medicaid enrollees*. Explainer. Commonwealth Fund. Available at: https://doi.org/10.26099/wk0h-dq24 [Accessed: 6 November 2023].

Coleman, K.J. (2014) *The Voting Rights Act of 1965: Background and overview (No. R43626)*. CRS Report. Washington, DC: Congressional Research Service.

Collins, C. and McCartney, G. (2011) 'The impact of neoliberal political attack on health: The case of the Scottish effect', *International Journal of Health Services*, 41(3), pp 501–23.

Corporation for National & Community Service Office of Research & Evaluation (2018) *VISTA 50-year review*. Available at: https://americorps.gov/sites/default/files/evidenceexchange/VISTA_Evaluation_and_Impact_Final%20Report_Edited_053118_FINAL_508v2_1.pdf [Accessed: 6 November 2023].

Costa-Font, J. and Knust, N. (2023) 'Does exposure to democracy decrease health inequality?', *Journal of Public Policy*, 43, pp 741–60.

Coube, M., Nikoloski, Z., Mrejen, M. and Mossialos, E. (2023) 'Inequalities in unmet need for healthcare services and medications in Brazil: A decomposition analysis', *The Lancet Regional Health – Americas*, 19.

Currie, J. and Cole, N. (1993) 'Welfare and child health: The link between AFDC participation and birth weight', *The American Economic Review*, 83(4), pp 971–85.

Currie, J. and Duque, V. (2019) 'Medicaid: What does it do, and can we do it better?', *The Annals of the American Academy of Political and Social Science*, 686, pp 148–79.

Davis, J. and Tallis, R. (eds) (2013) *NHS SOS: How the NHS was betrayed and how we can save it*. London: Oneworld.

De Almeida, T. (2020) *Trust and populism: The vote for Bolsonaro*. PhD thesis. Georgia State University. Available at: https://scholarworks.gsu.edu/cgi/viewcontent.cgi?article=1080&context=political_science_theses [Accessed: 27 June 2024].

de Jong, Greta. (2005) 'Staying in place: Black migration, the Civil Rights Movement, and the War on Poverty in the rural South', *The Journal of African American History*, 90(4), p 387.

Deaton, A. (1999) 'Inequalities in income and inequalities in health', in F. Welch (ed) *The causes and consequences of increasing inequality*. Chicago, IL, and London: The University of Chicago Press.

Deming, D. (2009) 'Early childhood intervention and life-cycle skill development: Evidence from Head Start', *American Economic Journal Applied Economics*, 1(3), pp 111–34.

De Oliveira Andrade, R. (2020) 'Covid-19 is causing the collapse of Brazil's national health service', *British Medical Journal*, 370, p m3032.

Department of Health (1997) *Press release: Public health strategy launched to tackle the root causes of ill-health*. London: Department of Health.

Department of Health (2000) *The NHS plan: A plan for investment, a plan for reform*. London: The Stationary Office.

Department of Health (2002) *Tackling health inequalities: 2002 cross-cutting review*. London: Department of Health.

Derenoncourt, E. and Montialoux, C. (2021) 'Minimum wages and racial inequality', *The Quarterly Journal of Economics*, 136, pp 169–228.

Dickman, S.L., Gaffney, A., McGregor, A., Himmelstein, D.U., McCormick, D., Bor, D.H. and Woolhandler, S. (2022) 'Trends in healthcare use among Black and White persons in the US, 1963–2019', *JAMA Network Open*, 5(6), pp e2217383.

Dilnot, A. and McCrae, J. (1999) *Family Credit and the Working Families' Tax Credit*. London, UK: Institute for Fiscal Studies. Available at: https://ifs.org.uk/sites/default/files/output_url_files/bn3.pdf [Accessed: 4 November 2023].

Donohue, J.J. and Heckman, J. (1991) 'Continuous versus episodic change: The impact of civil rights policy on the economic status of Blacks', *Journal of Economic Literature*, 29(4), pp 1603–43.

Dorling, D. (2012) *Fair play*. Bristol: Policy Press.

Dorling, D. (2014) *All that is solid: How the great housing disaster defines our times, and what we can do about it*. London: Penguin.

Dorling, D. (2018) *Peak inequality: Britain's ticking time bomb*, 1st edn. Bristol: Bristol University Press.

Dörr, M., Riemer, U., Christ, M., Bauersachs, J., Bosch, R., Laufs, U., Neumann, A., Scherer, M., Störk, S. and Wachter, R. (2021) 'Hospitalizations for heart failure: still major differences between East and West Germany 30 years after reunification', *ESC Heart Failure*, 8(4), pp 2546–55.

Downs, A. (1974) 'The successes and failures of federal housing policy', *The Public Interest*, 38, p 124.

Eikemo, T. and Bambra, C. (2008) 'The welfare state: A glossary for public health', *Journal of Epidemiology & Community Health*, 62, pp 3–6.

Ellen, I.G. and Steil, J.P. (eds) (2019) *The dream revisited: Contemporary debates about housing, segregation, and opportunity in the twenty-first century*. New York: Columbia University Press.

End Child Poverty (2024) Children are living in families impacted by the two-child limit everywhere in the UK, available at: https://endchildpoverty.org.uk/two_child_limit/ [Accessed: 2 August 2024].

Enenkel, K. and Rösel, F. (2023) *German reunification: Lessons from the German approach to closing regional economic divides*, Resolution Foundation and the Centre for Economic Performance at the London School of Economics. Available at: https://economy2030.resolutionfoundation.org/wp-content/uploads/2022/12/German-reunification.pdf [Accessed: 4 December 2023].

Ericson, A., Eriksson, H., Kisllin, B. and Zetterstrom, R. (1993) 'Secular trends in the effect of socio-economic factors on birth weight arid infant survival in Sweden', *Scandinavian Journal of Social Medicine*, 21, pp 10–16.

Esping-Andersen, G. (1990). *The three worlds of welfare capitalism*. London: Polity.

Estivaleti, J.M., Guzman-Habinger, J., Lobos, J., Azeredo, C.M., Claro, R., Ferrari, G., Adami, F. and Rezende, L.F. (2022) 'Time trends and projected obesity epidemic in Brazilian adults between 2006 and 2030', *Scientific Reports*, 12, p 12699.

Eurostat (2023) *Regions in Europe – 2023 edition*. Available at: https://ec.europa.eu/eurostat/web/interactive-publications/regions-2023#economy [Accessed: 5 December 2023].

Even, D., Abdalla, S.M., Maani, N., Galea, S. (2024) 'News media as a commercial determinant of health', *The Lancet Global Health*, 12(8), pp e1365–9.

Fearnside, P. (1984) 'Brazil's Amazon settlement schemes: Conflicting objectives and human carrying capacity', *Habitat International*, 8, pp 45–61.

Federal Government Commissioner for the New Federal States (2018) *Annual Report of the Federal Government on the Status of German Unity 2018*. Available at: https://www.bmwk.de/Redaktion/EN/Publikationen/jahresbericht-zum-stand-der-deutschen-einheit-2018.pdf?__blob=publicationFile&v=3 [Accessed: 2 December 2023].

Ferreira, F.H.G., Firpo, S.P. and Messina, J. (2016) 'Understanding recent dynamics of earnings inequality in Brazil', in B.R. Schneider (ed) *New order and progress: Development and democracy in Brazil.* New York: Oxford University Press.

Finzel, E. (2003) '"Equality" for women, child rearing, and the state in the former German Democratic Republic', *Women's Studies International Forum*, 26, pp 47–56.

Fisher, R., Allen, L., Malhotra, A.M. and Alderwick, H. (2022) *Tackling the inverse care law.* London: The Health Foundation.

Fishlow, A. (1973) 'Brazil's Economic Miracle', *The World Today*, 29(11), pp 474–81. Available at: http://www.jstor.org/stable/40394674

Fontes, P. and de Macedo, F.B. (2013) 'Strikes and pickets in Brazil: Working-class mobilization in the 'old' and 'new' unionism, the strikes of 1957 and 1980', *International Labour and Working-Class History*, 83, pp 86–111. Available at: doi:10.1017/S0147547913000161.

Fordham, G. (2010) *The New Deal for Communities programme: Achieving a neighbourhood focus for regeneration. The New Deal for Communities National Evaluation: Final report – Volume 1.* London, UK: Department for Communities and Local Government. Available at: https://extra.shu.ac.uk/ndc/downloads/general/Volume%20one%20-%20Achieving%20a%20neighbourhood%20focus%20for%20regeneration.pdf [Accessed: 14 November 2023].

Foster, M. (1998) *Black teachers on teaching.* New York: The New York Press.

Frieden, I., Peichl, A. & Schüle, P. (2023) 'Regional income inequality in Germany', *EconPol Forum*, 24, pp 50–55.

Friel, S., Townsend, B., Fisher, M., Harris, P., Freeman, T. and Baum, F. (2021) Power and the people's health', *Social Science & Medicine*, 282, p 114173.

Frisvold, D.E. (2015) 'Nutrition and cognitive achievement: An evaluation of the School Breakfast Programme', *Journal of Public Economics*, 124, pp 91–104.

Fukuyama, F. (2006) *The end of history and the last man.* Reissue edition. New York: Free Press.

Fulbrook, M. (2005) *The people's state: East German society from Hitler to Honecker.* Yale: Yale University Press.

Galvão, J. (2005) 'Brazil and access to HIV/AIDS drugs: A question of human rights and public health', *American Journal of Public Health*, 95(7), pp 1110–16.

Gamble, A. (1994) *Theate.* London: Macmillan.

Gamble, A. (2009) *The spectre at the feast: Capital crisis and the politics of recession.* Basingstoke: Palgrave.

Garces, E., Thomas, D. and Currie, J. (2002) 'Longer-term effects of Head Start', *The American Economic Review*, 92(4), pp 999–1012.

Garfield, S. (2001) *Indigenous struggle at the heart of Brazil state policy, frontier expansion, and the Xavante Indians, 1937–1988*. Durham, NC: Duke University Press.

Gibbs, C., Ludwig, J. and Miller, D.A. (2013) 'Head Start origins and impacts', in M.J. Bailey and S. Danziger (eds) *Legacies of the War on Poverty*. New York: Russell Sage Foundation, pp 39–65.

Gibson, M., Petticrew, M., Bambra, C., Sowden, A.J., Wright, K.E. and Whitehead, M. (2011) 'Housing and health inequalities: A synthesis of systematic reviews of interventions aimed at different pathways linking housing and health', *Health Place*, 17, pp 175–84.

Gibson, M., Thomson, H., Banas, K., Lutje,, V., Mckee,, M., Martin, S., Fenton, C., Bambra, C. and Bond, L. (2018) 'Welfare to work interventions and their effects on the health and well-being of lone parents and their children', *Cochrane Database System Review*, (2)2, p CD009820.

Gilens, M. (1999) *Why Americans hate welfare: Race, media, and the politics of antipoverty policy*. Chicago, IL: University of Chicago Press.

Ginsburg, N. (1992) *Divisions of welfare: A critical introduction to comparative social policy*. London: Sage.

Gjonça, A., Brockmann, H. and Maier, H. (2000) 'Old-age mortality in Germany prior to and after reunification', *Demographic Research*, 3(1).

Goodman-Bacon, A. (2018) 'Public insurance and mortality: Evidence from Medicaid implementation', *Journal of Political Economy*, 126, pp 216–62.

Goodman-Bacon, A. (2021) 'The long-run effects of childhood insurance coverage: Medicaid implementation, adult health, and labour market outcomes', *American Economic Review*, 111(8), pp 2550–93.

Gornick, M.E. (2000) 'Disparities in Medicare services: Potential causes, plausible explanations, and recommendations', *Healthcare Financing Review*, 21(4), pp 23–43.

Gornick, M.E. (2008) 'A decade of research on disparities in Medicare utilization: Lessons for the health and healthcare of vulnerable men', *American Journal of Public Health*, 98(Suppl 1), pp S162–8.

Gornick, M.E., Warren, J.L., Eggers, P.W., Lubitz, J.D., De Lew, N., Davis, M.H. and Cooper, B.S. (1996) 'Thirty years of Medicare: Impact on the covered population', *Healthcare Financing Review*, 18(2), pp 179–237.

Gornig, M. and Häussermann, H. (2002) 'Berlin: Economic and spatial change', *European Urban and Regional Studies*, 9(4), pp 331–41.

Graham, G.G. (1985) 'Poverty, hunger, malnutrition, prematurity, and infant mortality in the United States', *Pediatrics*, 75, pp 117–25.

Graham, H. (2009) 'The challenge of health inequalities', in H. Graham (ed) *Understanding health inequalities*. Maidenhead: Open University Press, pp 1–21.

Gregg, P., Harkness, S. and Smith, S. (2009) 'Welfare reform and lone parents in the UK'. *The Economic Journal*, 119(535), pp F38–65.

Grigoriev, P. and Pechholdová, M. (2017) 'Health convergence between East and West Germany as reflected in long-term cause-specific mortality trends: To What extent was it due to reunification?', *European Journal of Population*, 33(5), pp 701–31. Available at: 10.1007/s10680-017-9455-z.

Guanais, F.C. (2013) 'The combined effects of the expansion of primary healthcare and conditional cash transfers on infant mortality in Brazil, 1998–2010', *American Journal of Public Health*, 103, pp 2000–6.

Gundersen, C., Kreider, B. and Pepper, J. (2012) 'The impact of the National School Lunch Programme on child health: A nonparametric bounds analysis', *Journal of Econometrics*, 166, pp 79–91.

Gupta, R.P., De Wit, M.L. and Mckeown, D. (2007) 'The impact of poverty on the current and future health status of children', *Paediatrics & Child Health*, 12, pp 667–72.

Habibov, N., Auchynnikava, A. and Luo, R. (2019) 'Poverty does make us sick', *Annals of Global Health*, 85, Art. 33.

Hacking, J.M., Muller, S. and Buchan, I.E. (2011) 'Trends in mortality from 1965 to 2008 across the English north-south divide: Comparative observational study', *British Medical Journal*, 342, d508.

Hahn, R.A., Truman, B.I. and Williams, D.R. (2018) 'Civil rights as determinants of public health and racial and ethnic health equity: Healthcare, education, employment, and housing in the United States', *SSM – Population Health*, 4, pp 17–24.

Hale, J.N. (2011) 'The freedom schools, the civil rights movement, and refocusing the goals of American education', *The Journal of Social Studies Research*, 35(2), pp 259–76.

Hall, A. (2006) 'From *Fome Zero* to *Bolsa Família*: Social policies and poverty alleviation under Lula', *Journal of Latin American Studies*, 38(4), pp 689–709.

Hall, J. and Ludwig, U. (1994) 'East Germany's transitional economy', *Challenge*, 37(5), pp 26–32. Available at:10.1080/05775132.1994.11471768.

Hall, S. and Jacques, M. (1983) *The politics of Thatcherism*. London: Lawrence and Wishart.

Haller, A.O., Torrecilha, R.S., Del Peloso Haller, M.C. and Tourinho, M.M. (1996) 'The socioeconomic development levels of the people of Amazonian Brazil: 1970 and 1980', *The Journal of Developing Areas*, 30(3), pp 293–316.

Hare, B. (2006) 'Going under', *The Guardian*, 13 September 2006. https://www.theguardian.com/society/2006/sep/13/socialexclusion.guardiansocietysupplement [Accessed: 29 June 2024].

Harr, E. (2020) 'The militarization of police in favelas: Effects of an underlying authoritarian regime on the Brazilian political system', *Global Africana Review*, 4, p 85.

Hart, J.T. (1971) 'The inverse care law', *The Lancet*, 297(7696), pp 405–12.

Haurin, D.R., Herbert, C.E. and Rosenthal, S.S. (2007) 'Homeownership gaps among low-income and minority households', *Cityscape*, 9(2), pp 5–51.

Haveman, R., Blank, R., Moffitt, R., Smeeding, T. and Wallace, G. (2015) 'The War on Poverty: Measurement, trends, and policy', *Journal of Policy Analysis and Management*, 34(3), pp 593–638.

Health Foundation (2021) *How does UK health spending compare across Europe over the past decade?* Available at: https://www.health.org.uk/news-and-comment/charts-and-infographics/how-does-uk-health-spending-compare-across-europe-over-the-past-decade [Accessed: 16 November 2023].

Heckman, J.J. and Payner, B.S. (1989) 'Determining the impact of federal antidiscrimination policy on the economic status of Blacks: A study of South Carolina ', *The American Economic Review*, 79, pp 138–77.

Hiam, L., Dorling, D. and McKee, M. (2023) 'Falling down the global ranks: Life expectancy in the UK, 1952–2021', *Journal of the Royal Society of Medicine*, 116(3), pp 89–92.

Hicks, B.E. (2010) *Germany after the fall: Migration, gender and East–West identities*. Doctoral thesis, University of Michigan. Available at: https://doi.org/doi:10.25335/y8xn-j353 [Accessed: 23 December 2023].

Hiepko, K.A. (2019) *'Conditionally healthy and able to work': Diabetes prevention, care and research in the German democratic republic (GDR), c. 1949–1990*. PhD thesis. University of Manchester. Available at: https://www.proquest.com/dissertations-theses/conditionally-healthy-able-work-diabetes/docview/2498524515/se-2 [Accessed: 16 November 2023].

Highsmith, A.R. (2022) 'Health and inequality in the postwar metropolis', in M. Halliwell (ed) *The Edinburgh companion to the politics of American health*. Edinburgh: Edinburgh University Press, pp 15–32.

Hill, S., Amos, A., Clifford, H. and Platt, S. (2014) 'Impact of tobacco control interventions on socioeconomic inequalities in smoking: Review of the evidence', *Tobacco Control*, 23(e2), pp e89–97.

Hiltzik, M. (2011) *The new deal: A modern history*. New York: Free Press.

Hing, A. (2020) 'The right to vote, the right to health: Voter suppression as a determinant of racial health disparities', *Journal of Health Disparities Research and Practice*, 12(6), p 5.

Hirono, K. (2023) *Participation for health equity: A comparison of citizens' juries and health impact assessment*. PhD thesis. University of Edinburgh. Available at: https://era.ed.ac.uk/bitstream/handle/1842/40687/Hirono2023.pdf?sequence=1&isAllowed=y [Accessed: 26 June 2024].

Hiscock, R. and Bauld, L. (2013) Stop smoking services and health inequalities. *National Centre for Smoking Cessation and Training (NCSCT) Briefing 10.* URL: https://www.ncsct.co.uk/library/view/pdf/NCSCT_briefing_effect_of_SSS_on_health_inequalities.pdf [Accessed: 26 June 2024].

HMD (2023) *Human Mortality Database*. Max Planck Institute for Demographic Research (Germany), University of California, Berkeley (USA), and French Institute for Demographic Studies (France). Available at: https://www.mortality.org [Accessed: 4 December 2023].

HM Government (2012) *Welfare Reform Act 2012*. [Online]. Available at: https://www.legislation.gov.uk/ukpga/2012/5/contents/enacted [Accessed: 16 November 2023].

HM Government (2016) *Welfare Reform and Work Act 2016*. [Online]. Available at: https://www.legislation.gov.uk/ukpga/2016/7/section/17/enacted [Accessed: 16 November 2023].

HM Treasury (2004) *2004 spending review: Public service agreements 2005–2008*. London: The Stationary Office.

Hochstetler, K. (2017) 'Tracking presidents and policies: Environmental politics from Lula to Dilma', *Policy Studies*, 38(3), pp 262–76.

Hockenos, P. (2023) 'Germany is thinking of simply banning the far right', *Foreign Policy*, 13 December. Available at: https://foreignpolicy.com/2023/12/13/germany-afd-far-right-ban-populism/ [Accessed: 26 June 2024].

Hoebel, J., Nowossadeck, E., Michalski, N., Baumert, J., Wachtler, B. and Tetzlaff, F. (2024) 'Socioeconomic deprivation and premature mortality in Germany 1998–2021', *Federal Health Gazette*, 67, pp 528–37.

Hoffmann, R., Hu, Y., De Gelder, R., Menvielle, G., Bopp, M. and Mackenbach, J.P. (2016) 'The impact of increasing income inequalities on educational inequalities in mortality: An analysis of six European countries', *International Journal for Equity in Health*, 15, p 103.

Holdroyd, I., Vodden, A., Srinivasan, A., Kuhn, I., Bambra, C. and Ford, J. (2022) 'Systematic review of the effectiveness of the Health Inequalities Strategy in England between 1999 and 2010', *BMJ Open*, 12(9), p e063137.

Holzer, H. (2013) 'Workforce development programmes', in M.J. Bailey and S. Danziger (eds) *Legacies of the War on Poverty*. New York: Russell Sage Foundation, pp 121–50.

Hood, C. (2006) 'Gaming in Target world: The targets approach to managing British public services', *Public Administration Review*, 66(4), pp 515–21.

Hooks, B. (1981) *Ain't I a woman Black women and feminism*. Cambridge: South End Press.

Hopkin, J. and Lynch, J. (2016) 'Winner-take-all politics in Europe? European inequality in comparative perspective', *Politics & Society*, 44(3), pp 335–43.

Horton, R. (1997) 'Health inequality: The UK's biggest issue', *Lancet*, 349, p 1185.

House of Commons (2009) Health Committee - Third Report: Health Inequalities. Available at: https://publications.parliament.uk/pa/cm200809/cmselect/cmhealth/286/28602.htm [Accessed: 6 November 24].

House of Commons Library (2024) *The benefit cap*. Available at: https://commonslibrary.parliament.uk/benefit-cap/ [Accessed: 2 August 2024].

Houweling, T.A., Jayasinghe, S. and Chandola, T. (2007) 'The social determinants of childhood mortality in Sri Lanka: Time-trends and comparisons across South Asia', *Indian Journal of Medical Research*, 126(4), pp 239–48.

Hoynes, H.W. and Schanzenbach, D.W. (2018) 'Safety net investments in children', *Brookings Papers on Economic Activity*, Spring 2018, pp 89–32.

Hoynes, H.W., Page, M.E. and Stevens, A.H. (2009) *Is a WIC start a better start? Evaluating WIC's impact on infant health using programme introduction.* National Bureau of Economic Research Working Paper No. 15589. Cambridge, MA: NBER. Available at: https://doi.org/10.3386/w15589 [Accessed: 26 May 2024].

Hoynes, H.W., Schanzenbach, D.W. and Almond, D. (2016) 'Long-run impacts of childhood access to the safety net', *American Economic Review*, 106(4), pp 903–34.

Huang, J., Kim, Y. and Barnidge, E. (2016) 'Seasonal Difference in National School Lunch Programme participation and its impacts on household food security', *Health & Social Work*, 41(4), pp 235–43.

Hunter, D. (2008) *The health debate*. Bristol: Policy Press.

Hunter, W. and Sugiyama, N.B. (2009) 'Democracy and social policy in Brazil: Advancing basic needs, preserving privileged interests', *Latin American Politics and Society*, 51(2), pp 29–58. Available at: doi:10.1111/j.1548-2456.2009.00047.x.

International Tobacco Control Project (2022) *Brazil: Timeline of tobacco control policies and ITC surveys (BR)*. URL: https://itcproject.org/countries/brazil/ [Accessed: 23 January 2024].

Institute for Fiscal Studies (2018) *Inequality review*. Available at: https://ifs.org.uk/inequality/ [Accessed: 16 November 2023].

James, D.B. (1972) 'The limits of liberal reform', *Politics & Society*, 2(3), pp 309–22.

James, W. and Cossman, J.S. (2017) 'Long-term trends in Black and White mortality in the rural United States: Evidence of a race-specific rural mortality penalty', *The Journal of Rural Health*, 33(1), pp 21–31.

Jenkins, R., Vamos, E.P., Mason, K.E., Daras, K., Taylor-Robinson, D., Bambra, C., Millett, C. and Laverty, A.A. (2022) 'Local area public sector spending and nutritional anaemia hospital admissions in England: A longitudinal ecological study', *BMJ Open*, 12(9), p e059739.

Jessop, B. (1991) 'The welfare state in transition from Fordism to post-Fordism', in B. Jessop, H. Kastendiek, K. Nielsen and O.K. Pedersen (eds) *The politics of flexibility: Restructuring state and industry in Britain, Germany and Scandinavia*. Aldershot: Edward Elgar, pp 82–105.

Johnson, L.B. (1964a) *Remarks at the University of Michigan*. Available at: https://www.presidency.ucsb.edu/node/239689 [Accessed: 16 November 2023].

Johnson, L.B. (1964b) *Economic report of the president 1964*. Washington, DC: United States Government Printing Office. Available at: https://www.presidency.ucsb.edu/sites/default/files/books/presidential-documents-archive-guidebook/the-economic-report-of-the-president-truman-1947-obama-2017/1964.pdf [Accessed: 16 November 2023].

Judge, K. and Bauld, L. (2006) 'Learning from policy failure? Health action zones in England', *European Journal of Public Health*, 16(4), pp 341–3.

Junge, B., Mitchell, S.T., Jarrín, A. and Cantero, L. (eds) (2021) *Precarious democracy: Ethnographies of hope, despair, and resistance in Brazil*. New Brunswick: Rutgers University Press.

Kapilashrami, A., Hill, S. and Meer, N. (2015) 'What can health inequalities researchers learn from an intersectionality perspective? Understanding social dynamics with an inter-categorical approach?', *Social Theory & Health*, 13, pp 288–307.

Kelly-Irving, M., Ball, W.P., Bambra, C., Delpierre, C., Dundas, R., Lynch, J., Smith, K. (2022) 'Falling down the rabbit hole? Methodological, conceptual and policy issues in current health inequalities research', *Critical Public Health*, 33(1), pp 37–47.

Kido, E. (2019) 'The legacies of the uranium mining company "Wismut" in east Germany', *Asian Journal of Peacebuilding*, 7, pp 55–72.

King, L., Scheiring, G. and Nosrati, E. (2022) 'Deaths of despair in comparative perspective', *Annual Review of Sociology*, 48, pp 299–317.

Kolling, M. (2019) 'Becoming favela: Forced resettlement and reverse transitions of urban space in Brazil', *City & Society*, 31, pp 413–35.

Kopper, M. (2021) 'Withering dreams: Material hope and apathy among Brazil's once rising poor', in B. Junge, S.T. Mitchell, A. Jarrín and L. Cantero (eds) *Precarious democracy: Ethnographies of hope, despair, and resistance in Brazil*. New Brunswick: Rutgers University Press, pp 155–68.

Krieger, J. and Jacobs, D.E. (2011) 'Healthy homes', in A.L. Dannenberg, H. Frumkin and R.J. Jackson (eds) *Making healthy places: Designing and building for health, well-being, and sustainability*. Washington, DC: Island Press, pp 170–87.

Krieger, N., Rehkopf, D.H., Chen, J.T., Waterman, P.D., Marcelli, E. and Kennedy, M. (2008) 'The fall and rise of US inequities in premature mortality: 1960–2002', *PLoS Medicine*, 5(2), p e46.

Krieger, N., Chen, J.T., Coull, B., Waterman, P.D. and Beckfield, J. (2013) 'The unique impact of abolition of Jim Crow Laws on reducing inequities in infant death rates and implications for choice of comparison groups in analyzing societal determinants of health', *American Journal of Public Health*, 103(12), pp 2234–44.

Krieger, N., Chen, J.T., Coull, B.A., Beckfield, J., Kiang, M.V., Waterman, P.D. (2014) 'Jim Crow and premature mortality among the US Black and White population, 1960–2009: An age–period–cohort analysis', *Epidemiology*, 25(4), pp 494–504.

Krueger, A.B. and Pischke, J.-S. (1992) *A comparative analysis of East and West German labour markets: Before and after unification*. National Bureau of Economic Research Working Papers No. 4154. Cambridge, MA: NBER. Available at: https://www.nber.org/system/files/working_papers/w4154/w4154.pdf [Accessed: 23 November 2023].

Lampert, T., Müters, S., Kuntz, B., Dahm, S. and Nowossadeck, E. (2019) '30 years after the fall of the Berlin Wall: Regional health differences in Germany', *Journal of Health Monitoring*, 4(Suppl 2), pp 2–23.

Lamont, N. (1991) Hansard House of Commons, May 16, 1991. Available at: https://hansard.parliament.uk/%E2%80%8CCommons/1991-05-16 [Accessed: 6 November 2024].

Lee, K., Chagas, L.C. and Novotny, T.E. (2010) 'Brazil and the framework convention on tobacco control: Global health diplomacy as soft power', *PLoS Med*, 7(4), p e1000232.

Lee, R., Zhai, F., Han, W.-J., Brooks-Gunn, J. and Waldfogel, J. (2013) 'Head Start and children's nutrition, weight, and healthcare receipt', *Early Childhood Research Quarterly*, 28(4), pp 723–33.

Leifheit, K.M., Linton, S.L, Raifman, J., Schwartz, G.L., Benfer, E.A., Zimmerman, F.J. and Pollack, C.E. (2021) 'Expiring eviction moratoriums and COVID-19 incidence and mortality', *American Journal of Epidemiology*, 190(12), p 25032510.

Leighley, J.E. and Nagler, N. (2014) *Who votes now?: Demographics, issues, inequality and turnout in the United States*. Princeton, NJ: Princeton University Press.

Leinsalu, M., Vågerö, D. and Kunst, A.E. (2003) 'Estonia 1989–2000: Enormous increase in mortality differences by education', *International Journal of Epidemiology*, 32(6), pp 1081–7.

Lenhart, O. (2019) 'The effects of health shocks on labour market outcomes: Evidence from UK panel data', *The European Journal of Health Economics*, 20, pp 83–98.

Leon, D.A., Chenet, L., Shkolnikov, V.M., Zakharov, S., Shapiro, J., Rakhmanova, G., Vassin, S. and McKee, M. (1997) 'Huge variation in Russian mortality rates 1984–94: Artefact, alcohol, or what?', *Lancet*, 350(9075), pp 383–8.

Leyland, A.H. (2004) 'Increasing inequalities in premature mortality in Great Britain', *Journal of Epidemiology and Community Health*, 58(4), pp 296–302.

Link, B.G. and Phelan, J. (1995) 'Social conditions as fundamental causes of disease', *Journal of Health and Social Behavior*, 1995(Extra Issue), pp 80–94.

Loveland, I. (1993) 'The politics, law and practice of 'intentional homelessness': Abandonment of existing housing', *Journal of Social Welfare and Family Law*, 15, pp 185–99.

Lubotsky, D., Mazumder, B. and Seeskin, Z. (2010) *New perspectives on health and healthcare policy*. Chicago Fed Letter No. 276. Chicago, IL: Federal Reserve Bank of Chicago, pp 1–4. Available at: https://www.chicagofed.org/publications/chicago-fed-letter/2010/july-276 [Accessed: 16 November 2023].

Luy, M. (2004) 'Mortality differences between Western and Eastern Germany before and after reunification: A macro and micro level analysis of developments and responsible factors', *Genus*, 60(3/4), pp 99–141.

Lynch, J. (2020) *Regimes of inequality: The political economy of health and wealth.* Cambridge: Cambridge University Press.

Lynch, J. and Perera, I.M. (2017) 'Framing health equity: US health disparities in comparative perspective', *Journal of Health Politics, Policy and Law*, 42(5), pp 803–39.

Macinko, J., Guanais, F.C., De Fátima, M. and De Souza, M. (2006) 'Evaluation of the impact of the Family Health Programme on infant mortality in Brazil, 1990–2002', *Journal of Epidemiology and Community Health*, 60, pp 13–19.

Mackenbach, J.P. (2011) 'Can we reduce health inequalities? An analysis of the English strategy (1997–2010)', *Journal of Epidemiology and Community Health*, 65(5), pp 1282–8.

Mackenbach, J.P., Stirbu, I., Roskam, A.J.R., Schaap, M.M., Menvielle, G., Leinsalu, M. and Kunst, A.E. (2008) 'Socioeconomic inequalities in health in 22 European countries', *New England Journal of Medicine*, 359(12), p E14.

Mackenbach, J.P., Kulhánová, I., Artnik, B., Bopp, M., Borrell, C., Clemens, T. et al (2016) 'Changes in mortality inequalities over two decades: Register based study of European countries', *British Medical Journal*, 353, p i1732.

Mackenbach, J.P., Hu, Y., Artnik, B., Bopp, M., Costa, G., Kalediene, R., Martikainen, P., Menvielle, G., Strand, B.H., Wojtyniak, B. and Nusselder, W.J. (2017) 'Trends in inequalities in mortality amenable to healthcare in 17 European countries', *Health Affairs (Millwood)*, 36, pp 1110–18.

Mackenbach, J.P., Rubio Valverdea, J., Artnikb, B. et al (2018) 'Trends in health inequalities in 27 European countries', *PNAS*, 115(25), pp 6440–5.

MacLeavy, J. (2011) 'A "new politics" of austerity, workfare and gender? The UK coalition government's welfare reform proposals', *Cambridge Journal of Regions Economy and Society*, 4(3), pp 355–67.

Malta, M., Murray, L., da Silva, C.M.F.P. and Strathdee, S.A. (2020) 'Coronavirus in Brazil: The heavy weight of inequality and unsound leadership', *EClinicalMedicine*, 25, p 100472.

Marmot, M. (2020) *Health equity in England: The Marmot Review 10 years on.* London: Institute of Health Equity. Available at: https://www.health.org.uk/publications/reports/the-marmot-review-10-years-on [Accessed: 6 November 2023].

Marmot, M. and Bambra, C. (2024) 'Health and Society', in A Seldon (ed) *14 years: The conservative effect.* Cambridge: Cambridge University Press.

Martine, G. and McGranahan, G. (2012) 'The legacy of inequality and negligence in Brazil's unfinished urban transition: Lessons for other developing regions', *International Journal of Urban Sustainable Development*, 5(1), pp 7–24.

Mask, J.W. (1991) Interview with J.W. Mask, February 15, 1991. Interviewer Goldie F. Wells. Interview M-0013. *Southern Oral History Programme Collection* (#4007). Available at: docsouth.unc.edu/sohp/M-0013/M-0013.html [Accessed: 28 June 2024].

Massuda, A., Hone, T., Leles, F.A.G., De Castro, M.C. and Atun, R. (2018) 'The Brazilian health system at crossroads: Progress, crisis and resilience', *BMJ Global Health*, 3, p e000829.

Masters, R.K., Hummer, R.A., Powers, D.A., Beck, A., Lin, S.-F. and Finch, B.K. (2014) 'Long-term trends in adult mortality for US Blacks and Whites: An examination of period- and cohort-based changes', *Demography*, 51(6), pp 2047–73.

McCartney, G., Dickie, E., Escobar, O. and Collins, C. (2021) 'Health inequalities, fundamental causes and power: Towards the practice of good theory', *Sociology of Health & Illness*, 43(1), pp 20–39.

McCartney, G., McMaster, R., Popham, F., Dundas, R. and Walsh, D. (2022) 'Is austerity a cause of slower improvements in mortality in high-income countries? A panel analysis', *Social Science & Medicine*, 313, p 115397.

McCartney, G., Popham, F., McMaster, R. and Cumbers, A. (2019) 'Defining health and health inequalities', *Public Health*, 172, pp 22–30.

McGowan, V.J., Buckner, S., Mead, R., McGill, E., Ronzi, S., Beyer, F. and Bambra, C. (2021) Examining the effectiveness of place-based interventions to improve public health and reduce health inequalities: An umbrella review. *BMC Public Health*, 21, p 1888.

McKinley, J. (1975) 'The case for refocusing upstream: The political economy of illness', in A.J. Enelow and J.B. Henderson (eds) *Applying behavioral science to cardiovascular risk*. New York: American Heart Association.

McSorley, A.-M.M., Thomas Tobin, C.S. and Kuhn, R. (2023) 'The relationship between political efficacy and self-rated health: An analysis of Mexican, Puerto Rican, and Cuban subgroups compared to non-Latinx Whites in the United States', *SSM Population Health*, 22, p 101390.

Medeiros, M. (2016) 'Income inequality in Brazil: New evidence from combined tax and survey data', in ISSC, IDS and UNESCO's *World Social Science Report 2016, challenging inequalities: Pathways to a just world.* Paris: UNESCO Publishing, pp 107–111. Available at: https://doi.org/10.54678/QTOK7532 [Accessed: 28 June 2024].

Melhuish, E., Belsky, J., Leyland, A.H. and Barnes, J. (2008) 'Effects of fully-established Sure Start Local Programmes on 3-year-old children and their families living in England: a quasi-experimental observational study', *The Lancet*, 372(9650), pp 1641–7.

Melo, M.A. (2016) 'Political malaise and the new politics of accountability: Representation, taxation, and the social contract', in B.R. Schneider (ed) *New order and progress: Development and democracy in Brazil.* New York: Oxford University Press.

Mendeloff, J. (2015) *Workplace accidents in Brazil are significantly underreported: Inspection issues and informal workplaces make it difficult to determine true safety levels*. Santa Monica, CA: RAND Corporation. https://www.rand.org/pubs/research_briefs/RB9851.html [Accessed: 28 June 2024].

Menvielle, G., Chastang, J., Luce, D. and Leclerc, A. (2007) 'Évolution temporelle des inégalités sociales de mortalité en France entre 1968 et 1996. Étude en fonction du niveau d'études par cause de décès', *Revue d'Épidémiologie et de Santé Publique*, 55(2), pp 97–105.

Meyer, B.D. and Sullivan, J.X. (2012) *Winning the war: Poverty from the Great Society to the Great Recession*. Brookings Papers on Economic Activity. Washington: Brookings Institution. Available at: https://www.brookings.edu/articles/winning-the-war-poverty-from-the-great-society-to-the-great-recession/ [Accessed: 4 November 2023].

Michelsen, C. and Weiß, D. (2010) 'What happened to the East German housing market? A historical perspective on the role of public funding', *Post-Communist Economies*, 22(3), pp 387–409.

Miethe, I. (2019) 'Difference and dominance between East and West: A plea for a nationwide reappraisal of the German unification and transformation', *Brolly*, 2(3), pp 43–67.

Ministério das Cidades (2010) *Urbanização de favelas: a experiência do PAC*. Brasília: Ministry of Cities – SNH. URL: https://antigo.mdr.gov.br/images/stories/ArquivosSNH/ArquivosPDF/PAC_Urbanizacao_de_Favelas_Web.pdf [Accessed: 3 March 2024].

Möller, H., Haigh, F., Harwood, C., Kinsella, T. and Pope, D. (2013) 'Rising unemployment and increasing spatial health inequalities in England: Further extension of the North–South divide', *Journal of Public Health*, 35(2), pp 313–21.

Moran, M. (1999) *Governing the healthcare state: A comparative study of the UK, the USA and Germany*. Manchester: Manchester University Press.

Morey, B.N., García, S.J., Nieri, T., Bruckner, T.A. and Link, B.G. (2021) 'Symbolic disempowerment and Donald Trump's 2016 presidential election: Mental health responses among Latinx and White populations', *Social Science & Medicine*, 289, p 114417.

Muñoz, C. (2017) Brazil's disappointing human rights policies, human rights watch. URL: https://www.hrw.org/news/2017/05/04/brazils-disappointing-human-rights-policies [Accessed: 23 March 2024].

Musen, K. (2023) *Minimum wages and racial infant health inequality: Evidence from the Fair Labour Standards Act of 1966*. Available at: http://katemusen.com/uploads/FLSA_paper.pdf [Accessed: 23 December 2023].

Nadasen, P. (2007) 'From widow to "welfare queen": Welfare and the politics of race', *Black Women, Gender + Families*, 1(2), pp 52–77.

Nannan, N., Timaeus, I.M. and Laubscher, R. (2007) 'Levels and differentials in childhood mortality in South Africa, 1977–1998', *Journal of Biosocial Science*, 39(4), pp 613–32.

National Audit Office (2018) *Financial sustainability of local authorities 2018*. Available at: https://www.nao.org.uk/wp-content/uploads/2018/03/Financial-sustainabilty-of-local-authorites-2018-Summary.pdf [Accessed: 4 November 2023].

Navarro, V., Borrell, C., Benach, J. and Muntaner, C. (2003) 'The importance of the political and the social in explaining mortality differentials among the countries of the OECD, 1950–1998', *International Journal of Health Services Research*, 33(3), pp 419–94.

Navarro, V., Muntaner, C., Borrell, C. and Benach, J. (2006) 'Politics and health outcomes', *Lancet,* 368(9540), pp 1033–7.

Nazroo, J. (2022) *Race/ethnic inequalities in health: Moving beyond confusion to focus on fundamental causes*, Institute for Fiscal Studies Deaton Review of Inequality. https://ifs.org.uk/inequality/race-ethnic-inequalities-in-health-moving-beyond-confusion-to-focus-on-fundamental-causes [Accessed: 4 November 2023].

Nery, JS., Rodrigues, LC., Rasella, D. et al (2017) 'Effect of Brazil's conditional cash transfer programme on tuberculosis incidence', *International Journal of Tuberculosis and Lung Disease*, 21, pp 790–6.

Neuendorf, U.L. (2017) *Surveillance and control: An ethnographic study of the legacy of the Stasi and its impact on wellbeing*. PhD thesis. University College London. Available at: https://discovery.ucl.ac.uk/id/eprint/10040339/3/Neuendorf_10040339_thesis.pdf [Accessed: 16 November 2023].

Neumark, D. (2023) *The effects of minimum wages on (almost) everything? A review of recent evidence on health and related behaviors*. National Bureau of Economic Research Working Paper No. 31191. Cambridge, MA: NBER. Available at: https://doi.org/10.3386/w31191 [Accessed: 28 June 2024].

Nicholls, J. (2012) Time for reform? Alcohol policy and cultural change in England since 2000. *British Politics*, 7, 250–71.

Noghanibehambari, H. (2022) 'Intergenerational health effects of Medicaid', *Economics & Human Biology*, 45, p 101114.

Noll, H.-H. and Weick, S. (2014) 'Housing in Germany: Expensive, comfortable and usually rented. Analysis of the housing conditions and quality in comparison to other European countries' Informationsdienst Soziale Indikatoren. Selected English Articles. 1–6. Available at: https://www.gesis.org/fileadmin/upload/forschung/publikationen/zeitschriften/isi/isi41-NollWeick-English.pdf [Accessed: 5 December 2023].

Nolte, E. and McKee, M. (2000) 'Ten years of German unification', *British Medical Journal*, 321(7269), pp 1094–5.

Nolte, E. and M. McKee (2011) 'Variations in amenable mortality: Trends in 16 high-income nations', *Health Policy*, 103, pp 47–52.

Nolte, E., Scholz, R., Shkolnikov, V. and McKee, M. (2002) 'The contribution of medical care to changing life expectancy in Germany and Poland', *Social Science & Medicine*, 55(11), pp 1905–21.

Norman, P., Boyle, P., Exeter, D., Feng, Z. and Popham, F. (2011) 'Rising premature mortality in the UK's persistently deprived areas: Only a Scottish phenomenon?', *Social Science & Medicine*, 73(11), pp 1575–84.

Nuffield Trust (2023) *Building a resilient social care system in England: What can be learnt from the first wave of Covid-19?* p 21. Available at: https://www.nuffieldtrust.org.uk/sites/default/files/2023-05/Building%20a%20resilient%20social%20care%20system%20in%20England.pdf [Accessed: 5 November 2023].

OECD (2021) *OECD reviews of health systems: Brazil 2021.* Available at: https://doi.org/10.1787/146d0dea-en [Accessed: 2 November 2024].

Office for National Statistics (2021a) *Health state life expectancies by Index of Multiple Deprivation (IMD 2015 and IMD 2019), England, at birth and age 65 years.* Available at: https://www.ons.gov.uk/peoplepopulationandcommunity/healthandsocialcare/healthinequalities/datasets/healthstatelifeexpectanciesbyindexofmultipledeprivationengland [Accessed: 29 October 2023].

Office for National Statistics (2021b) *Health state life expectancies by national deprivation deciles, England: 2017 to 2019.* Available at: https://www.ons.gov.uk/peoplepopulationandcommunity/healthandsocialcare/healthinequalities/bulletins/healthstatelifeexpectanciesbyindexofmultipledeprivationimd/2017to2019#life-expectancy-at-birth-in-england-by-the-index-of-multiple-deprivation [Accessed: 29 October 2023].

Olsen, E.O. and Ludwig, J. (2013) 'Performance and legacy of housing policies', in M.J. Bailey and S. Danziger (eds) *Legacies of the War on Poverty.* New York: Russell Sage Foundation, pp 206–34.

O'Neil, A. (2022a) *Trends in IMR in Sweden.* Statista. Available at: https://www.statista.com/statistics/1042729/sweden-all-time-infant-mortality-rate/ [Accessed: 21 November 2023].

O'Neil, A. (2022b) *Trends in IMR in the USA.* Statista. Available at: https://www.statista.com/statistics/1042370/united-states-all-time-infant-mortality-rate/ [Accessed: 21 November 2023].

Orfield, G. (2015) 'Ending Jim Crow, attacking ghetto walls', in R.H. Wilson, N.J. Glickman, and L.E. Lynn (eds) *LBJ's neglected legacy: How Lyndon Johnson reshaped domestic policy and government.* New York: University of Texas Press, pp 31–97.

Ortega, F. and Pele, A. (2023) 'Brazil's unified health system: 35 years and future challenges', *The Lancet Regional Health – Americas*, 28, p 100631.

Oyèkọ́lá, O. (2023) 'Democracy does improve health', *Social Indicators Research*, 166, pp 105–32.

Palma, N., Papadia, A., Pereira, T. and Weller, L. (2021) 'Slavery and development in nineteenth century Brazil', *Capitalism*, 2(2), pp 372–426.

Parkes, K.S. (1997) *Understanding contemporary Germany.* London: Taylor & Francis.

Parkhurst, J.O., and Abeysinghe, S. (2016). 'What constitutes "good" evidence for public health and social policy-making? From hierarchies to appropriateness', *Social Epistemology*, 30(5–6), pp 665–79.

Pearce, J. and Dorling, D. (2006) 'Increasing geographical inequalities in health in New Zealand, 1980–2001', *International Journal of Epidemiology*, 35(3), pp 597–603.

Pearce, J., Dorling, D., Wheeler, B., Barnett, R. and Rigby, J. (2006) 'Geographical inequalities in health in New Zealand, 1980–2001: The gap widens', *Australian and New Zealand Journal of Public Health*, 30(5), pp 461–66.

Da Silva Pereira, R. (2023) '"Protect the children, save the family"– "gender ideology" in the classroom: a case study of moral panic in Brazil', University of British Columbia Thesis. URL: https://open.library.ubc.ca/soa/cIRcle/collections/ubctheses/24/items/1.0431597 [Accessed: 20 April 2024]

Perz, S.G., Caldas, M.M., Arima, E. and Walker, R.J. (2007) 'Unofficial road building in the Amazon: Socioeconomic and biophysical explanations', *Development and Change*, 38, pp 529–51.

Pescarini, J.M., Campbell, D., Amorim, L.D., Falcão, I.R., Ferreira, A.J.F., Allik, M., Shaw, R.J., Malta, D.C., Ali, M.S., Smeeth, L., Barreto, M.L., Leyland, A., Craig, P., Aquino, E.M.L. and Katikireddi, S.V. (2022) 'Impact of Brazil's Bolsa Família Programme on cardiovascular and all-cause mortality: A natural experiment study using the 100 Million Brazilian Cohort', *Int J Epidemiol*, 51, pp 1847–61.

Pickett, K.E. and Wilkinson, R.G. (2015) 'Income inequality and health: A causal review', *Social Science & Medicine*, 128, pp 316–26.

Pierson, P. (1993) 'When effect becomes cause: policy feedback and political change', *World Politics*, 45(4), pp 595–628.

Piketty, T. (2014) *Capital in the twenty-first century*. Cambridge, MA: Harvard University Press.

Pinho, C.E.S. (2021) 'Welfare state and epistemic communities of fiscal austerity in Brazil: from Lula da Silva to Jair Bolsonaro (2003–2020)', *Sociedade E Estado*, 36(1), pp 195–216.

Platt, J., Prins, S., Bates, L. and Keyes, K. (2016) 'Unequal depression for equal work? How the wage gap explains gendered disparities in mood disorders', *Social Science & Medicine*, 149, pp 1–8.

Popay, J., Whitehead, M., Carr-Hill, R., Dibden, C., Dixon, P., Halliday, E., Nazroo, J., Peart, E., Povall, S., Stafford, M., Turner, J and Walthery, P. (2015) *The impact on health inequalities of approaches to community engagement in the New Deal for Communities regeneration initiative: A mixed-methods evaluation*. Southampton: NIHR Journals Library. Available at: https://doi.org/10.3310/phr03120 [Accessed: 7 April 2024].

Popay, J., Whitehead, M., Ponsford, R., Egan, M. and Mead, R. (2021) 'Power, control, communities and health inequalities I: Theories, concepts and analytical frameworks', *Health Promotion International*, 36(5), pp 1253–63.

Portes, L.H., Machado, C.V., Turci, S.R.B., Figueiredo, V.C., Cavalcante, T.M. and da Costa E Silva, V.L. (2018) 'Tobacco control policies in Brazil: A 30-year assessment', *Ciência & Saúde Coletiva*, 23(6), pp 1837–48.

Powell, M. (2019) 'The English National Health Service in a cold climate: A decade of austerity', in E. Heins, J. Rees and C. Needham (eds) *Social policy review 31: Analysis and debate in social policy, 2019*. Bristol: Policy Press, pp 7–28.

Quadagno, J. (1994) *The colour of welfare: How racism undermined the war on poverty*. New York: Oxford University Press.

Quadagno, J. (2022) 'Medicare and Medicaid after the Great Society: Containing costs, expanding coverage', in M Halliwell (ed) *The Edinburgh companion to the politics of American health*. Edinburgh: Edinburgh University Press, pp 375–88.

Raalte, A., Klüsener, S., Oksuzyan, A. and Grigoriev, P. (2020) 'Declining regional disparities in mortality in the context of persisting large inequalities in economic conditions: The case of Germany', *International Journal of Epidemiology*, 49, pp 486–96.

Rasella, D., Aquino, R., Santos, CA. et al (2013) 'Effect of a conditional cash transfer programme on childhood mortality: A nationwide analysis of Brazilian municipalities', *Lancet*, 382, pp 57–64.

Ratchick, I. (1968) 'Evaluation of school health services for disadvantaged children under Title I, Elementary and Secondary Education Act', *Journal of School Health*, 38(3), pp 140–46.

Reardon, S. F. and Owens, A. (2014) '60 years after Brown: Trends and consequences of school segregation', *Annual Review of Sociology*, 40, 199–218.

Regenstein, A.C. (1985) *Healthcare in the two Germanys: A comparison with emphasis on maternal and infant healthcare*. Yale Medicine Thesis Digital Library. 3057. Available at: http://elischolar.library.yale.edu/ymtdl/3057 [Accessed: 7 April 2024].

Rehnberg, C. (2020) *The East German phenomenon: The development of public health and healthcare provision after the fall of the Berlin Wall*. Stockholm: Timbro. Available at: https://www.epicentrenetwork.eu/wp-content/uploads/2024/01/Rehnberg-2020-The-East-German-Phenomenon.pdf [Accessed: 14 November 2023].

Reiser, M. and Reiter, R. (2022) 'A (new) East–West-divide? Representative democracy in Germany 30 years after unification', *German Politics*, 32(1), pp 1–19.

Rhodes, J.H. (2017) *Ballot blocked: The political erosion of the Voting Rights Act*, 1st edn. Stanford: Stanford University Press.

Rios, F. (2020) 'Cycles of democracy and the racial issue in Brazil (1978–2019)', in B. Bianchi, J. Chaloub, P. Rangel and F.O. Wolf (eds) *Democracy and Brazil*. UK: Routledge, pp 26–40.

Rita, R.A. (2010) The Indigenous movement in Brazil: A quarter century of ups and downs, *Cultural Survival*. URL: https://www.culturalsurvival.org/publications/cultural-survival-quarterly/indigenous-movement-brazil-quarter-century-ups-and-downs [Accessed: 7 April 2024].

Robinson, T., Brown, H., Norman, P.D., Fraser, L.K., Barr, B. and Bambra, C. (2019) 'The impact of New Labour's English Health Inequalities Strategy on geographical inequalities in infant mortality: A time-trend analysis', *Journal of Epidemiology and Community Health*, 73(6), pp 564–8.

Rodriguez, J., Bae, B., Geronimus, A. and Bound, J. (2022) 'The political realignment of health: How partisan power shaped infant health in the United States, 1915–2017', *Journal of Health Politics, Policy and Law*, 47(2), pp 201–24.

Rojas, D., Olival, A.D.A. and Olival, A.A.S. (2021) 'Despairing hopes (and hopeful despair) in Amazonia, Chapter 9', in B. Junge, S.T. Mitchell, A. Jarrín, and L. Cantero (eds) *Precarious democracy: Ethnographies of hope, despair, and resistance in Brazil*. New Brunswick: Rutgers University Press.

Roman, A. (2023) 'A closer look into Brazil's healthcare system: What can we learn?', *Cureus*, 15, p e38390.

Romanello, M. (2017) 'The transition of Brazilian workers to formality: Evidences from duration analysis', *Economía, Sociedad y Territorio*, 17(54), pp 309–35.

Rosenfeld, R.A., Trappe, H. and Gornick, J.C. (2004) 'Gender and work in Germany: Before and after reunification', *Annual Review of Sociology*, 30, pp 103–24.

Rubin, L.B. (1969) 'Maximum feasible participation: The origins, implications, and present status', *The Annals of the American Academy of Political and Social Science*, 385, pp 14–29.

Rushovich, T., Nethery, R.C., White, A. and Krieger, N. (2024) '1965 US Voting Rights Act impact on Black and Black versus White infant death rates in Jim Crow States, 1959–1980 and 2017–2021', *American Journal of Public Health*, 114(3), pp 300–8.

Saboia, J. (2007) 'Salário minimo e distribução da renda no Brasil no periodo 1995–2005', *Econômica*, 9(2), pp 265–85.

Saez, E. and Zucman, G. (2020) 'The rise of income and wealth inequality in America: Evidence from distributional macroeconomic accounts', *Journal of Economic Perspectives*, 34(4), pp 3–26.

Safaei, J. (2006) 'Is democracy good for health?', *International Journal of Health Services*, 36(4), pp 767–86.

Sant'Anna, A.L. de O. de, Castro, A. de C. and Jacó-Vilela, A.M. (2018) 'Ditadura militar e práticas disciplinares no controle de Índios: Perspectivas psicossociais no relatório figuiredo', *Psicologia & Sociedade*, 30, p e188045.

Santos, R., Welch, J., Pontes, A., Garnelo, L., Moreira Cardoso, A., & Coimbra Jr., C. (2022, August 15). Health of Indigenous peoples in Brazil: Inequities and the uneven trajectory of public policies. *Oxford Research Encyclopedia of Global Public Health*. Available at: https://oxfordre.com/publichealth/view/10.1093/acrefore/9780190632366.001.0001/acrefore-9780190632366-e-33 [Accessed: 29 June 2024].

Satcher, D., Fryer, G.E., McCann, J., Troutman, A., Woolf, S.H. and Rust, G. (2005) 'What if we were equal? A comparison of the Black–White mortality gap in 1960 and 2000', *Health Affairs*, 24, pp 459–64.

Scheidel, W. (2017) *The great leveler: Violence and the history of inequality from the stone age to the twenty-first century*. Princeton, NJ: Princeton University Press.

Scheiring, G., Irdam, D. and King, L.P. (2019) 'Cross-country evidence on the social determinants of the post-socialist mortality crisis in Europe: A review and performance-based hierarchy of variables', *Sociology of Health & Illness*, 41(4), pp 673–91.

Scheiring, G., Azarova, A., Irdam, D., Doniec, K., McKee, M., Stuckler, D. and King, L. (2023) 'Deindustrialisation and the post-socialist mortality crisis', *Cambridge Journal of Economics*, 47(2), pp 341–72.

Schneider, N. (2020) 'Bolsonaro in power: Failed memory politics in post-authoritarian Brazil?' *Modern Languages Open*, (1)25, pp 1–11.

Schochet, P.Z., Burghardt, J. and McConnell, S. (2008) 'Does job corps work? Impact findings from the national job corps study', *American Economic Review*, 98(5), pp 1864–86.

Schrecker, T. and Bambra, C. (2015) *How politics makes us sick: Neoliberal epidemics*, 1st edn. London: Palgrave Macmillan.

Schrecker, T. and Bambra, C. (2025) *How politics makes us sick: Neoliberal epidemics*, 2nd edn. London: Palgrave Macmillan.

Schroeder, K. and Deutz-Schröder, M. (2008) *Soziales Paradies oder Stasi-Staat? Das DDR-Bild von Schülern-Ein Ost-West-Vergleich*. Munich: Verlag Ernst Vögel.

Schulz, C., Conrad, A., Becker, K., Kolossa-Gehring, M., Seiwert, M. and Seifert, B. (2007) 'Twenty years of the German Environmental Survey (GerES): Human biomonitoring–temporal and spatial (West Germany/East Germany) differences in population exposure', *International Journal of Hygiene and Environmental Health*, 210(3–4), pp 271–97.

Scott-Samuel, A., Bambra, C., Collins, C., Hunter, DJ., McCartney, G., and Smith, K. (2014) 'The impact of Thatcherism on health and wellbeing in Britain', *International Journal of Health Services*, 44, pp 53–71.

Scruggs, L., Jahn, D. and Kuitto, K. (2014) *Comparative welfare entitlements dataset 2 (Version 2014–03)*. Storrs and Greifswald: University of Connecticut and University of Greifswald. Available at: http://cwed2.org/ [Accessed: 16 November 2023].

Secretary of State for Health (2004) *Choosing health: Making healthy choices easier*. London: The Stationary Office.

Seligman, H.K., Laraia, B.A. and Kushel, M.B. (2010) 'Food insecurity is associated with chronic disease among low-income NHANES participants', *The Journal of Nutrition*, 140(2), pp 304–10.

Shahidi, F.V., Muntaner, C., Shankardass, K., Quiñonez, C. and Siddiqi, A. (2020) 'The effect of welfare reform on the health of the unemployed: Evidence from a natural experiment in Germany', *Journal of Epidemiology and Community Health*, 74(3), pp 211–18.

Shaw, C., Blakely, T., Atkinson, J. and Crampton, P. (2005) 'Do social and economic reforms change socioeconomic inequalities in child mortality? A case study: New Zealand 1981–1999', *Journal of Epidemiology and Community Health*, 59(8), pp 638–44.

Shei, A., Costa, F., Reis, M.G. and Ko, A.I. (2014) 'The impact of Brazil's Bolsa Família conditional cash transfer programme on children's healthcare utilization and health outcomes', *BMC International Health & Human Rights*, 14, p 10.

Shkolnikov, V.M., Leon, D.A., Adamets, S., Andreev, E. and Deev, A. (1998) 'Educational level and adult mortality in Russia: An analysis of routine data 1979 to 1994', *Social Science & Medicine*, 47(3), pp 357–69.

Shkolnikov, V.M., Andreev, E.M., Jasilionis, D., Leinsalu, M., Antonova, O.I. and McKee, M. (2006) 'The changing relation between education and life expectancy in central and eastern Europe in the 1990s', *Journal of Epidemiology and Community Health*, 60(10), pp 875–81.

Simpson, J., Bambra, C., Bell, Z., Albani, V., and Brown, H. (2021) 'Effects of social security policy reforms on mental health and inequalities: A systematic review of observational studies in high-income countries', *Social Science & Medicine*, 272, p 113717.

Simpson, J., Albani, V., Kingston, A. and Bambra, C. (2024) 'Closing the life expectancy gap: An ecological study of the factors associated with smaller regional health inequalities in post-reunification Germany', *Social Science & Medicine*, 362, p 117436.

Singh, G.K. and Yu, S.M. (1995) 'Infant mortality in the United States: Trends, differentials, and projections, 1950 through 2010', *American Journal of Public Health*, 85(7), pp 957–64.

Singh, G.K., Daus, G.P., Allender, M., Ramey, C.T., Martin, E.K., Perry, C., De Los Reyes, A.A. and Vedamuthu, I.P. (2017) 'Social determinants of health in the United States: Addressing major health inequality trends for the nation, 1935–2016', *International Journal of MCH and AIDS*, 6(2), pp 139–64.

Siqueira, C.E. and Haiama-Neurohr, N. (2006) 'The sinking of the neoliberal p-36 platform in Brazil', in V. Mogensen (ed) *Worker safety under siege: Labour, capital, and the politics of workplace safety in a deregulated world*. Abingdon and New York: Routledge, pp 187–203.

Smith, C. (2018) 'Lingering trauma in Brazil: Police violence against Black Women: Black women disproportionately experience the trauma of police aggression in Brazil. Understanding how requires complicating and expanding our definitions of state violence', *NACLA Report on the Americas*, 50(4), pp 369–76. Available at: https://doi.org/10.1080/10714839.2018.1550979 [Accessed: 7 April 2024].

Smith, D.B. (1990) 'Population ecology and the racial integration of hospitals and nursing homes in the United States', *The Milbank Quarterly*, 68(4), pp 561–96.

Smith, G.D., Morris, J.N. and Shaw, M. (1998) 'The independent inquiry into inequalities in health: Is welcome, but its recommendations are too cautious and vague', *British Medical Journal*, 317(7171), pp 1465–6.

Smith, K.E., Hill, S. and Bambra, C. (2015) 'Background and introduction: UK experiences of health inequalities', in K.E. Smith, S. Hill and C. Bambra (eds) *Health inequalities: Critical perspectives*. Oxford: Oxford University Press, 1–21.

Smith, K.E., Hunter, D.J., Blackman, T., Elliott, E., Greene, A., Harrington, B.E., Marks, L., McKee, L. and Williams, G.H. (2009) 'Divergence or convergence? Health inequalities and policy in a devolved Britain', *Critical Social Policy*, 29(2), pp 216–42.

Smith, K.E. and Stewart, E. (2024) 'Under attack? Public accounts of health inequalities and the social determinants of health in Scotland', *Journal of Critical Public Health*, 2, pp 5–23.

Snider, C.M. (2018) ' "The perfection of democracy cannot dispense with dealing with the past": Dictatorship, memory, and the politics of the present in Brazil', *The Latin Americanist*, 62, pp 55–79.

Snower, D.J. and Merkl, C. (2006) 'The caring hand that cripples: The East German labour market after reunification', *American Economic Review*, 96(2), pp 375–82.

Soares, F.V., Ribas, R.P. and Osório, R.G. (2010) 'Evaluating the impact of Brazil's Bolsa Família: Cash Transfer programmes in comparative perspective', *Latin American Research Review*, 45(2), pp 173–90.

Social Exclusion Unit (2001) *A new commitment to neighbourhood renewal: National strategy action plan*. London: The Cabinet Office.

Souza, C. (2001) 'Participatory budgeting in Brazilian cities: Limits and possibilities in building democratic institutions', *Environment and Urbanization*, 13(1), pp 159–84.

Stone, J. (2022) *Local indicators of child poverty after housing costs, 2020/21*. Loughborough: Centre for Research in Social Policy Loughborough University. Available at: https://endchildpoverty.org.uk/wp-content/uploads/2022/07/Local-child-poverty-indicators-report-2022_FINAL.pdf [Accessed: 4 November 2023].

Stuckler, D. and Basu, S. (2013) *The body economic: Eight experiments in economic recovery, from Iceland to Greece*. London: Penguin.

Stuckler, D., King, L. and McKee, M. (2009) 'Mass privatisation and the post-communist mortality crisis: A cross-national analysis', *The Lancet*, 373(9661), pp 399–407.

Szwarcwald, C.L., Almeida, W.D., Júnior, P.R.B., Rodrigues, R.M. and Romero, D.A. (2022) 'Socio-spatial inequalities in healthy life expectancy in the elderly, Brazil, 2013 and 2019', *Cadernos de Saúde Pública*, 38(Suppl 1), e00124421.

Szwarcwald, C.L., Almeida, W.D.S.D., Teixeira, R.A., França, E.B., de Miranda, M.J. and Malta, D.C. (2020) 'Inequalities in infant mortality in Brazil at subnational levels in Brazil, 1990 to 2015', *Population Health Metrics*, 18(Suppl 1), p 4.

Taylor, K. Y. (2012). 'Back story to the neoliberal moment: Race taxes and the political economy of Black urban housing in the 1960s', *Souls*, 14(3–4), pp 185–206.

Taylor-Robinson, D., Lai, E.T., Wickham, S., Rose, T., Norman, P., Bambra, C., Whitehead, M. and Barr, B. (2019) 'Assessing the impact of rising child poverty on the unprecedented rise in infant mortality in England, 2000–2017: Time trend analysis', *BMJ Open*, 9(10), p e029424.

Tetzlaff, F., Soderberg, M., Grigoriev, P., Tetzlaff, J., Mühlichen, M., Baumert, J., Wengler, A., Nowossadeck,E. and Hoebel, J. (2024) 'Age-specific and cause-specific mortality contributions to the socioeconomic gap in life expectancy in Germany, 2003–21: An ecological study', *The Lancet Public Health*, 9(5), pp e295–305.

The King's Fund (2022) *The NHS budget and how it has changed*. Available at: https://www.kingsfund.org.uk/projects/nhs-in-a-nutshell/nhs-budget [Accessed: 4 November 2023].

Thomas, B., Dorling, D. and Smith, GD. (2010) 'Inequalities in premature mortality in Britain: Observational study from 1921 to 2007', *British Medical Journal*, 341, p c3639.

Thomson, K., Hillier-Brown, F., Todd, A. et al (2018) 'The effects of public health policies on health inequalities in high-income countries: An umbrella review', *BMC Public Health*, 18, p 869.

Thorlby, R., Gardner, T. and Turton, C. (2019) *NHS performance and waiting times: Priorities for the new government*. London: The Health Foundation. Available at: https://www.health.org.uk/publications/long-reads/nhs-performance-and-waiting-times?gad_source=1&gclid=CjwKCAjwm_SzBhAsEiwAXE2CvwUAXEKPLegBmEulmGoZgrNUIcTUgL-SuW q9uacPH46Ffp952-ON2RoCw2EQAvD_BwEn [Accessed: 27 June 2024].

Thorlby, R. and Maybin, J. (2010) *A high-performing NHS? A review of progress 1997–2010*. The King's Fund. Available at: https://assets.kingsfund.org.uk/f/256914/x/54a86c88b5/high_performing_nhs_2010.pdf https://assets.kingsfund.org.uk/f/256914/x/54a86c88b5/high_performing_nhs_2010.pdf [Accessed: 27 June 2024].

Tombs, S. and Whyte, D. (2010) 'A deadly consensus: Worker safety and regulatory degradation under New Labour', *The British Journal of Criminology*, 50(1), pp 46–65,

# References

Toynbee, P. and Walker, D. (2011) *The verdict: Did labour change Britain?* London: Granta.

Turner, N., Danesh, K. and Moran, K. (2020) 'The evolution of infant mortality inequality in the United States, 1960–2016', *Science Advances*, 6(29), p eaba5908.

United States Census Bureau (1962) *1960 Census – population, supplementary reports: Educational attainment of the population of the United States, PC(S1)-37*. Washington, DC: US Department of Commerce. Available at: https://www.census.gov/library/publications/1962/dec/population-pc-s1-37.html [Accessed: 21 November 2023].

United States Census Bureau (1964) *1960 Census – population, supplementary reports: Low income families, PC(S1)-43*. Washington, DC: US Department of Commerce. Available at: https://www.census.gov/library/publications/1964/dec/population-pc-s1-43.html [Accessed: 21 November 2023].

US Department of Health and Human Services (2024) *Civic participation [WWW Document]*. Healthy People 2030. Available at: https://health.gov/healthypeople/priority-areas/social-determinants-health/literature-summaries/civic-participation [Accessed: 16 June 2024].

Vaizey, H. (2014) *Born in the GDR: Living in the shadow of the wall*. Oxford: Oxford University Press.

van Raalte, A.A., Klüsener, S., Oksuzyan, A. and Grigoriev, P. (2020) 'Declining regional disparities in mortality in the context of persisting large inequalities in economic conditions: the case of Germany', *International Journal of Epidemiology*, 49(2), pp 486–96.

Vineis, P., Delpierre, C., Castagné, R., Fiorito, G., McCrory, C., Kivimaki, M., Stringhini, S., Carmeli, C. and Kelly-Irving, M. (2020) 'Health inequalities: Embodied evidence across biological layers', *Social Science & Medicine*, 246, Art. 112781.

Virtanen, P., Vahtera, J., Kivimäki, M., Pentti, J. and Ferrie, J. (2002) 'Employment security and health', *Journal of Epidemiology and Community Health*, 56(8), pp 569–74.

Vogt, T., van Raalte, A., Grigoriev, P. and Myrskylä, M. (2017) 'The German East–West mortality difference: Two crossovers driven by smoking', *Demography*, 54(3), pp 1051–71.

Vogt, T.C. and Kluge, F.A. (2015) 'Can public spending reduce mortality disparities? Findings from East Germany after reunification', *The Journal of the Economics of Ageing*, 5, pp 7–13.

Vogt, T.C. and Vaupel, J.W. (2015) 'The importance of regional availability of healthcare for old age survival: Findings from German reunification', *Population Health Metrics*, 13, p 26.

Wacquant, L. (2007) 'Territorial stigmatization in the age of advanced marginality', *Thesis Eleven*, 91(1), pp 66–77.

Walsh, D. and McCartney, G. (2024) *Social murder? Austerity and life expectancy in the UK*. Bristol: Bristol Policy Press.

Walsh, D., Dundas, R., McCartney, G., Gibson, M. and Seaman, R. (2022) 'Bearing the burden of austerity: How do changing mortality rates in the UK compare between men and women?' *Journal of Epidemiol Community Health*, 76(12), pp 1027–33.

Wampler, B. (2012) 'Entering the state: Civil society activism and participatory governance in Brazil', *Political Studies*, 60(2), pp 341–62.

Wampler, B. and Avritzer, L. (2005) 'The spread of participatory democracy in Brazil: From radical democracy to good government', *Journal of Latin American Urban Studies*, 7, pp 37–52.

Wang, G., Schwartz, G.L., Kershaw, K.N., McGowan, C., Kim, M.H. and Hamad, R. (2022) 'The association of residential racial segregation with health among US children: A nationwide longitudinal study', *SSM Population Health*, 19, p 101250.

Wang, Y.T., Mechkova, V., and Andersson, F. (2019) 'Does democracy enhance health? New empirical evidence 1900–2012', *Political Research Quarterly*, 72(3), pp 554–69.

Ward, K. and England, K. (2007) 'Introduction: Reading Neoliberalization', in K. England and K. Ward (eds) *Neoliberalization: States, networks, people*. Oxford: Blackwell, pp 1–22.

Watson, P. (1998) 'Health difference in Eastern Europe: Preliminary findings from the Nowa Huta study', *Social Science & Medicine*, 46(4–5), pp 549–58.

Watt, G. (2013) 'What can the NHS do to prevent and reduce health inequalities?', *British Journal of General Practice*, 63, pp 494–5.

Watts, J. (2013) Brazil's Bolsa Familia scheme: Political tool or social welfare success? *The Guardian*, 19 December 2013. Available at: https://www.theguardian.com/global-development/2013/dec/19/brazil-bolsa-familia-political-tool-social-welfare [Accessed: 19 June 2024]

Weaver, R.K. (2000) *Ending welfare as we know it*. Washington, DC: Brookings Institution Press. Available at: https://www.jstor.org/stable/10.7864/j.ctvdmwzqn [Accessed: 19 June 2024].

Weisskircher, M. (2020) 'The strength of Far-Right AfD in Eastern Germany: The East–West divide and the multiple causes behind "populism"', *The Political Quarterly*, 91, pp 614–22.

Whitehead, M. (2007) 'A typology of actions to tackle inequalities in health', *Journal of Epidemiology and Community Health*, 61(6), pp 473–8.

Whitehead, M. and J. Popay (2010) 'Swimming upstream? Taking action on the social determinants of health inequalities', *Social Science & Medicine*, 71(7), pp 1234–6.

Whyte, B. and T. Ajetunmobi (2012) *Still the 'sick man of Europe'? Scottish mortality in a European context 1950–2010. An analysis of comparative mortality trends.* Glasgow: Glasgow Centre for Population Health. Available at: https://www.gcph.co.uk/assets/000/000/231/Scottish_Mortality_in_a_European_Context_2012_v11_FINAL_bw_original.pdf?1700036397 [Accessed: 4 November 2023].

Wickham, S., Whitehead, M., Taylor-Robinson, D. and Barr, B. (2017) 'The effect of a transition into poverty on child and maternal mental health: A longitudinal analysis of the UK Millennium Cohort Study', *Lancet Public Health*, 2(3), E141–8.

Wickham, S., Bentley, L., Rose, T., Whitehead, M., Taylor-Robinson, D. and Barr, B. (2020) 'Effects on mental health of a UK welfare reform, Universal Credit: a longitudinal controlled study', *Lancet Public Health*, 5(3), pp E157–64.

Williams, D.R. and Collins, C. (2001) 'Racial residential segregation: A fundamental cause of racial disparities in health', *Public Health Reports*, 116(5), pp 404–16.

Williams, D.R., Lawrence, J.A., Davis, B.A. and Vu, C. (2019) 'Understanding how discrimination can affect health', *Health Services Research*, 54(Suppl 2), pp 1374–88.

Winkler, G., Brasche, S. and Heinrich, J. (1997) 'Trends in food intake in adults from the city of Erfurt before and after the German reunification', *Annals of Nutrition and Metabolism*, 41(5), pp 283–90.

Wise, M. and Sainsbury, P. (2007) 'Democracy: The forgotten determinant of mental health', *Health Promotion Journal of Australia*, 18, pp 177–83.

Wolle, S. (2019) *The ideal world of dictatorship: Daily life and party rule in the GDR, 1971–1989.* Berlin: CH Links Verlag.

Woolf, S.H. and Schoomaker, H. (2019) 'Life expectancy and mortality rates in the United States, 1959–2017', *JAMA*, 322(20), pp 1996–2016.

World Bank Group (2001) *Brazil – Assessment of the Bolsa Escola programmes* (English). Washington, DC: World Bank Group. Available at: http://documents.worldbank.org/curated/en/148031468743736711/Brazil-Assessment-of-the-Bolsa-Escola-Programmes [Accessed: 16 December 2023].

World Bank Group (2024) *World Bank open data.* Washington, DC: World Bank Group. Available at: https://data.worldbank.org/ [Accessed: 16 December 2023].

World Health Organization (2008) *Closing the gap in a generation: Health equity through action on the social determinants of health.* Available at: https://www.who.int/publications/i/item/WHO-IER-CSDH-08.1 [Accessed: 16 December 2023].

World Health Organization (2012) *Health for all database.* Available at: https://gateway.euro.who.int/en/datasets/european-health-for-all-database/ [Accessed: 12 June 2024].

Yearby, R. (2018) 'Racial disparities in health status and access to healthcare: The continuation of inequality in the United States due to structural racism', *The American Journal of Economics and Sociology*, 77(3–4), pp 1113–52.

Yearby, R., Clark, B. and Figueroa, J.F. (2022) 'Structural racism in historical and modern US healthcare policy', *Health Affairs (Millwood)*, 41(2), pp 187–94.

Yuan, B., Målqvist, M., Trygg, N. Qian, X., Ng, N. and Thomsen, A. (2014) 'What interventions are effective on reducing inequalities in maternal and child health in low- and middle-income settings? A systematic review', *BMC Public Health*, 14, p 634.

Zeevaert, M. (2020) *The Legacy of Germany's Reunification*. New Haven, CT: The Yale Review of International Studies. Available at: http://yris.yira.org/comments/4473#_ftn6 [Accessed: 4 December 2023].

# Index

References to figures are in *italics* and to tables are in **bold**; references to notes are the page number followed by the note and chapter number (131n6 (ch3)).

## A

Acheson Report, UK 77, 78–9, 90
Affordable Care Act (ACA, 2008, USA) 102
Aid to Families with Dependent Children (AFDC), USA 27, 99
air pollution **24**, 25, 56, 62, 89
alcohol consumption 58, 63, 67, 70
alcohol regulation 48, 49, 89
alcohol-related mortality 76–7
all-cause mortality rates 9, 10, 46, 76, 86, 120
*Alternative für Deutschland* (Alternative for Germany, AfD) 108–9
anti-retroviral drugs (ARVs) 44, 49
austerity policies
 Brazil 104, 119, 121
 Europe 111
 Germany 108, 119, 121, 122
 UK 91, 111–15, 119, 120–1, 123
Australia 3, **66**
Austria 55, **66**
Avis, M. et al. 87

## B

Bambra, C. **117**
Barr, B. et al 84
Bartley, M. 4
Baum, Fran 124
Beatty, C. 113
Beckfield, J. 65
bedroom tax (Under Occupancy Charge), UK 112, 131n4 (ch6)
Belarus *68*, *69*
Bennett, N. et al. 85
Berg, J. 46
Besley, T. 65
birth weights 28, 67
Black Report, UK 77–9, 90
Boing, A.F. et al. 41
*Bolsa Escola* (School Grant) 44–5, **51**, 53, 119
*Bolsa Família* 45, 48, **51**, 105, 119, 121
Bolsonaro, Jair 36, 103, 104, 107, 124
Brazil 35–53, 93–4, 103–8
 1988 Constitution 40–1, 43–4, 47, **51**, 93, 105, 129
 democratisation 39–40, 47–8, 50–2, **51**, 93–4, 106, 108, 124
 Gross Domestic Product (GDP) 38, 43

housing 38, 49, **51**, 53, 105–6, 107, 126
income inequalities 36, 38, *42–3*, 44–6, **51**, 52, 123
land reform 40, 105, 123, 126
military dictatorship (1964–84) 35, 36–40, 103–4, 107–8, 124
Burstrom, B. 8, 10, 11
Bush, George H.W. 119

## C

Canada 3, **66**
cancer 80, 86
car safety **24**, 25
cardiovascular disease 32, 45, 46, 59, 63, 64, 86
Cardoso, Fernando Henrique 44
Case, A. 9
census data 18–19, 41
Charlton, T.L. et al. 16
Child Benefit, UK 112
child labour 45
child poverty 28, 78, 80–1, **81**, 85, 113, 114
Child Tax Credit, UK **81**, 111, 112
childcare 7, 60–1, **81**, 122
childhood mortality rates 32, 45, 64, 65
Christian Democrats, Germany 64
Chung, H. 67
civil rights 15, 19, 39–40, 65, 98, 119, 127, 129
Civil Rights Act (1957 and 1960, USA) 20, 21
Civil Rights Act (1964, USA) **23–4**, 26, 29, 33, 93
Clarke, Kenneth 18
class *see* socio-economic groups
Clinton, Bill 100
Coburn, D. 67
Coelho, V.S.P. *42*, *43*, 50
Cohen, Stanley 107
*Comissão Nacional da Verdade* (National Truth Commission) report (2014) 38
commercial determinants of health
 Brazil 48–9, **51**, 93
 cross-national discussion 126
 USA **24**, 25
 *see also* tobacco regulation
Community Action Programmes (CAPs) **23**, 30, 32
Community Health Centers (CHCs) 21, 26, 31, 32–3, 102, 121

169

Conservative Party, UK 77–8, 91, 95, 111
COVID-19
  Brazil 53, 103, 104, 121
  cross-national discussion 1, 12
  Germany 108
  UK 112, 115
  USA 119
Czech Republic 70

## D

Da Silva Pereira, R. 107
De Jong, G. 17
Deaton, A. 9
deindustrialisation 60, 62, 70, 74, 75, 94
Democratic Party, USA 15, 98, 100
democratisation
  Brazil 39–40, 47–8, 50–2, **51**, 93–4, 106, 108, 124
  Germany 55, 64–7, 94, 98, 124
  UK, reversal 74, 98
Denmark 8, **66**
deregulation 72, 73, 74, 89, 99, 101, 120
desegregation **23**, **24**, 29–33, 93, 99, 101
Dias, M. *42*, *43*, 50
disability
  Germany 57
  UK 74, 78, 89
  USA 20, **22**, 23, 32, 93, 99, 120
Doha Declaration (2010) 44
drinking water, access to 10, 43, 56

## E

Earned Income Tax Credits (EITC), USA 100
East Germany (German Democratic Republic/GDR) 54–9, *58*, 60, 62, 64, 110
Eastern bloc 54–5, 60, 67, *68*, *69*, 70, 95
Economic Opportunity Act (1964, USA) 20, 99
economic policy
  Brazil 38, 47–8, **51**, 93, 97, 123, 124
  cross-national discussion 65, 97, 98, 127–8
  Germany 55–6, 57, 59–61, 109
  UK 72–7, 79, 89–90, 123, 127–8
  USA 93, 97, 98–9, 128
education
  Brazil 44–5, 46, 50, **51**, 53, 93, 105
  cross-national discussion 9, 70, 96, 122
  England/UK 74, 78, 80, 81, 87
  Germany 55
  USA 16, 18–21, **22**–**3**, 28–31, 96, 100–1
Elementary and Secondary Education Act (ESEA, 1965, USA) 20, **23**, 30–1
employment
  job creation and training 20, **23**, 29, 32, 87
  *see also* manual workers; minimum wage; occupational groups; professionals; salaries; wage disparities

employment security
  Brazil 46, **51**, 52, 53, 93, 123
  cross-national discussion 97
  Germany 61
  UK 73, 75, 131n2 (ch5)
England 9–10, 110–15, 120–1, 123
  *see also* Health Inequalities Strategy for England
enslavement 36–7, 40
environmental issues
  Brazil 39, 53
  climate change 12, 108
  Germany 56, 60, 61, 62, 94, 126
  UK 89, 112
  USA **24**, 25
Equal Pay Act (1963, USA) **22**, 29
Estonia *68*, *69*, 70
Europe 8–12, 111, 122, 125

## F

Fair Housing Act (1968, USA) **22**, 27, 29, 98
Fair Labour Standards Act (1966, USA) **22**, 29
far-right, the
  Brazil 103, 107, 124, 127
  cross-national discussion 128
  Germany 108–9, 110, 124, 127
  UK 127
Federal Republic of Germany (FRG/West Germany) 54–5, *58*, 62
Finland **66**, 70
Fleming, Cora 16
food stamps **22**, 28, 100
Foster, M. 19
Fothergill, S. 113
Framework Convention on Tobacco Control (FCTC) 49, **51**, **82**, 83
France 9, 10, **66**
Franco, Marielle 107
Fukuyama, F. 127
Fulbrook, M. 55–8

## G

gender
  Brazil 39–40, 50, 107
  Eastern bloc *68*, *69*, 70
  England 84–8, 113–14
  Germany 54, 58–9, *58*, 60–3, 94
  overview 1, 3, 7, 65, 66, 115, 128
  USA 27, 28, 29–30, 93, 99, 101
George, Eddie 76
German Democratic Republic (GDR/East Germany) 54–9, *58*, 60, 62, 64, 110
Germany 54–67, 94–5, 108–10
  democratisation 55, 64–7, 94, 98, 124
  economic policy 55–6, 57, 59–61, 109
  far-right 108–9, 110, 124, 127
  Gross Domestic Product (GDP) 56, 60, 61

healthcare access 57, 63–4, 120
housing 56, 61, 62–3, 94, 109
Gini coefficient 36, 38, 131n1 (ch3)
Global Financial Crisis (2007–08) 12, 111, 114–15
Goulart, João 38
Great Society, USA
  need for 15–20, 92
  outcomes 21, 25–34, *25*, *26*, 101, 103, 120, 121
  programmes 15, 20–1, **22–4**, 96
  subsequent era 34, 98–103
Grigoriev, P. 64
Gross Domestic Product (GDP)
  Brazil 38, 43
  Germany 56, 60, 61
  UK 61, 90
  USA 16
  and welfare state types 67
Guanais, F.C. 121

### H

Head Start, USA **22**, 30, 99
Health Action Zones, England 81, **81**, 83, 87, 95
health and safety standards
  Brazil 39, 46, 53, 105, 126
  cross-national discussion 97
  Germany 56, 126
  UK 89, 126
  USA 126
health behaviours 58, 59, 63, 67, 70, 87–9
health disparities, definition 3
health inequalities, overview 3, 4–9, 128–30
Health Inequalities Strategy for England
  description of 72, 78–81, **81–2**, 118–19
  evaluation of 83–9
  targets 79–80, **82**, 83, 86, 117
  unravelling of 95, 123, 129
health inequities, definition 3
health insurance 19, 21, **23**, 66, 119, 120–1
  *see also* Medicaid, USA; Medicare, USA
healthcare access
  Brazil 45, **51**, 120, 121
  cross-national discussion 96, 97, 122
  England/UK 74, 81, 120–1
  Germany 57, 63–4, 120
  levelling mechanism 2, 96–7, 120–2
  USA 19, 21, **23**, 27, 31–3, 97, 102–3, 120, 121
healthcare funding
  Brazil 41, 43, **51**, 93, 120, 129
  Germany 57, 63, 71, 121
  UK 78, 85, 86, 120–1
healthy life expectancy 65, 86, 113, 132n8 (ch6)
heart disease 6, 32, 64, 80

High/Scope Perry Pre-School programme 86
Holdroyd, I. et al. 86
Honecker, Erich 57
household benefit cap, UK 112
housing
  Brazil 38, 49, **51**, 53, 105–6, 107, 126
  cross-national discussion 11, 66, 96, 129
  England/UK 11, 74–5, 77, 80–1, 112, 114
  Germany 56, 61, 62–3, 94, 109
  New Zealand 120
  USA 17–18, 20–1, **22**, 27, 28–9, 100–1, 119, 127
Housing Benefit, UK 131n6 (ch3)
Human Mortality Database 58–9
human rights violations 38–40, 53, 55
Hungary 55, 70
Hunter, W. 105

### I

Iceland **66**, 114
income inequalities
  Brazil 36, 38, *42–3*, 44–6, **51**, 52, 123
  cross-national discussion 4, 10–12, 96–7, 131n1 (ch3)
  Eastern bloc 67
  Germany 61, 109, 122
  levelling mechanism 2, 96–7, 122–4
  UK 73–4, 76–8, 89, *90*, 123
  USA 8–9, 11, 33–4, 93–4, 100, 119, 121–2
income tax **22**, 71, 100, 123
Indian Civil Rights Act (1968, USA) **24**
Indigenous populations
  Brazil 36–7, 39, 48, 106, 107
  cross-national discussion 65
infant mortality rates (IMR)
  Brazil 36–7, 40–1, *42*, 43–4, 45, 50, 119, 121
  cross-national discussion 8–9, 10, 64–5, 67
  England 9, 79, 83, 85, *85*, 88, 114
  Germany 59
  USA 8, 16, 25–6, 30, 33, 65, 93, 103, 119
International American Development Bank 45
International Monetary Fund (IMF) 45, 111

### J

James, D.B. 99
Jenkins, Patrick 78
Job Corps programme, USA **23**, 29
Johnson, Alan 84
Johnson, Lyndon B. 11, 15, 98
Jowell, Tessa 77

### K

Kennedy, John F. 15
Keynesian economics 11, 12, 66, 73

King, Martin Luther, Jr. 98
Kluge, F.A. 62
Kohl, Helmut 11, 71
Kopper, M. 106
Krieger, N. et al. 8, 9, 65
Krueger, A.B. 56
Kudamatsu, M. 65

## L

Labour Party, UK 77–9, 86, 89, 90, 96, 117, 123
Lamont, Norman 76
land reform 40, 105, 123, 126
Latvia *68*, *69*
Le Grand, Julian 84
levelling mechanisms 95–8, 115, 118–30
  healthcare access 2, 96–7, 120–2
  income inequality reduction 2, 96–7, 122–4
  political participation 2, 97–8, 124–5, 126–7, 129–30
  welfare state 2, 96, 118–20, 122, 123, 125
LGBTQ+ groups 1, 3, 128
Liberal Democrat Party, UK 111
life expectancy
  Brazil 1, 36, 40–1, *43*, 50, 103, 119
  cross-national discussion 64–5, 67, *68*, *69*, 70, 115
  Eastern bloc 67, *68*, *69*, 70
  England/UK 9–10, 77, 79, 84–5, 88, 113–14
  Germany 54, 58–9, *58*, 62, 64, 94, 108, 119
  USA 1, 9–10, 16, 25, 103
  *see also* mortality rates
Lithuania *68*, *69*
London 89, 113, 114
low-income people
  Brazil 44, 47, 49–50
  England 83, 96, 112–13, 114
  overview 5, 6
  USA 17–18, 20–1, **22**–3, 25–30, *26*, 32, 34, 99–102, *100*
Lucke, Bernd 108
Lula da Silva, Luiz Inácio
  military dictatorship, resistance to 40
  presidency (2003–11) 44–8, **51**, 52–3, 106, 124
  presidency (2023) 103, 108, 124

## M

Macinko, J. et al 43–4
Mackenbach, J.P. et al 9, 84
manual workers 1, 19, 56, 70, 79, 96
manufacturing 39, 48, 60, 74, 75, 89, 109
marketisation 72, 73, 74, 75, 89–90, 128
Marks, Etta Joan 19
Mask, J.W. 18–19

McGowan, V.J. et al. **117**
media 52, 53, 107, 109–10, 129
Medicaid, USA
  impact of 26, 31–3, 97
  introduction of 21, **23**, 120, 121
  resistance 101–2
Medicare, USA **23**, 31–3, 97, 101, 120
medications
  Brazil 43–4, 49, **51**, 93, 129
  cross-national discussion 97
  Germany 57, 63
mental health 1, 29, 86, 87, 88, 114
Miethe, I. 109
migration 1, **24**, 38, 57, 61, 110, 128
*Minha Casa, Minha Vida* 49, **51**, 106
Minimum Income Guarantee for Pensions **81**, 86, 87, 89
minimum wage
  Brazil 46, **51**, 93, 123
  cross-national discussion 97, 122
  UK 81, 89, 95
  USA 20, **22**, 27, 29–30
mining 39, 56, 60, 74
Mississippi 17, 19, 20
mortality rates
  Brazil 44, 45–6
  cross-national discussion 1, 115
  Eastern bloc 67, 70
  England/UK 76–7, 80, 85–6, 88, 114, 115
  Germany 58–9, 62, 63, 108
  USA 32
  *see also* all-cause mortality rates; infant mortality rates (IMR); life expectancy; premature mortality rates
Mourão Filho, Olímpio 38
Muntaner, C. 67

## N

National Health Service (NHS)
  austerity (2010–24) 111, 120–1
  Labour government (1997–2010) 80–1, **82**, 85, 86, 88, 89
  Thatcherism (1979–97) 74, 75
National Programme for Tobacco Control (NTCP) 48, **51**
National Truth Commission (*Comissão Nacional da Verdade*) report (2014) 38
Navarro, V. et al. 66–7
neoliberalism
  cross-national discussion 96, 128
  UK 11, 72–7, 89–91, 98, 119
  USA 34, 99–100, 119
  welfare state, stage of *10*, 11–12, 72
Neuendorf, U.L. 55
Neves, Tancredo 40
New Deal for Communities 81, **82**, 86, 87–8, 89, 95
New Zealand 3, *66*, 119–20

# Index

NHS *see* National Health Service (NHS)
NHS Plan 2000 **82**
Nixon, Richard 99, 101
Norway 1, 8, **66**
nutrition
  Brazil 45, 48, 49
  cross-national discussion 4, 6
  Germany 56, 59, 62, 63, 64, 94
  UK 78, 80
  USA 17, **22**, 28, 93

## O

Obama, Barack 102
obesity 28, 30, 32, 49, 53, 63
occupational groups 77, 83
  *see also* manual workers; professionals
Office of Economic Opportunity (OEO), UK 20, 33, 93, 99
older adults
  Germany 57, 58, 59, 61, 64
  UK 78, **81**, 89, 111–12
  USA 18, 20, 21, **23**, 31–2, 92–3, 101, 120
O'Neil, A. 8

## P

participatory budgeting 47–8, **51**, 93, 124
*Partido dos Trabalhadores* (Workers' Party, PT) 47, 104, 105
Patient Protection and Affordable Care Act (ACA, 2008, USA) 102
Pechholdová, M. 64
pensions
  Germany 59, 61–2, 109
  UK 81, **81**, 86, 87, 89, 95
  USA 20
Pickett, K.E. 123
Pischke, J.-S. 56
Poland 70
political participation
  cross-national discussion 64–5, 97–8, 122, 125
  levelling mechanism 2, 97, 124–5, 126–7, 129–30
  USA 20–1, **23–4**, 25, 33–4, 93, 97–9, 102, 124
  *see also* democratisation
Portugal 61, 114
poverty
  Brazil 44–5, 47, 50, 94, 104, 105
  Eastern bloc 67, 70
  England/UK 73–4, 76–8, 80–1, **81–2**, 83–9, 123
  Germany 61, 62, 95
  overview 6–7, 11–12, 96, 98, 122–4, 125
  USA 15–18, 20–1, **22–3**, 27–8, 92–3, 99–101, *100*
premature mortality rates
  Brazil 46

cross-national discussion 9, 10, 67
Eastern bloc 70
England 9, 10, 88
USA 9, 10, 11, *25*, *26*, 119
prisons 106–7
privatisation 60, 67, 70, 72–4, 101, 120
pro-poor policies, Brazil
  cash transfer programmes 36, 44–6, **51**, 93, 94, 123
  failures of 104, 105
professionals 1, 5, 29, 70, 96, 110
*Programa Saude da Famiia* (Family Health Programme, PSF) 43–4, 121
public policy management councils (*conselhos*) 47, **51**
Public Policy Management System (*Sistema de Gestão de Políticas Públicas*) 47, 48, **51**

## R

race/ethnicity, non-USA
  Brazil 36–7, 39–40, 48, 106–7
  cross-national discussion 5, 65
  UK 78, 83, 113
race/ethnicity, USA
  political participation 20–1, **23–4**, 25, 33–4, 93, 97–9, 102, 124
  segregation/desegregation 17–21, **23**, **24**, 29–33, 93, 99, 101
  trends and context 7–11
  *see also* Great Society, USA
Rasella, D. et al. 45
Reagan, Ronald 11, 99, 101, 119
redistributive tax systems 66, 97, 120–1
Regenstein, A.C. 57
Republican Party, USA 15, 98, 100
'right to buy' policy, UK 74–5
'right to health' policy, Brazil 41, 43–4, 93, 129
Robinson, T. et al. 85
Rodriguez, J. et al. 8
Roosevelt, Franklin D. 11
Rousseff, Dilma 48, 52, 104
Russia 67, *68*, *69*, 70

## S

Safaei, J. 65
salaries 56, 60, 73, 94
  *see also* minimum wage; wage disparities
Sarney, José 40
Scheidel, Walter 2
Scheiring, G. et al. 70
School Grant (*Bolsa Escola*) 44–5, **51**, 53, 119
school meals **22**, 28, 49
Scotland 77, 78
segregation 17–21, 101
  *see also* desegregation
SIMPLES law, Brazil 46
Simpson, J. et al. 62

*Sistema de Gestão de Políticas Públicas* (Public Policy Management System) 47, 48, **51**
*Sistema Único de Saúde (SUS)* 41, 43, **51**, 120, 121
smoking 58, 63, 87–9
  *see also* tobacco regulation
social care 111–12, 114, 115
social housing 10, 11, 12, 74, 106, 120, 131n4 (ch6)
social media 53, 107, 129
social security
  Eastern bloc 67, 70
  Germany 61, 62, 94, 120
  UK 78, **81**, 89, 112
  USA 20, **22**, 27
  *see also* unemployment benefits
Socialist Unity Party of Germany (SED) 55, 64
socio-economic groups
  Brazil 35, 39–40, 46
  cross-national discussion 1, 3, 4, 10, 116
  Germany 58
  UK 3, 10, 77, 78, 82, 83, 88
  USA 10, 17, 20, **23**, 102
  *see also* manual workers; occupational groups; professionals
South Africa 65
Souza, C. 47
Soviet Union 67, 127
state violence 38, 104, 106–7, 127
strikes 39, 40, 74
Stuckler, D. et al. 70
Sugiyama, N.B. 113
suicide 77, 114
Sure Start, England **81**, 85, 86–7, 89, 111
Sweden 8, 10–11, **66**
Szwarcwald, C.L. et al 41, *42*

**T**

tax credits **81**, 86–7, 89, 100, 111, 112, 113
taxation
  Brazil 41, 45–6, 49, **51**, 93, 120, 123, 129
  Germany 57, 71, 109
  UK 90, 111, 120–1
  USA **22**, 98, 99–100
  welfare state types 66, 97, 122
Taylor, K.Y. 18
Temer, Michel 104
Thatcherism 11, 72–7, 89–91, 98, 119
Thomas, B. et al. 9
Thomson, K. et al. **117**
tobacco regulation
  Brazil 48–9, **51**, 93–4
  Germany 63, 126
  UK **82**, 83, 88, 89, 96, 126
  USA **24**, 25, 96, 126
Trade-Related Aspects of Intellectual Property Rights (TRIPS Agreement) 44, 49, **51**

trade unions
  Brazil 39, 40, 46, 48, **51**, 53, 93, 124
  cross-national discussion 97, 122, 127
  UK 73, 75, 98
  USA 100

**U**

Ukraine *68, 69*
*Uma Ponta para a Futuro* (A Bridge to the Future) 104
Under Occupancy Charge (bedroom tax), UK 112, 131n4 (ch6)
unemployment benefits
  Eastern bloc 70
  Germany 61, 62, 108, 119
  UK 76, 114
  USA 11, 18, 99
unemployment rates
  Eastern bloc 67
  Germany 60–2, 94, 108, 109
  UK 12, 73–4, 75–6, 77, 80, 111, 114
  USA 18, 111
*União das Nações Indígenas* 39
Union of Indian Nations 39
United Kingdom (UK) 72–91, 95, 110–15
  Gross Domestic Product (GDP) 61, 90
  historical trends 8, 9–10, 11–12
  income inequalities 73–4, 76–8, 89, *90*, 123
  socio-economic groups 3, 10, 77, 78, 82, 83, 88
  Thatcherism 11, 72–7, 89–91, 98, 119
  *see also* England; Health Inequalities Strategy for England
United States of America (USA) 15–34, 92–3, 98–103
  and Brazil 38, 44
  evidence-based research 117, 118
  Global Financial Crisis (2007–08) 12, 111
  Gross Domestic Product (GDP) 16
  poverty 15–18, 20–1, **22–3**, 27–8, 92–3, 99–101, *100*
  *see also* Great Society, USA; race/ethnicity, USA
Universal Credit, UK 112, 114

**V**

vaccinations 43, 45, 93
Vaupel, J.W. 64
Vineis, P. et al. 116
violence 77, 109
  *see also* state violence
Vogt, T.C. 62, 64
Volunteers in Service to America (VISTA) **23**, 33
Voting Rights Act (1965, USA) 21, **24**, 25, 33–4, 93, 102, 124

## W

wage disparities  21, 29–30, 33, 60, 93, 96–7, 100
Wales  77, 78
Wang, Y.T. et al.  65
War on Poverty, USA  20, 21, 99–100, 119
water pollution  **24**, 25, 43, 56
Watt, Graham  121–2
wealth inequalities
  Brazil  36
  cross-national discussion  64, 67, 122, 123–4, 127, 131n1 (ch3)
  UK  74–6, **82**, 89–90, *90*
  USA  101–2
Welfare Reform Act 2012 (UK)  112
Welfare Reform and Work Act 2016 (UK)  112
welfare state
  Brazil  104, 119
  Germany  62, 66, **66**, 67, 94, 119
  levelling mechanism  2, 96, 118–20, 122, 123, 125
  stages of  10–12, *10*, 72, 73
  types of  66–7, **66**, 125
  UK  11–12, **66**, 73–4, 78, 90, 111–15, 118–19, 123
  USA  **66**, 93, 99, 119
West Germany (Federal Republic of Germany/FRG)  54–5, *58*, 62
Wilkinson, R.G.  123
Winkler, G. et al.  63
Workers' Party (*Partido dos Trabalhadores/PT*)  47, 104, 105
Working Tax Credit, UK  **81**, 111, 112
World Bank  36, 44, 45
World Health Organization (WHO)  3, 5, 49, **51**
World Trade Organization  44

## Y

Yuan, B. et al.  **117**

## Z

Zika virus  53, 104, 121

www.ingramcontent.com/pod-product-compliance
Lightning Source LLC
Chambersburg PA
CBHW051549020426
42333CB00016B/2169